essential guide to

maui

LĀNA'I AND MOLOKA'I

Virginia Wageman

 ISLAND HERITAGE PUBLISHING

Published and
distributed by Island
Heritage Publishing
ISBN 0-89610-443-5

Designed by Jim Wageman

Address orders and
correspondence to:
Island Heritage Publishing
94-411 Kō'aki Street
Waipahu, HI 96797
Fax 808-564-8888
Phone 800-468-2800;
808-564-8800
www.islandheritage.com

Printed in Hong Kong
First edition, second printing, 2002

Pages 2–3: Sunrise from the
summit of Haleakalā.
Pages 6–7: Replica of an
ancient Hawaiian ki'i (tiki),
Kā'anapali Beach Hotel.

contents

maps

top ten **essentials**
for a great maui vacation

If you do anything other than swim, sun, and play golf, we recommend the following as essential to a great Maui vacation.

Top to bottom: The pool at the Ritz-Carlton, Kapalua; the road to Hāna; Hulopoʻe Beach on Lānaʻi; Hāliʻimaile General Store; and the theatrical production ʻUlalena.

Opposite, top to bottom: A whale exhibit in the Maui Ocean Center; hiking in Haleakalā; horseback riding in Kula; Molokaʻi's north coast; and snorkeling off Molokini.

● Stay at one of the grand resort hotels, if only for two nights (one isn't enough). Our choices: the Ritz-Carlton, Kapalua (pages 218–19), for the ultimate in luxury in an environment hospitable to Hawaiian culture, or the Four Seasons Resort Maui (pages 214–15), for ultra friendly service and a magnificent spa.

● Spend a few days in heavenly Hāna, at the far east side of the island. Stay at the wonderful Hotel Hāna-Maui (page 215) or at one of the many guesthouses or cottages in the area. To get there, take the famous Hāna Highway (page 104), and return via the scenic Piʻilani Highway (page 122), 37 miles from Hāna to ʻUlupalakua.

● Visit Molokaʻi or Lānaʻi (or both), both part of Maui County. While these islands are just a short distance from Maui in miles, they offer the visitor a totally different experience. Molokaʻi is low key and down home (pages 247–68), while fantasies come true at Lānaʻi's luxury resorts (pages 269–89).

- Eat at several of the great restaurants: Hāli'imaile General Store in Upcountry Maui, Pacific'o or I'o in Lahaina, Chez Paul in Olowalu, A Pacific Café in Honokōwai or Kīhei, then back to Hāli'imaile General Store (our favorite). See Dining, pages 233–44.

- Go to see 'Ulalena, a show presented by the Maui Myth and Magic Theatre in Lahaina (page 202). This dazzling performance tells in music and dance the history of the Hawaiian islands. Audiences of all ages are spellbound by the spectacular costumes and visual effects of this colorful, fast-paced production.

- Visit the Maui Ocean Center (page 74), Maui's newest must-see attraction. A huge tropical aquarium, the Ocean Center is dedicated to preserving Hawai'i's indigenous and endemic marine life. Plan to stay the day or stop for an hour or so on the way to the airport. Whatever you do, don't miss it!

- Take a hike in Haleakalā crater (page 101). The true grandeur of this mighty mountain, over 10,000 feet above sea level at its summit, can best be experienced by descending into the crater. With 27 miles of trails, there are easy strolls as well as demanding hikes of a day or more.

- Ride a horse over land unchanged since before Westerners set foot on Maui. Mākena Stables (page 185), at the end of the road near La Pérouse Bay, offers awesome rides across 'Ulupalakua ranchlands. You'll feel like you're exploring lands where no person has been since the Hawaiians lived here centuries ago.

- Explore Maui from the air on a heli-copter that will take you into deep valleys and over majestic mountains, then over the Pailolo Channel to the 3,000-foot cliffs of Moloka'i, the world's highest sea cliffs. Blue Hawaiian Helicopters (page 196) sets the standard, with knowledgeable and skilled pilots.

- Snorkel in the tidepools of 'Āhihi-Kīna'u Natural Area Reserve (pages 80, 82), on Maui's southern coast, or at Molokini (pages 169–70), a magnificent marine preserve and seabird sanctuary located 2.5 miles off the southern coast. Both are teeming with colorful fish.

maui *history, culture, geography*

"I went to Maui to stay a week and remained five. I never spent so pleasant a month before, or bade any place good-bye so regretfully. I have not once thought of business, or care or human toil or trouble or sorrow or weariness . . . and the memory of it will remain with me always." —MARK TWAIN, 1866

Maui stands out as a brilliant, spectacularly diverse jewel in the strand of beautiful islands that make up Hawai'i. From the towering grandeur of the volcano Haleakalā—still considered active though it's been over two hundred years since it erupted—to the sweeping beaches of Kā'anapali, Maui in all its variety truly fulfills the dreamer's fantasy of what an idyllic tropical paradise should be. It is here that the visitor may discover both the charming, sleepy village of Hāna and the fast-paced resort area of West Maui. Bustling Lahaina, the center of the whaling industry of yesteryear and today the capital of the whale-watching industry, reflects how Maui's rich past has evolved into a different, though no less fascinating, present.

Maui commands a significant place in Hawai'i's colorful and occasionally turbulent history. Here Hawaiian chiefs played out important events, waging fierce battles and vying for power over all the islands.

Included in Maui County are the islands of Moloka'i, Lāna'i, and Kaho'olawe, which lie off Maui's leeward coast. Until recently, the 45-square-mile Kaho'olawe was used by the military as a target for bombing practice. On May 8, 1994, in a historic ceremony at Palauea Beach near Mākena on Maui, ownership of the island was officially transferred by the U.S. Navy to the state of Hawai'i, specifically to people of native Hawaiian descent. Workers are now removing ordnance from enough of the island so that it might at least be visited. The eventual use of the island has yet to be determined, though many native Hawaiians are hopeful that it will become a place for a separate nation of Hawai'i to exist.

Page 10: *Men of the Sandwich Islands Dancing,* 1822, detail from a lithograph by Louis Choris (Russian, 1795–1828).

Page 11: A dancer performs hula *kahiko.*

Opposite: A replica of a Polynesian sailing canoe during the Celebration of Canoes, a festival held in Lahaina every May.

Maui History

MORE THAN TWO CENTURIES AGO, King Kahekili ruled all of Maui except for the Hāna area, which fell under the de facto control of Kalaniʻōpuʻu, a powerful ruler on the neighboring island of Hawaiʻi. In 1776 Kalaniʻōpuʻu's armies invaded Maui, but Kahekili's warriors annihilated them in a famous battle near Wailuku. Kahekili, justly famous as a mighty king in his own right, also may have been the father of Kamehameha, who was destined to unite all the islands in his kingdom.

On May 29, 1786, a French expedition led by Captain Jean-François de Galaup, comte de La Pérouse, anchored in a sheltered bay at Keoneʻōʻio, just south of Wailea and Mākena. The next day La Pérouse became the first non-Hawaiian to set foot on Maui. (Captain James Cook had seen Maui in 1778 but sailed by after failing to find anchorage.) Maui soon became a regular port of call.

The comte de la Pérouse, 1797

A view of Lahainaluna Seminary in the mid-19th century. The school, founded by missionaries in 1831, is today a public high school.

Four years after La Pérouse's arrival, Kamehameha's forces defeated the army of Kahekili, and Kamehameha, who became known as the Napoleon of the Pacific, brought Maui under his control. In 1793 Captain George Vancouver sailed into Lahaina and confirmed La Pérouse's earlier report of a fine anchorage. In less than a dozen years, Kamehameha's fleet of *peleleu* canoes—twin-hulled canoes with a covered platform, some of them rigged with a main sail and a jib—lingered on West Maui beaches before he sailed on to conquer Oʻahu. The first whaling vessel to reach the islands, the *Balaena* out of Massachusetts, stopped off in Lahaina in 1819, a harbinger of the vast fleets to come.

Of more lasting impact, Christians built their first mission in Lahaina in 1823, and the great conversion of Maui—and Hawaiʻi—gained impetus. At the same time, the standard of education on the island improved, attracting the children of the wealthy from other islands and even from the U.S. mainland.

The Hawaiian and Commercial Sugar Company plant in Puʻunēnē, early 20th century.

With the decline of whaling, George Wilfong started the first sugar plantation on Maui in 1849, in Hāna. A dozen years later, James Campbell built the first great sugar mill on the island, Pioneer Mill in Lahaina. By 1900 more than half the population on Maui was comprised of Chinese and Japanese citizens working the eleven sugar plantation fields. Through the efforts of such men as Harry P. Baldwin and Samuel Thomas Alexander, the sugar industry gained preeminence. Claus Spreckels had large holdings on Maui, and he built an enormous irrigation ditch that brought 50 million gallons of water a day from Haʻikū (in Upcountry) to the area of Puʻunēnē in the central valley so that sugar could flourish. Maui's center of focus shifted from Lahaina to Pāʻia, a sugar town with a nearby mill.

Not far away, near the governmental seat at Wailuku, the port of Kahului developed into the island's principal seaport; it also was headquarters for a prosperous railroad operation, with narrow-gauge passenger and freight trains underway between Wailuku–Kahului and Spreckelsville–Pāʻia.

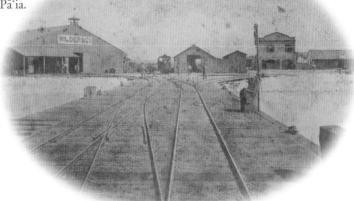

The Wailuku–Kahului railroad terminus at Kahului Landing, early 20th century.

A Sikorsky aircraft operated by Inter-Island Airways flies over Haleakalā, carrying U.S. Mail, ca. 1930. In the background are the slopes of Mauna Loa and Mauna Kea on the island of Hawai'i.

By 1930 transportation on Maui and between islands had improved considerably. There were some five thousand automobiles on Maui streets and roads. Inter-Island Airways landed its first Sikorsky aircraft on Maui in 1929 and began regular service from the airport at Māʻalaea in the central valley.

The Japanese attack on Pearl Harbor on December 7, 1941, shocked the residents of all the islands, Mauians included. Maui responded by contributing manpower to the war effort and bought more than its share of war bonds.

Postwar Maui took part in the gradual, then rapid, development of the islands, spurred by jet travel. With its stunning scenery, its splendid beaches and lush pastures, and perhaps the best climate of all the Hawaiian islands, Maui is the fastest growing of any of the islands. Its population more than doubled in the three decades between 1970 and 1990 and increased by nearly 28 percent in the last decade. It now stands at over 128,000. This is not counting the 40,000 tourists who are on Maui each day or the thousands of "snowbirds" who come for the winter season.

Cultural Background

IN ANONYMITY AND OUT OF ASIA, the ancestors of the Hawaiians began millennia ago to work their way across the vast, trackless Pacific. They journeyed from central Asia to Southeast Asia, poised on the brink of a great adventure: the people of the land were about to become the people of the sea and ultimately the people of "many islands," for that is what the word Polynesia means. As they moved, they changed, altering their gods to the demands of new places, subtly reworking their myths and legends and genealogies to make them compatible with the enormous seas and the evolution of their canoes. Their mode of dress changed; their physical statures altered as they adapted to life on, and in, the water.

At some point during these long and epic voyages, the Polynesians stood offshore in the lee of a group of islands at the apex of a triangle formed by New Zealand, Tahiti, and Hawai'i. Some anonymous Polynesian sailor, more than eleven centuries ago, shouted excitedly to the rest of the crew and pointed out islands that would mark the crowning achievement of the long voyages. That sailor and the rest of the crew are believed to have been from the Marquesas island group far to the southeast, though new theories as to the origins of the original settlers are still being put forth.

Dietrich Varez, *Wa'a Kaulua,* linocut. The *wa'a kaulua,* or double canoe, was capable of withstanding heavy seas. This type of canoe was used by Polynesians for long voyages of discovery and migration.

More voyages back and forth followed. One day, a new group of energetic islanders, the Polynesians from Tahiti, made the journey. In all likelihood they came to escape war or famine. Or perhaps it was merely the dominance of a strong, aggressive race that led to their voyage. Whatever the cause, by about A.D. 1100 the people from Tahiti had surfaced as the unquestioned masters in a magnificent new home. They gave it a name: Hawai'i. Later some would say the name had no significance, while others believed it was a variation of Hawaiki, the legendary homeland of all Polynesians.

Other newcomers had made landfall here over the centuries. Seeds came in the bellies of birds; coconuts washed ashore on the beaches and took hold. Windblown pollen and insects bumped up against the islands' high mountains. Natural springs and rivers formed.

The Polynesians added variety to the indigenous plants, introducing bananas, sweet potatoes, bamboo, ginger, yams, breadfruit, and *kukui* trees. They also brought dogs, chickens, and pigs to Hawai'i. In time, a new civilization developed as the settlers adapted to their new home.

The life of the average Hawaiian was ordered, and he was often powerless to change it. The *ali'i*, or royalty, were absolute masters. A second group, the *kāhuna*, or priests, cast a long shadow, dealing in both the natural and supernatural worlds. As *kāhuna*, the priests were known to talk with the gods and interpret their powers. The ordinary men and women were *maka'aīnana*, in many cases born to a time and place that locked them into a pattern from which they could not escape.

But it was not an altogether grim life. The *maka'aīnana* lived in a healthy, uncrowded, and stunningly beautiful archipelago where they arose to brilliant mornings and retired awash in sunsets of great beauty. They had their *makahiki*, a festival time following the fall harvest when they played traditional games, and they revered their old people, the *kūpuna*. They cared about the family unit and about their *'ohana*, or extended family. By the time Westerners arrived, Hawaiian society had become complex and colorful, yet infused with a strict sense of order.

The great English explorer and navigator Captain James Cook came upon these remote north Pacific islands on January 18, 1778. European diseases and Western weapons followed, dramatically changing the lives of the Hawaiians.

The islands impressed Cook, who was surprised to find that the inhabitants spoke a variation of the languages he had heard earlier in the South Pacific. He wrote of the natives' generosity and worried over their tendency to steal; he watched with both understanding and dismay as native girls, the *wāhine*, came aboard his two

Captain James Cook

ships. He knew such liaisons with his men were inevitable, but he also knew some of his sailors were infected with venereal disease.

Cook was killed by Hawaiians on the beach at Kealakekua, on the southernmost island, after a misunderstanding. Had he lived, he would have seen diseases decimate the Hawaiian population from an estimated 800,000 in 1778 to fewer than 40,000 a century later. And by 1878 other forces had diminished the influence of the Hawaiians in their own land.

In Kamehameha's lifetime, Hawaiian power reached its zenith. Tough and energetic, intelligent and implacable, Kamehameha had inherited as his personal god the war god Kūkāʻilimoku from his uncle, Kalaniʻōpuʻu, ranking chief at Kealakekua. He also inherited a tall frame and a tactician's approach to problem solving. When Kamehameha saw the superior firepower of European guns and the logic of European tactics in war, he immediately appropriated English advisors and set out to buy guns. He wanted to become the person who linked the islands, each under one or more chieftains, into a true kingdom with himself as its head. By craft and treachery, by bravery and a modicum of luck, Kamehameha fulfilled his dream. A series of bloody wars and a bit of diplomacy with the king of Kauaʻi brought all the islands under his rule.

Under Kamehameha, trade and interaction with the West were extensive. When he allowed, ships from abroad filled Hawaiian harbors. But he also was careful to maintain the old ways among his people. The *kapu* system that allowed the *aliʻi* to lay an edict over any person, place, or thing remained in effect at Kamehameha's death. If the Hawaiians did not fully understand the concept of nationhood, they certainly understood the power of authority. Kamehameha ruled as much by force of personality as by force of arms.

Upon his death on May 8, 1819, at the end of years of peace and stability, Kamehameha was buried in a secret place. It is a secret that endures. Today no one knows the burial site of the greatest of all Hawaiians.

Almost immediately Kamehameha's influence began to dissipate. A week after the king's death, his favorite wife, Kaʻahumanu, declared Kamehameha's son, Liholiho, the next ruler, adding, however, that she would rule with him. In time she pressured Liholiho into abandoning the *kapu* system and the old religion, and momentous changes inevitably followed.

Louis Choris, *Kamehameha in Red Vest*, 1816, watercolor. Honolulu Academy of Arts, gift of Edith B. Williams.

Below: Image of the war god Kūkāʻilimoku, known as Kū.

About the time Kamehameha died, word flashed around the maritime nations that there were enormous herds of whales in the Pacific. The news galvanized seamen, who knew the Atlantic grounds held fewer and fewer whales, and Hawai'i assumed a new importance. Within three years, up to sixty whaling ships at a time anchored in Honolulu Harbor alone, and the waters of Lahaina were dark with the timbers of ships. Sailors came to rely on Hawai'i's ports for women, grog, and provisions. There was, they said, "no God west of the Horn," and they seemed bent on proving it. Whaling became an important industry to Hawai'i; whaling men became a prime nuisance.

Whaling meant money. Goods were transshipped, ships were repaired, and the activity attracted nonwhaling merchant vessels as well. Whaling also brought bewilderment and confusion to the *maka'aīnana*, who saw the sailors indulging themselves without punishment. By now the Hawaiians had no strong system of their own to turn to for faith, and they were finding it difficult to make sense of their lives and times.

A second group of foreigners, or *haole*, brought more than a little confusion to the Hawaiians as well. The missionaries had arrived in 1819 with their stern visages and rigid life styles as well as their talk of Trinity and damnation. Between the whalers and the missionaries, battles raged over the land, bodies, and souls of the native Hawaiians.

In their way, the missionaries turned out to be as tough as the oak planking of the whaling ships. Arriving first on the brig *Thaddeus* on October 23, 1819, the missionaries found Hawaiian society in chaos following Kamehameha's death. They also found a dearth of new ideas and moved quickly to fill the vacuum. Liholiho came to be regarded as a friend. The missionaries converted Keōpūolani, the queen mother, then the powerful chiefess Kapi'olani. Within two years, the missionaries created a written form of Hawaiian, printed Bibles, and opened schools. They became a powerful force in the islands, and their descendants would become powerful leaders of Hawai'i society, business, and industry.

Hawai'i attracted more and more foreigners. Americans, Britons, French, Germans, and Scots traveled to Hawai'i, drawn to the image of a tropical paradise, held by the opportunities they found.

Liholiho, who became Kamehameha II

In the United States in 1859, an oil well went into production in Pennsylvania, signaling the end of the whaling industry, with whales no longer the only source of precious oil, for which they were slaughtered. War broke out between the Union and the Confederacy, and many whaling ships were pressed into service as merchantmen, decreasing markedly the whaling fleet. Finally, in the fall of 1871, ice trapped thirty-three whaling ships in Arctic waters north of the Bering Strait and remorselessly crushed the last hope of a whaling industry.

In Hawai'i, new industries flourished, one of them sugar. Planters needed cheap agricultural labor and had to look to foreign countries because diseases had vastly reduced the Hawaiian population. Plantation owners turned first to China, then Japan, then Portugal, the Philippines, and other places. This marked the beginning of Hawai'i as a multiethnic society.

Land ownership, which before Cook's arrival was reserved only for the *ali'i*, became an increasingly perplexing problem. The Hawaiian government ultimately gave up rights to all property except certain lands set aside for the king and the government. Commoners now were permitted to buy land, and foreigners could lease it. The *haole*, having come from civilizations that prized land ownership, reached for as much as they could get. The average Hawaiian, at sea with all the attendant bureaucracy, just got more confused. On the one hand, he could lease or cultivate his land, rights he never before possessed, while on the other hand, it became easy to sell land to the *haole*. The Great Mahele, the movement that began in the 1840s with attempts to tie the Hawaiians closer to their land by reapportioning it among various groups, ended in them losing it in great quantities.

Immigrant laborers harvesting sugarcane and loading it onto a waiting train at the Spreckelsville plantation, ca. 1900.

In the 1890s conflicts grew between Queen Lili'uokalani, destined to be the last Hawaiian monarch, and a group of businessmen who objected to the queen's push for a new constitution that would have restored much of the Hawaiian royalty's lost powers. On January 17, 1893, the monarchy was toppled, and the Republic of Hawai'i was formed with a new constitution.

Five years later, on August 12, 1898, spectators jammed the area around 'Iolani Palace in Honolulu to hear the Hawaiian national anthem played and watch the Hawaiian flag slowly lowered to the ground and the American flag raised in its place. America's national anthem was played, and Sanford Ballard Dole, a leader in the monarchy's overthrow, was sworn in as first chief executive officer of the Territory of Hawai'i, a possession of the United States.

Stability and social change followed. A society emerged in which racial groups were proud of their ancestry but also proud of their Americanization. It seemed there was a little Hawaiian blood in almost everyone. For more than four decades, the largely agricultural society went about its business, attracted a few visitors, and never dreamed it would be the target of a sudden attack that became the impetus for the United States to enter World War II.

On Sunday, December 7, 1941, Japanese aircraft swarmed in from a fleet that had crept unseen and unheard across the Pacific to a point north of the islands. The devastating raid on Pearl Harbor plunged America into the war and brought quick changes to Hawai'i. Martial law was declared, a military government was installed in 'Iolani Palace, and thousands of young servicemen turned up in the islands. Some never left. The number of intermarriages soared. By the end of the war, the whole fabric of Hawai'i society had changed with the interweaving of the new *haole* immigrants. The end of the war also saw the return of the young *nisei*— the second-generation Japanese—who had fought bravely for their new country and who now thirsted for political power. They were determined to put an end to the long rule of the entrenched Republican establishment of the day.

With their GI Bill for education, the veterans went off to colleges and came back as lawyers, doctors, accountants, and other professionals. They were politically oriented and hard working, and their enthusiasm inspired other young men in Hawai'i equally fired by ambition. In 1954, in a thunderous victory, the Democrats, led by the veterans, took over the top political positions in Hawai'i and forced a new equality on the establishment.

In another five years statehood marked the beginning of still another era of change. Statehood meant stability for investments. The advent of the jet plane, a surge in the influx of tourists, and international publicity about America's newest state turned Hawai'i into a magnet for those seeking a new life in a paradisiacal setting. Tourism edged out agriculture as the primary source of revenue, which it remains to this day. Nearly 7 million visitors are drawn to Hawai'i's islands each year, spending over $10 billion a year. About a quarter of the local labor force has jobs in the visitor industry; by contrast, agriculture—which once dominated Hawai'i's economy—today claims only 2 percent of the total workforce.

Geography

FAIRLY RECENTLY IN THE HISTORY OF THE EARTH (only 25 million years ago), a series of cracks began to open in the ocean floor of the north Pacific. In tumultuous explosions followed by fiery rivers of magma and molten lava, land began to build up underneath the surface of the sea. In time, the land broke the surface and lay barren and exposed to winds and the pounding sea. The rise and fall of ice caps thousands of miles away helped raise or lower the level of the sea. Still the land remained, buffeted by winds, clawed by seas that broke over the exposed shoreline. Then there was a time of quiet.

In a thundering end to the silence, lava explosions began again. Lava flows tumbled and rolled down the sides of mountains and, in astonishing pyrotechnics, more land was born. As the land increased, so did its diversity, as wind and waves continued to carve coves and valleys. Algae and coral polyps began to build reefs around the land. With the seeding of the land by birds, drifting coconuts, and other material, the land began to turn green.

Maui is the second largest island in Hawai'i, which consists of a string of islands in the north Pacific about a thousand miles from its nearest neighbors— the Line Islands at the equator to the south and the Marshall Islands to the southwest. Nothing but ocean lies between Hawai'i and California, 2,390 miles to the east-northeast; Japan, 3,850 miles to the west-northwest; and Alaska, 2,800 miles to the north. The Marquesas—from which at least some of the early Polynesian migrants came—are 2,400 miles to the south-southeast.

When the Polynesians arrived in the Hawaiian islands, they brought their own versions of how the land came to be. In one account, a mischievous Polynesian demigod named Māui fished the land up from the bottom of the ocean. A myth common to much of Polynesia holds that the islands were the children of the gods Papa and Wākea, earth mother and sky father.

Dietrich Varez, *Māui the Fisherman,* linocut. With a hook made from a jawbone he had obtained in the underworld, baited with a sacred *'alae* bird, Māui hooked the great fish Kaunihokahi . . . and pulled up all the islands from the bed of the ocean.

The Hawaiian archipelago spans 1,523 miles and includes 132 islands, reefs, and shoals strewn across the Tropic of Cancer—from Kure Atoll in the north to Nīhoa in the south. Many of the northwestern islands are uncharted, and reefs can rip out the bottoms of unsuspecting ships. The 84 million underwater acres of the northwestern islands are the largest nature preserve in the U.S., with fishing and other activities limited to help conserve the area's coral reefs and wildlife.

A new island, Loʻihi—which means "prolonged in time"—is being created by volcanic eruptions southeast of Hawaiʻi island; visitors ten thousand or so years from now are likely to find that island. All the islands are included in the state of Hawaiʻi except the Midway Islands, which are administered by the U.S. Fish and Wildlife Service. Hawaiʻi's major islands share their tropical latitudes with such urban centers as Mexico City, Havana, Mecca, Calcutta, Hanoi, and Hong Kong.

While Hawaiʻi's land surface adds up to only 6,425 square miles (at that, still larger than Connecticut, Delaware, or Rhode Island), the archipelago, including its territorial waters, covers a total of about 654,500 square miles—an area considerably larger than Alaska and more than twice the size of Texas.

Maui is one of eight main islands in the Hawaiian chain. One of the islands, Kahoʻolawe, is not inhabited. The tiny island of Niʻihau is privately owned and can be visited by nonresidents only by invitation. Niʻihau, owing to its fierce protection from outside influence, is the last stronghold of Hawaiian culture (its entire population is of at least part-Hawaiian blood), and it is the only place on earth where Hawaiian is still spoken as the mother tongue.

That leaves the islands of Kauaʻi, Oʻahu, Molokaʻi, Lānaʻi, Maui, and Hawaiʻi (commonly known as the Big Island)—in that order, northwest to southeast and chronologically in age—for visitors to explore.

Maui once was two islands, each with a volcanic peak soaring above the surface of the sea like tips of icebergs. Scientists believe that the first eruptions were between 120,000 and 145,000 years ago. Over eons, erosion wore down the flanks of the volcanoes until they connected in an isthmus, which today is referred to as the central valley. Maui's commercial centers of Kahului and Wailuku are here. Other distinct regions are West Maui, where the old whaling port of Lahaina is found; Kapalua, a sleepy tropical area at the far west of the island; the sunny and dry areas of Kīhei, Wailea, and Mākena along the southern coast; the Upcountry area, a place of lush pastures and cattle ranches on the slopes of Haleakalā; and, at the extreme east end, the lush, lovely Hāna.

maui *at a glance*

Maui is considered by many to be the best island in the world. It's not hard to see why. There are miles of pristine beaches, the largest dormant volcano anywhere, hiking trails to challenge even the most experienced outdoors person, lush valleys, and cool, green pastureland. And, there are nightclubs, world-class golf courses, luxury hotels, superb restaurants, art galleries, and plenty of opportunities for shopping. Each year 2.3 million visitors come to this idyllic island.

Wherever you stay, unless it's Hāna, you'll be able to visit any part of the island on a day trip. West Maui, from Lahaina to Kapalua (including Kāʻanapali), is the most popular area, followed by the older beach town of Kīhei and the manicured resorts at Wailea and Mākena, along the sunny leeward coast. There are few places to stay other than B&Bs and vacation rentals in the area called Upcountry, on the slopes of Haleakalā—not the beachgoer's favorite destination unless you want to surf or windsurf on the north shore. Hāna, isolated on Maui's eastern coast by a 2.5-hour drive along a narrow, winding road, is a tropical paradise.

Here is a summary of the various areas to help you decide where to visit:

The island of Moloka'i looms across the Pailolo Channel from Nāpili Bay in West Maui.

Kāʻanapali. Ten minutes from Lahaina, Kāʻanapali was the first planned resort destination in Hawaiʻi. Included are six beachfront hotels, numerous condos, two golf courses, a deluxe restaurant/shopping complex, and 3 miles of spectacular white sand beach. The historic old whaling town of Lahaina offers affordable accommodations amid the bustle of a lively community.

Kapalua. Farther up the northwest coast is the planned golf resort community of Kapalua, with two premier hotels on the edge of gorgeous beaches. The resorts offer luxurious amenities amid beautiful surroundings carved and hacked out of lava and scrub brush. Between here and Kāʻanapali are numerous condominiums of varying price ranges in the towns of Nāpili, Kahana, and Honokōwai, providing a beachgoer's haven.

Kīhei/Wailea/Mākena. Wailea Resort, on the sun-drenched southern gold coast, has six luxury hotels, three championship golf courses, and a variety of low-rise condo units. The newly opened Shops at Wailea provides upscale shopping and fine dining. Condominiums, located either on the beach or close by, abound along this coast. Farther south, the beautiful beaches of Mākena contribute to Maui's idyllic reputation.

Hāna. This area on the far eastern tip of Maui is one of the most enchanting places in the world. When you arrive in heavenly Hāna, you'll feel as if you've reached the end of the earth. Here you can experience old Hawai'i at its unspoiled best. There's not much to do but relax and enjoy the most isolated, most tropical, most friendly community on Maui. Although accommodations are somewhat limited, advance planning can get you a deluxe hotel room at the luxurious Hotel Hāna-Maui, a condominium, a private cottage, a bed and breakfast lodging, or even a rustic cabin.

Upcountry. On the slopes of Haleakalā, nights are cool and mornings crisp, and outstanding views abound. Here you'll smell the sweet fragrance of eucalyptus trees or catch whiffs of smoke from fireplaces on winter mornings. If you don't mind being located away from the ocean, this is an ideal vacation spot for hiking, horseback riding, visiting art galleries, and fine dining.

Central valley. The Kahului-Wailuku area has few beaches, but it does provide history and character for the visitor who prefers to be out of the tourist mainstream and in the heart of an unfamiliar place. Wailuku is the capital of the island, the seat of government, and a charming old town that is taking its restoration seriously. It is home to a number of historic sites as well as the intriguing 'Iao Valley Park and 'Iao Needle.

Telephone

MAUI'S AREA CODE IS 808, as for the rest of Hawai'i. However, when calling from another island, it is necessary to dial the area code along with the number. Toll-free numbers have the area code 800 or 888. For emergency calls, dial 911. Public coin telephones require 25¢ for local calls (except for emergency calls to 911, which are free).

Climate *and* Weather

CURRENT MAUI WEATHER CONDITIONS are available by calling 877-5111. For a recreational forecast from the National Weather Service, call 871-5054. Also, Maui weather is available on the Worldwide Web: **www.hawaiiweathertoday.com/mwt**.

Maui's pleasant climate doesn't change much throughout the year—at sea level. The temperature ranges between a daytime high near 90°F (about 30°C) in "summer" and a nighttime low near 60°F (about 18°C) in "winter." There are no distinct seasons

According to an ancient legend, the clever demigod Māui wanted days to be longer so the fishermen would have more time to fish, the farmers more time to care for their crops, and his mother more time to dry her *kapa*. So from the summit of Haleakalā he lassoed the sun's rays as it passed over the giant volcano and caused the sun to slow down. (Some stories say that he used a huge net—he was a fisherman of renown—and caught the sun as it streaked overhead.) Because the sun was very angry at being slowed, Māui relented and allowed the sun to go at its regular pace for half the year and at a more leisurely pace for the other half. Thus the long days of summer permit extra time for work, while the shorter winter days allow long nights for talking and watching the stars.

as such. Even in winter the daytime temperature is usually in the 80s. The comfort factor that this involves depends on what you're used to. Residents start to shiver and bundle up when the mercury plummets to 75°F (24°C). The coldest months are February and March and the hottest August and September.

Despite this lack of strong seasonal variation, Hawai'i is home to an extraordinary diversity of microclimates—from desert to rainforest. The temperature drops about 3°F for every thousand feet of increased altitude, a factor that sometimes produces seasonal snow on the upper slopes of Haleakalā and the Big Island's Mauna Kea.

Rainfall varies dramatically in different parts of each island. All the lush tropical foliage requires a lot of rain, yet drought is not unheard of—there was a prolonged period of drought in the late 1990s. The state's heaviest rains are brought by storms between October and April. Fortunately, most local rain showers are short, except in the upper reaches of valleys where the rain clouds never leave for long. The windward areas get far more rain than their leeward counterparts.

There have been only a few damaging storms in Hawai'i, the most devastating in recent years being Hurricane 'Iniki ("strong wind"), in September 1992. 'Iniki hit the island of Kaua'i dead on with winds measuring up to 175 m.p.h. and left behind a path of destruction and property loss estimated at one billion dollars. Hurricane Iwa in 1982 brought gusts of 100 m.p.h. to the islands.

A *kalo* field in Kahaku-loa Valley, a remote area of western Maui. *Kalo* (taro) was once the staple starch food of Hawaiians and is still cultivated in areas where the old ways hold strong.

While most natural disaster–type events such as hurricanes and tsunamis and even volcanic flows are usually predicted well in advance, the one natural event that is unpredictable is a tsunami caused by an earthquake in the immediate area. If you happen to be near the coast and you feel the earth start to shake, leave immediately for higher ground. This means run, and don't stop for anything. Such disasters are rare—just one or two in a century—but they can happen.

Time *and* Daylight

BECAUSE OF HAWAI'I'S TROPICAL LOCATION, the length of daylight doesn't vary greatly from one time of year to the next, and so Hawai'i has never felt a need to save daylight time. Hawai'i Standard Time is in effect year round. In June, with the longest days, the sun rises about 5:45 A.M. and sets about 7 P.M. In the shorter days of December, sunrise is about 7 A.M. and sunset about 5:45 P.M.

Hawai'i Standard Time is 5 hours behind New York, 4 hours behind Chicago, 3 hours behind Denver, and 2 hours behind San Francisco. It is also 11 hours behind London, 19 hours behind Tokyo, 20 hours behind Sydney, and 22 hours behind Auckland and Suva. Add an hour to all of these when daylight savings time is in effect elsewhere.

For the current time on Maui, call (808) 242-0212.

Plant *and* Animal Life

ABUNDANT, HIGH-QUALITY WATER AND CLEAN AIR bless this environmental wonderland. Plant life in Hawai'i also is a naturalist's dream. More than 2,500 kinds of plants grow only in Hawai'i. Because of Hawai'i's long isolation, evolution of plant life was rapid and diverse. Conversely, many plants that are found throughout the Pacific were not present in Hawai'i until man brought them—such as the banyan, *kalo,* and figs. Most of the myriad orchids that grace Hawai'i today came from other places. Of the many varieties found here, there is only one native palm tree.

Because Hawai'i is so far from other land, very few animals arrived under their own power. The hoary bat *(Lasiurus)* is an exception. The Hawaiian bat is smaller than its distant relatives but strong enough to fly long distances. The Hawaiian monk seal *(Monachus schauinslandi),* a species related to seals in the Caribbean and the

A Hawaiian monk seal, an endangered species, rests on Kaihalulu Beach in Hāna. Known by locals as Red Sand Beach, it is the only red sand beach in Hawai'i.

Mediterranean, also arrived from afar. It may have been the first mammal to live in Hawai'i and today is found nowhere else. The Polynesian rat *(Rattus)* stowed away aboard Polynesian voyaging canoes and, like the Polynesians themselves, originated in Asia. The Polynesians valued the domestic dog *(Canis)* as pet, food source, and a part of religious rituals. By all accounts, the Polynesian dog was highly dependent and non-aggressive; as new breeds of dogs came to the islands, the original version disappeared.

The importation of pigs *(Sus scrofa)* to the islands turned out to be a mixed blessing. They were an important food source, but when they began to run wild in the lush forests, they became a nuisance. Today feral pigs are blamed for destroying much of the islands' watershed areas by digging up the forest floor and the aquifer, the natural filter through which a lot of island water flows.

Captain Cook released goats in Hawai'i, and others who came after him brought sheep, cattle, and horses. These large animals were extremely destructive to Hawaiian plants. By 1900 many native plants below roughly the 1,200-foot level had been eradicated, some replaced by heartier species. Today these large animals are considered an asset, not a menace.

Hawai'i's isolation also gave rise to a unique bird life. Today, however, more than half the native birds have become extinct in Hawai'i. They have succumbed to hunters, to introduced predators such as the swift mongooses brought to Hawai'i to combat rats, and to urban encroachment.

Many birds live near streams, marshes, or ponds; the largest number inhabit the deep forests. Perhaps the most dramatic to watch are the long-winged seabirds. Twenty-two different species spend their nonbreeding time flying over the open ocean, scavenging for food and resting on the water, coming back to Hawai'i to breed. Millions of them nest in the sanctuary of uninhabited small islands northwest of the occupied islands of Hawai'i. Some birds that were introduced to the islands from elsewhere and thrive here include pigeons, doves, mynahs, cardinals, and sparrows.

The state bird is the *nēnē (Branta sandvicensis),* a goose that lives high on the rugged slopes of the volcanoes. The *nēnē* has battled back from near extinction. Many of Hawai'i's native birds are found only on specific islands; the *'io,* or hawk *(Buteo solitarius),* for example, is found only on the island of Hawai'i.

Long before any land mammals came, before plants or even birds, marine mammals swam in the surrounding seas. In fact, the ancestors of some of the whales and dolphins now found in Hawaiian waters may have been here even before the islands arose from the sea. They include the humpback whales, which are seasonal visitors, several varieties of dolphins, killer whales, sperm whales—in all, at least twenty types. Today the most popular marine mammal is the humpback whale, important enough to Maui to deserve singling out (see below).

The *nēnē* is the Hawai'i state bird.

Other marine life became important to the Hawaiians not only for food but in rituals, legends, myths, and *mele* (chants). Hawaiian fishermen had their own god, Ku'ulakai, and small fishing shrines *(ko'a)* near the ocean were dedicated to the god. The shrines often were no more than stacked rocks, but they were significant to the fishermen, who offered the first of their catch at the *ko'a.* A fish—particularly a shark—that frequented the waters near their homes was often considered an *'aumakua,* or family god, by the Hawaiians.

Each wave of newcomers brought its own fishing mystique, taste, and style. Today the fishing practices of Hawai'i's people reflect the state's multiracial populace and preserve the islands' reputation as a top marine center.

Whales

EACH YEAR, ABOUT TWO-THIRDS OF THE HUMPBACK WHALES of the northern Pacific come to Maui seeking waters that are about 75°F (24°C) and the shelter of the leeward shores and quiet bays. They come down from the Arctic to breed, generally in late November, covering some 2,800 miles in an estimated eighty to one hundred days. While in Hawaiian waters they fast.

In early May they return to the cool northern waters near Alaska, where fish are plentiful.

They do not arrive in herds but flow in and out of the breeding grounds individually (or in small groups) through the winter months, some staying as late as July. The newly pregnant females leave first for northern waters, followed by younger whales and then the more mature of both sexes.

Intelligence, size, gentleness—all have endeared the humpback whales to the people of Maui, who have been in the forefront of efforts to protect the whales. Not until recently did man pay much attention to the whales' sensitivity and intelligence. They have a communications system that produces sounds of haunting beauty—and specific intent. Whales also have a highly developed sense of direction and good eyesight, both above and below the water (they are known to surface to look at passing ships).

Humpback whales ply Maui's waters from November through May. When they breach, or leap out of the water, their distinctive tail flukes can be seen.

Calves are not only conceived in Hawaiian waters; many are born here. To discourage predators, mother whales give birth in relatively shallow waters of about 150 feet. They produce up to 130 gallons of milk a day for their offspring.

The whales' annual journey here allows the visitor to Maui a unique opportunity to see these massive ocean creatures at fairly close range—an experience possible in relatively few other places in the world.

For more on the humpback whale and whale watching, see pages 179–80.

The State Flag *and* **Anthem**

THE HAWAIʻI STATE FLAG has
served kingdom, republic, and
state. It was designed sometime
prior to 1816 for King Kamehameha I, who had been presented
with a British Union Jack in 1794
by Captain Vancouver. It is said
that Kamehameha combined the
Union Jack, found in the upper-
left quadrant of Hawaiʻi's flag, with
the stripes of the United States flag
so that pirates at sea might mistake

Hawaiian ships for either British or American and allow them to pass without inci-
dent. The eight horizontal stripes represent the archipelago's eight main islands.

The Hawaiʻi state flag
flies with the flag of
the United States.

Hawaiʻi's state anthem, "Hawaiʻi Ponoʻī," is its former national anthem and was
composed by King David Kalākaua, a gifted musician who reigned from 1874 to 1891.

Language

ENGLISH BECAME THE COMMON LANGUAGE of Hawaiian commerce very early in
the era of immigration and economic investment by Americans and other foreigners.
And so it has remained. The missionaries made sweeping and now irreversible
changes in the Hawaiian language when they hurriedly transliterated and transcribed
it for print in order to produce Bibles. Subsequent efforts to suppress the native
tongue were very successful. By the second half of the 20th century, only a few
hundred native speakers were left, most of whom were either very old or from
Niʻihau. However, a strong grass-roots movement to save the language has taken
hold, and a few schools even offer Hawaiian-language immersion programs.

Virtually everyone in the islands today speaks the American variety of English,
with a few local variations on the theme. Perhaps the most important variation for
tourists is the local way of giving directions. The cardinal points of the compass on

an island are far less relevant than the obvious "toward the mountain" and "toward the sea." A contracted form of the Hawaiian words for these directions is universally used in Hawai'i. "Toward the upland *(uka)*" is *mauka*; "toward the sea *(kai)*" is *makai*. For the other directions, major landmarks are used.

Some people have difficulty with Hawaiian place names and street names. The Hawaiian language is beautiful and only looks intimidating to non-Polynesians who are not accustomed to seeing so many vowels in a row. Basically, if you just pronounce all the letters individually, you'll be fine. The glottal stop (written ') is a pause created by stopping between vowel sounds; for example, a double "o" is pronounced like "oh-oh" in English. In Hawaiian, this is called an *'okina*. Just stop talking, then start immediately again. The macron (written as a long mark over a vowel), called a *kahakō* in Hawaiian, simply means that the vowel is held a little longer. The meaning of many words varies according to the presence or absence of a *kahakō*.

Consonants are pronounced the same as in English except that "w" sounds like "v" when it immediately precedes a final single vowel and occasionally at other times. Vowels are pronounced as in Spanish or Italian (ah, eh, ee, oh, oo). The vowel combinations—ai, ae, ao, au, ei, eu, oi, and ou—are stressed on the first member and sounded as single units, though the second vowel in the set is truly pronounced and not lost in the combination.

Multisyllabic words are almost always accented or stressed on the next-to-last syllable. No matter how many times you hear it differently along the tourist trail, the very special and wonderfully soft Hawaiian word "aloha" is not correctly pronounced with the accent on the last syllable.

You will often see Hawaiian words written without the *kahakō* or *'okina*. This was the custom of English-speaking people who first transcribed the language and was common practice until fairly recently. The markings are necessary for correct pronunciation of many words and for discerning between similarly spelled words with quite different meanings.

The other feature of local language that visitors are bound to encounter is Hawai'i's own brand of pidgin English. It is spiced with words from the rich linguistic heritage brought by people of many lands, but, basically, it is English with a bit of Hawaiian, and, if you listen carefully, you'll catch on. The idiom and the lilt are peculiar to Hawai'i, but the pronunciation of most words is recognizable.

A list of commonly used Hawaiian and pidgin English words along with their meanings is in the glossary at the end of this book.

Opposite:
H. P. Baldwin Park, Pā'ia, is a favorite among locals as well as tourists.

exploring *maui*

HAWAII VISITORS BUREAU MARKER

Crashing waves batter the rocky coast at isolated Ke'anae Peninsula, halfway between Pā'ia and Hāna.

*V*isitors could hurry around this lovely island in a day or two, but that would be a waste, and most of their time would be spent driving in the car. There is simply too much to see on Maui to rush. Like the other islands, Maui enjoys not only great scenic beauty but a colorful history as well. Sights you will want to see often combine beauty and a sense of the past, evoking a more gracious time.

As you travel, watch for the warrior signs put up by the Hawai'i Visitors Bureau to mark historic and cultural sites (above). Presumably, the signs were designed to point toward the attraction, but many have ended up pointing in the opposite direction.

Maui residents advise that the best way to see the island is to divide one's time among its distinct parts. For example, it's possible in a daylong tour to see the summit of Haleakalā, explore Kula and the Upcountry cowboy town of Makawao, and visit the sprawling 'Ulupalakua Ranch. Or one could see most of the Kapalua area in a day, while allowing for a leisurely lunch and perhaps some beach time. But this requires planning, and to that end we have divided this section into sightseeing districts comparable to the various regions of Maui: Lahaina/Kā'anapali/Kapalua; Mā'alaea/Kīhei/Wailea; Upcountry/Pā'ia; Hāna; and Kahului/Wailuku.

Included in addition to sightseeing aspects of each area are hikes that will take you beyond the beaten path and museums where you will learn more about Hawai'i's unique culture. We tell you about exceptional shopping opportunities, but we'll leave it to you, and your hotel concierge, to find your way to the Gap and Banana Republic. Check out the places mentioned here if you want something different. Maui is a mecca for craftspeople and artists, and prices are often quite affordable.

For in-depth descriptions of Maui's beaches, see pages 141–63.

Maui Facts and Figures

- *With a land area of 729 square miles, Maui is the second largest of the Hawaiian islands. It is 48 miles long and 26 miles across its widest point.*

- *The population of Maui County according to the 2000 census is 128,094.*

- *The largest dormant volcano in the world is Haleakalā on Maui.*

- *Haleakalā is large enough to hold the entire island of Manhattan in the crater at its summit.*

- *Tourism is Maui's major industry.*

- *The average daytime temperature on Maui is between 75°F and 85°F.*

- *With 120 miles of shoreline, Maui has more swimmable beaches than any other of the Hawaiian islands.*

- *About 1,500 whales winter in Maui's waters each year.*

0 Miles	4 Miles	8 Miles

0 Km	3 Km	6 Km

the island of **maui**

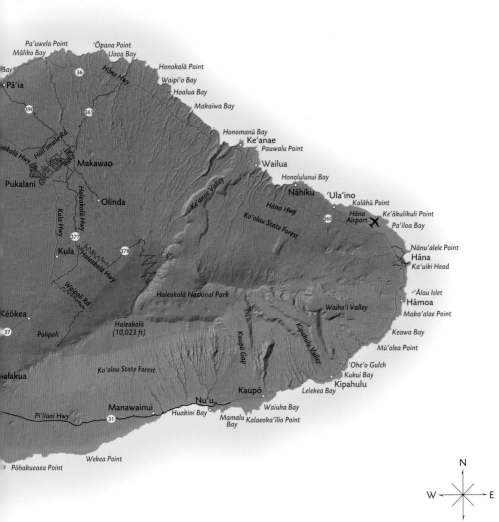

Pa'uwela Point
Māliko Bay
'Ōpana Point
Uaoa Bay
Bay
Honokalā Point
Hāna Hwy
Waipi'o Bay
Pā'ia
Hoalua Bay
Makaīwa Bay
Honomanū Bay
Ke'anae
Makawao
Pauwalu Point
Wailua
Pukalani
Honolulunui Bay
Nāhiku
'Ula'ino
Olinda
Kalāhū Point
Hāna Hwy
Hāna
Ke'ākulikuli Point
Airport
Ko'olau State Forest
Pa'iloa Bay
Kula
Nānu'alele Point
Hāna
Ka'uiki Head
'Ālau Islet
Hāmoa
Haleakalā National Park
Waiho'i Valley
Maka'alae Point
Kēōkea
Haleakalā
(10,023 ft)
Keawa Bay
Polipoli
Mū'olea Point
Ko'olau State Forest
'Ohe'o Gulch
alakua
Kukui Bay
Kipahulu
Kaupō
Lelekea Bay
Nu'u
Manawainui
Waiuha Bay
Pi'ilani Hwy
Huakini Bay
Mamalu
Kalaeoka'ilio Point
Bay
Wekea Point
Pōhakueaea Point

N
W   E
S

Lahaina/Kā'anapali/ Kapalua *area*

the **Lahaina** coast

ABOUT 25 MILES FROM KAHULUI AIRPORT or a short 6 miles from the commuter airport of Kapalua–West Maui, the area of Lahaina and Kā'anapali thrives as a resort region with heavy overtones of its colorful past. In many ways, this is Maui's heart. The great Kamehameha made this his seat of government after the conquest of Maui in a famous battle near 'Īao Needle, on the other side of the mountains. The missionaries settled here in the mid-1800s, launching their efforts to convert the Hawaiians to Christianity. Lahaina also was the magnet for whalers, with hundreds of ships anchoring off its shore when whaling was at its peak.

View of Part of Lahaina in Maui, engraving from a drawing made in 1825 by Robert Dampier (English, 1800–1874).

to Kā'anapali

Pu'unoa Point

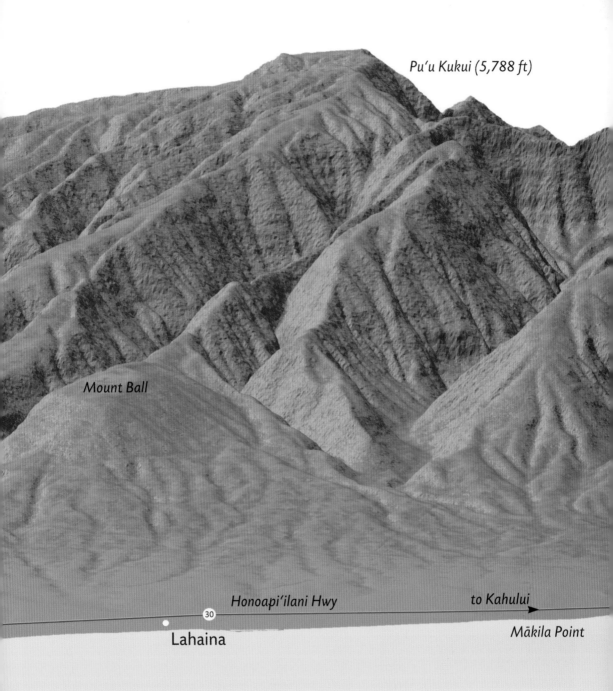

Pu'u Kukui (5,788 ft)

Mount Ball

Honoapi'ilani Hwy

to Kahului

30

Lahaina

Mākila Point

Kamehameha III was a resident of the area when he proclaimed new laws and Maui's first official constitution. A great Hawaiian intellectual, David Malo, studied and worked in Lahaina and is buried in the hills above the town. Lahaina's magnificent views of other islands, its beaches, and its fine climate (although its name means "merciless sun" in Hawaiian) have long attracted visitors. Today tourism is the lifeblood of the region.

Approaching Lahaina on Highway 30 from Kahului is a fine way to get into the mood of the area; the drive goes around a lava coastline and affords views of the islands of Kaho'olawe and Lāna'i, the islet of Molokini, and, in the distance, the island of Moloka'i.

There are several scenic points, and during the whale-watching season, from late November to May, these areas are crowded with cars.

Here also are small roadside parks with good ocean views: **Pāpalaua**, **Ukumehame**, **Launiupoko**, and **Puamana**. They offer a chance to stop, stretch, feel the sun, and enjoy the view. The road winds past **Olowalu**, a community of a few homes, a general store, and an excellent French restaurant, Chez Paul (see Dining).

From Olowalu to Lahaina, the road continues to curve between the sea and old sugarcane fields and finally leads on into the town itself. Some longtime residents look on Lahaina as a classic example of survival: the town has gone from

Friday night is Art Night in Lahaina (see page 57).

Olowalu is the site of a famous massacre. At the end of January 1790, the American merchantship *Eleanora* sailed to Maui's leeward coast, looking for fresh water and hoping to trade goods with the natives. One night while the *Eleanora* was anchored offshore of the village of Honua'ula, a group of Hawaiians crept aboard, killed a seaman, then stole a small cutter that had been tied astern of the ship. The next day the ship's captain, Simon Metcalf, killed several Hawaiians and set fire to the huts and *heiau* of Honua'ula before sailing farther down the coast to Olowalu. There Metcalf encouraged Hawaiian trading canoes to come out to the *Eleanora,* but once there he ordered the ship's guns and canons to fire on the canoes. More than one hundred Hawaiians died in the cannonade and more than two hundred were wounded, leaving the sea red with blood. The Olowalu massacre became known as "the day of spilled brains."

fishing village to whaling capital of the Pacific, then to supplier of goods and staples to the sugar plantations, and finally to the hub of Maui visitor activities that it is today.

Lahaina

Some of the old flavor remains in Lahaina—the narrow streets, the buildings hunched against each other, and of course the smell of the sea and the view across the harbor to other islands. The number of visitors walking the streets today at least rivals the crowds of a century ago when Hawaiians, whalers, missionaries, and beachcombers all gathered at Lahaina. Lahaina itself is a National Historic Landmark and also is protected as a Maui County Historic District. The **Lahaina Restoration Foundation** (662-0560), housed in the 1834 Masters' Reading Room at 120 Dickenson Street, is dedicated to the restoration of old buildings and landmarks.

The town is full of tourists and tee-shirt shops. Many Maui residents never go to Front Street, Lahaina's bustling main drag. However, this colorful town has a lot to offer, from fine restaurants (see Dining) to interesting historical sites. Hawai'i's royalty, or *ali'i*, once lived on this land, including Kamehameha the

Lahaina Harbor with the West Maui Mountains in the distance.

Front Street, Lahaina.

Opposite: The Sugar Cane Train (see page 197) chugs between Lahaina and Kāʻanapali, delighting visiting youngsters. Once steam locomotives on this line transported Pioneer Mill workers to the fields and hauled sugarcane to the mill for processing.

Great, who built the first brick house in Lahaina for his royal residence. During his reign (1790–1819), Kamehameha developed the prosperous sandalwood trade with China, harvesting the fragrant wood in the West Maui Mountains and shipping it out of Lahaina. The first American whaling ships came to Lahaina in 1819, followed a year later by the missionaries. By the middle of the century, Lahaina was a bustling, rowdy seaport, the center of the whaling trade in Hawaiʻi, indeed in the Pacific. In 1846, 395 whaling ships put into its harbor. A number of factors led to the decline of

the whaling industry, including over-zealous hunting of whales, and by 1869, when the transcontinental railway was completed, the port of San Francisco displaced Lahaina as the stopping off place for the few remaining whaling ships. The population of Lahaina declined drastically, though the town continued as an agricultural center, with the large Pioneer Mill on Lahainaluna Road dominating the landscape. The mill closed in 1999 after 139 years of sugar production. Today, as a mecca for tourists, Lahaina's streets are lined with art galleries and souvenir shops.

Parking in Lahaina

It can be difficult to find a parking spot in Lahaina unless you arrive early in the morning, but even then most free spaces have a 2-hour maximum. There are a number of conveniently located parking lots just one or two blocks off Front Street, with hourly rates. For those who don't mind walking a few blocks, a public lot is available free of charge (3 hours maximum), situated at the far south end of Front Street, between the banyan tree and 505 Front Street. Lahaina Center offers paid parking, which is free for 4 hours with validation of a purchase from one of their stores, restaurants, or movie theaters. Lahaina Shopping Center has free parking, but empty parking spaces are often elusive.

Historic Sites in Lahaina

The Lahaina Restoration Foundation has published a walking tour of the town. Brochures can be picked up at the **Visitors Center** in the old Courthouse, across from Lahaina Harbor, behind the great banyan tree on Front Street (next to Pioneer Inn). However, many of the places on the tour are either not open to the public or are unrestored sites of historic importance but offering little to see. If your time is limited, we suggest limiting your tour to the following places (note that it would be difficult to literally walk this entire tour; several of the sites are quite far from the town center):

Not merely a cultural event put on for the entertainment of visitors, the festival called In Celebration of Canoes, held every May in Lahaina, brings together indigenous peoples from throughout Polynesia. Master carvers create canoes using traditional methods and tools, then array them under the banyan tree for all to admire. Ancient rituals are reenacted, and there's a parade of flower-bedecked canoes down Front Street. In the Ben Abiera Memorial Race, outriggers contest with one another from the Kāʻanapali Beach Hotel, sponsor of the race, to Lahaina.

The Courthouse, 648 Wharf Street (#10 on walking tour). Built in 1859 of coral rock from a previous courthouse destroyed by a gale the year before, this building was for many years the seat of Maui's government. It is remembered as the place on Maui where, on August 12, 1898, the Hawaiian flag was lowered and the American flag raised, marking the end of the Hawaiian republic.

The building is now the home of the **Lahaina Arts Society**, which has galleries on the main floor and in the old jail downstairs. The Visitors Center in the Courthouse offers helpful information and also operates an excellent shop where books, postcards, and other souvenirs can be found. The banyan tree in the front of the building was planted more than 125 years ago. It now shades more than two-thirds of an acre and houses a noisy population of mynah birds.

Carthaginian II (#7A on walking tour). Docked at the wharf is a replica of a 19th-century sailing brig, typical of the type that dropped anchor in Lahaina's harbor during the golden age of whaling. Inside you can see just how small these ships were and imagine what it must have been like to sail the seas for months, even years at a time in such a boat. Inside is an exhibit on whales and an original whaleboat. The small admission fee allows you to wander the boat at will.

Immediately ashore of the *Carthaginian* is the historic **Pioneer Inn** (#8), built in 1901 and West Maui's major hotel until the 1950s (it's still in use; see Accommodations—and it serves a mean breakfast in a breakfast-starved town).

Carthaginian II in Lahaina Harbor.

Pioneer Inn in Lahaina.

Looking *mauka* in Lahaina, you can't help but see the giant "L" on Mount Ball, behind Lahainaluna School. The gravesite of the great Hawaiian intellectual David Malo is near here. Early on Malo, educated by the Protestant missionaries at Lahainaluna, had fears about how the Protestants would destroy his culture. "The white man's ships have arrived with clever men from the big countries," he wrote. "They know our people are few in number and our country is small, they will devour us." Before Malo died, in 1853, he asked to be buried on Mount Ball, to be far from the foreign invasion of his land.

The "L" engraved in the red dirt of Mount Ball was put there by Lahainaluna graduating students in 1904. Every spring at graduation, alumni come from all over Maui to hike up the mountain with canisters of fuel and set the "L" afire to clear away the brush, then sprinkle it with lime so it's visible from afar.

David Malo

Below: A giant banyan shades Lahaina's Courthouse Square.

The "L" on Mount Ball can be seen from nearly anyplace in Lahaina and Kā'anapali.

This sea captain guards the entrance to the Pioneer Inn.

The 19th-century Baldwin House on Front Street in Lahaina.

From 1899 to 1901, the family that then owned the island of Lāna'i, 9 miles offshore from Lahaina, unsuccessfully tried to grow sugarcane commercially on that island, forming a company called the Maunalei Sugar Company. They built the Keōmoku Hotel on Lāna'i's eastern shore to accommodate workers at the sugar plantation. When the company failed in 1901, the hotel was dismantled and shipped by barge across the 'Au'au Channel to Lahaina, where it became the Pioneer Inn on Wharf Street.

The **Hau'ola stone** (#5), just north of the *Carthaginian,* is a site where ancient Hawaiians practiced medical arts. According to legend, the stone is believed to have been a woman who was fleeing from her enemies when the gods turned her into a stone. The name Hau'ola means "dew of life," and it was at this site that Hawaiian women once gave birth, burying the umbilical cord, or *piko,* underneath the stone to ensure a healthy child.

Baldwin House, Front Street, across from the banyan tree (#2 on walking tour). This two-story house was erected in 1835. In 1836 it became the home of the missionary Dwight D. Baldwin, who was among the 112 foreigners living in Lahaina in 1846, when the first

census was taken; there were 3,445 native Hawaiians. Furnished with period pieces, several original to it, the house offers a glimpse of what life was like in the mid-19th century. Baldwin and his wife, Charlotte, had eight children; just imagine what it must have been like for ten people to live in that small abode. Knowledgeable guides make a visit to this home well worth the small admission fee.

Hale Pa'ahao, corner of Prison and Waine'e streets (#21 on walking tour). Built in the 1850s primarily to get rampaging sailors off the street, this prison held inmates whose offenses ranged from riding a horse on Sundays to murder. Open daily, with no admission fee, the prison, with its sense of minimum security (judging from the height of the walls it would have been pretty easy to break out), is a fun place for kids to visit.

Wo Hing Temple, Front Street between Lahainaluna Road and Pāpalaua Street (#29 on walking tour). Built in 1912, this is one of the few buildings in Lahaina that survived a 1919 fire. It served as a community meeting place for the Wo Hing Society, a chapter of the Freemasons of China. Exhibits, including a large lion for the lion dance, relate the history of Chinese immigrants in Hawai'i. Upstairs is the only public Taoist altar on Maui. And next door, in what was once the cook-house, you can watch films made in Hawai'i in 1898 and 1906 by Thomas Edison, showing Honolulu street scenes, Waikīkī Beach, and cattle hauling sugar-cane (15 minutes). Free.

Hale Pa'i, Lahainaluna School (#28 on walking tour). Drive up Lahainaluna Road 1.5 miles to the end, where you'll

A Taoist altar (above left) is in the Wo Hing Temple (above), built in 1912 by Chinese immigrants. This Front Street landmark was restored in 1984, and its gilded decorations (below) can now be seen in all their glory.

Jodo, or Pure Land, Buddhism is a sect of Buddhism that arose in Japan in A.D. 1175, founded by the monk Hōnen. Believing that the traditional Buddhist practices of meditation and observance of moral precepts weren't enough to attain enlightenment, Hōnen focused on the worship of the Amida Buddha. According to Hōnen's precepts, by simple invocation of the Amida-Buddha's name, Namu Amida Butsu, one achieves rebirth in Amida's paradise, the Western Paradise of the Pure Land.

The practice of nenbutsu, or recitation of the Amida Buddha's name, soon was taken up by all levels of Japanese society, commoners and members of the imperial family alike. The key point in Jodo Buddhism is the throwing away or transcending of the human intellect. Hōnen preached that one should "return to ignorance," or "become illiterate," emphasizing that detachment from things and ideas is necessary for enlightenment. Today Jodo Buddhism vies with Zen Buddhism—which maintains that man can attain enlightenment through his own power—as the predominant religion in Japan.

The Jodo Mission, a Buddhist shrine in Lahaina, includes a 90-foot-high pagoda where ashes of deceased members are kept in niches on the first floor. The great Amida Buddha (right) at the mission was cast in Kyoto in 1968. It is 12 feet high and weighs 3.5 tons.

come to **Lahainaluna School**, the oldest school west of the Rockies, opened in 1831 by missionaries. In its heyday the school accepted pupils from all the islands of Hawai'i and even from California. Today Lahainaluna is Lahaina's public high school. An adjunct of the school was Hale Pa'i (House of Printing), where Hawai'i's first newspaper, the *Torch of Hawaii*, was published. Restored in 1982, Hale Pa'i features a replica of the original press, on which visitors may print their own souvenir copy of the first Hawaiian primer. There is an excellent display, with vintage photographs, outlining the history of the written word in Hawai'i. The museum is open weekdays, 10 A.M.–4 P.M. You might want to call ahead, though, since hours do seem to vary (661-3262).

Jodo Mission, Māla Wharf (#31 on walking tour). You'll have to drive to get to this Buddhist shrine, at the northern end of town. In addition to its traditional Japanese temple architecture, the mission is famous for its immense copper and bronze image of the Amida

Buddha, unveiled in June 1968 to mark the centennial anniversary of Japanese immigration to Hawai'i. If you happen to be on Maui on the first Saturday in July, don't miss the mission's annual O'Bon festival, a colorful traditional Buddhist celebration honoring departed loved ones, held at sunset with a service, dancing, and a floating lanterns ceremony.

Other sites on the walking tour that will be of interest to the devoted history buff include **Malu'uluolele Park** (#16 on walking tour), which is unremarkable today but once was a significant area where powerful *ali'i* lived, including Kamehameha III; the site is in the process of restoration and eventually should be a valuable addition to Lahaina's historical points of interest. Also of interest are **Waiola Church** (#17), built in the 1950s on the site of Lahaina's first stone church, and nearby **Waine'e Cemetery** (#18), where amid the 19th-century gravestones is the burial place of Keōpūolani, a queen of Kamehameha the Great; the **Hongwanji Mission** (#19), a Buddhist meeting place since 1910; the **home site of David Malo** (#20), the Hawaiian intellectual who, having embraced many of the new *haole* teachings, then feared they would diminish the importance of ancient Hawaiian ways and ultimately fought against them; and the **Shingon Temple** (#24), built by and for Japanese laborers who came to Maui near the turn of the century to work in plantation fields.

Today playing fields and a parking lot, Malu'uluolele Park occupies some of Maui's most royal land. Once there was a fresh-water fishpond here. Called Loko o Mokuhinia, the pond was the site of an islet named Moku'ula, which was considered a center of spiritual power. Moku'ula was sacred to the great 16th-century Maui chief Pi'ilani, Kamehameha I revered the islet, and it is where Kamehameha III buried his beloved sister (see pages 54–55)

and lived for eight years after to be by her grave. The end of the monarchy, however, saw the significance of the area forgotten, and in 1914 the swampy land was filled in and Malu'uluolele Park was created. Looking at the park today, it is difficult to imagine that it once held royal residences. But a group of native Hawaiians with extraordinary vision have organized as the Friends of Moku'ula and are raising funds to restore the area.

Above: Artist's rendering of Moku'ula by Ed Kayton. Courtesy Friends of Moku'ula.

Luakini Street, a one-way road going off Waine'e Street and running parallel to Front Street (a street you're most likely to visit looking for a parking place), is significant as the route of the funeral procession of the tragic Princess Nāhi'ena'ena. She died at age twenty-one, a victim of the conflicts in 1837 that pitted the old Hawaiian ways against the new thought brought by the missionaries.

Nāhi'ena'ena had been in love with her brother since they were children together in Lahaina. When he became King Kamehameha III, Hawaiian tradition would allow Nāhi'ena'ena to marry him and bear royal children. To the Hawaiians, this was the natural and logical way of perpetuating a dynasty and ensuring stability throughout the land. To the new *haole* missionaries, however, it was an anathema. The king was torn between these viewpoints, loving his sister on the one hand, but greatly swayed by the teachings of the missionaries on the other. Further, he was somewhat of a drunkard and sexual predator; he slept with his sister and with many other women. Nāhi'ena'ena became dissolute and wretched. In December 1836 the young princess died, a few months after having given birth to Kamehameha III's son, who lived only several hours. Long after her death, the king could be found sitting quietly by her graveside on the anniversary of her death.

The story of Nāhiʻenaʻena and Kamehameha III became the classic tale of cultures in conflict, and all people of Hawaiʻi, whatever their beliefs, mourned her death. The first funeral ceremony for the princess was in Honolulu, where the king led a procession of great chiefs behind a simple cart draped in black silk; at the church, the service was conducted by the Reverend Hiram Bingham, the leader of the missionaries. Kamehameha III then fitted out a ship and sent his sister's body home to Lahaina, where a roadway was cut through groves of breadfruit and *kou* and named Alanui o Nāhiʻenaʻena (Nāhiʻenaʻena Street). The cortege, with its black-draped coffin, moved along the street, which was layered with sand, grass, and mats, accompanied by the lament of the *makaʻainana* along the route. Nāhiʻenaʻena was entombed in the royal mausoleum built by the king on Mokuʻula and remembered forever by her people.

Today, Alanui o Nāhiʻenaʻena is Luakini Street. *Luakini* are a type of places of worship, and the street was named this in recognition of the twelve churches that line it.

Shopping in Lahaina

Every Saturday local craftspeople set up tables under the spreading banyan tree (on Front Street, next to the Pioneer Inn). On the second and fourth Saturday of each month, members of the **Lahaina Arts Society** spread out their jewelry, paintings, and the like. On all other Saturdays, native Hawaiians are in attendance at what is called **He Uʻi Cultural Arts Festival** (*"he uʻi"* translates as "a youthful"). The participating artists encourage education in the language and culture of Hawaiʻi. This is a good place to pick up a woodcarving or a basket crafted from native materials and to spend some time "talking story" with native people who welcome the opportunity to share their love of the land.

The best place to go on Maui for a selection of arts, crafts, gifts, and clothing made by Hawaiians and reflecting the traditions of old is a small shop, **Nā Mea Hawaiʻi**, housed in the Masters' Reading Room, at the corner of Front and Dickenson (661-5707). They also have a fine selection of books about Hawaiʻi's history, culture, and language, and lei sellers are often on the front lawn, stringing their fragrant creations. The historic Masters' Reading Room building was used during the whaling era as an officers' club for ships' captains.

Opposite:
Robert Dampier, *Kamehameha III as a Boy (Kauikeaouli) and Nāhiʻenaʻena, Sister of Kamehameha III*, 1825, oil on canvas. Honolulu Academy of Arts, gifts of Mrs. C. Montague Cooke, Jr., Charles M. Cooke III, and Mrs. Heaton Wrenn in memory of Dr. C. Montague Cooke, Jr.

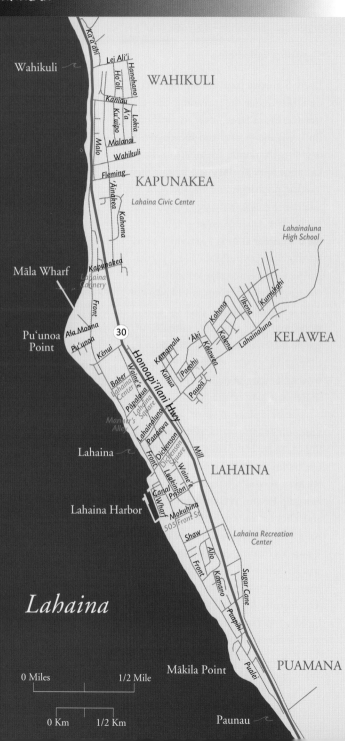

Wahikuli

Lei Aliʻi
Hanohano
Hoʻoi
Kaʻrahi

WAHIKULI

Kamau
Kuʻuipo
Aʻa
Lokia

Malo
Malanai
Wahikuli

Fleming
KAPUNAKEA
Ainakea

Lahaina Civic Center

Lahainaluna
High School

Māla Wharf

Kapunakea
Lahaina
Cannery

Kahoma

Puʻunoa
Point

Ala Moana
Puʻunoa

Front

30

Kaheng
ʻAki
Otena
Kumukahi

Kamamalu
Kahena
Lahainaluna

KELAWEA

Kēnui

Kuhua
Paohii
Pauoa

Baker
Waineʻe
Lahaina
Center

Honoapiʻilani Hwy

PanaIua

Lahainaluna
Lenging
Square

Panaewa

Mariner's
Alley

Dickenson
Front
Dickenson
Square

Waineʻe

Mill

Lahaina

Luakini
Prison

LAHAINA

Lahaina Harbor

Canal
Wharf
Mokuhina
505 Front St.

Shaw

Lahaina Recreation
Center

Alio
Kanano

Front

Sugar Cane

Puaphii

Lahaina

Lahaina

0 Miles   1/2 Mile

0 Km   1/2 Km

Mākila Point

Pualei

PUAMANA

Paunau

For an amazing selection of quality used books, go to the **Old Lahaina Book Emporium** at 505 Front Street (244-7777), where 20,000 books—from poolside reading to Hawaiiana, military history, literature, mysteries, children's books, cookbooks, and, reflecting the owner's interests, books by and about Africa and African Americans—fill every nook and cranny of the store. JoAnn Carroll, who presides over this collection, also fulfills another personal interest with her selection of 5,000 rental videos, with a heavy emphasis on pre-1950s and silent films.

Take Home Maui at 121 Dickenson Street (661-8067 or 661-6185) is where to go for freshly picked Maui pineapples, papayas, and onions packed for taking back to the mainland; if you wish, they'll deliver your order free to the airport or your hotel. To order from the mainland, call 800-545-6284.

No place is better than **Hilo Hattie** (667-7911), at Lahaina Center, for a great selection of aloha wear, including women's *muʻumuʻu* and men's aloha shirts. They also have a good selection of made-in-Hawaiʻi gifts. For beautiful and unique bracelets, necklaces, and earrings made from the tiny, delicate pink shells found only on the privately owned island of Niʻihau—a shell that is considered a gem —try Jack Ackerman's **Maui Divers** at 640 Front Street (661-0988). If you're hooked on humpbacks, you won't want to miss the Pacific Whale Foundation's **Ocean Store** at 143 Dickenson Street

(667-7447), where there are all sorts of good things related to whales and other marine creatures.

Lahaina Art Galleries

You can pick up a gallery map listing and describing about thirty galleries at the **Lahaina Arts Society**, 648 Wharf Street (661-0111), in the old Courthouse across from the boat dock. Here also are two galleries with excellent selections of work by both emerging and established Maui artists. **The Banyan Tree Gallery**, with craft and gift items as well as paintings, is on the main floor of the Courthouse. Downstairs is the **Old Jail Gallery**, some of its space still divided into small cells.

Village Galleries, with locations at 120 and 180 Dickenson Street (661-4402 and 661-5559), is the finest art gallery on Maui. Only local artists are featured, and all the best ones can be found here. The main gallery features traditional artworks, while the contemporary branch down the street displays paintings that are more abstract plus a lot of craftlike items, such as glass and ceramics. There is also an outlet for the Village Galleries at the Ritz-Carlton Hotel in Kapalua.

In the Pioneer Inn, facing Front Street, is the gallery of mazemaster **David Anson Russo**, a paper artist who constructs fascinating 3-D mazes. **Curtis Wilson Cost**, who has a gallery at 710 Front Street, paints exquisitely detailed Maui landscapes (he also has a gallery at Kula Lodge in the Upcountry area). **Island Woodcarving Gallery**, in the courtyard at 844 Front Street, has fine carved wooden reliefs of island-type scenes and offers other well-crafted wood items.

Maui to Go, at the other end of Front Street, at no. 505, is where artist Joelle C. Perz displays her accomplished prints as well as the artwork of other Hawai'i residents. Also at 505 Front Street is the **Elizabeth Doyle Gallery**, which features fine art glass from the studio of Dale Chihuly and the Pilchuck School of Glass. The Doyle Gallery is also in the Kapalua Shops.

Joyce Clark, West Maui Mountains, oil on canvas.

Most of the other Lahaina galleries offer touristy, saccharine paintings that you could buy anywhere or factory-produced seascapes with whale motifs.

Friday night is Art Night in Lahaina. The galleries stay open and artists are on hand, often demonstrating their skills. It can be fun to stroll around the galleries and chat with the artists.

Kāʻanapali

Kāʻanapali is an incredibly lush and comfortable resort area carved from lava, farmland, and scrub brush by one of Hawaiʻi's oldest companies, Amfac. A string of world-class hotels provides luxurious rooms and suites, surrounded by tennis courts, golf courses, and a long stretch of dazzling beach.

The area is anchored by the Whalers Village shopping complex, on the third floor of which is **Whalers Village Museum** (661-5992), which has what

has been called the largest collection of whaling memorabilia in the world, including a replica of the whaling bark *Sunbeam*, ships' log books, maps, and a scrimshaw collection. Its hours are 9:30 A.M. until 10 P.M. daily.

Whalers Village Museum displays a skeleton of a whale.

An interesting feature of Kāʻanapali Beach is **Black Rock**, a volcanic formation eroded by the sea. Black Rock was considered a holy place by early Hawaiians, who thought it was a place where spirits of the dead left the earth for the spirit world. Today Black Rock has been integrated into the design of the Sheraton Maui. It is an ideal spot for snorkeling, with colorful reef fish that are accustomed to visitors.

Shopping in Kāʻanapali

In the center of the hotel complexes is **Whalers Village**, an eight-acre shopping center containing art galleries, restaurants, and shops, in addition to the Whalers Village Museum. Galleries include **Lahaina Printsellers**, which specializes

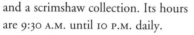

the **Kāʻanapali** coast

to Kapalua

Kekaʻa Poir

in antique maps and engravings of the Pacific area. There are upscale boutiques like Louis Vuitton and Chanel as well as several good Hawai'i-based chains, among them **Maui Clothing Co.**, **Blue Ginger**, and **Crazy Shirts**. For a broad selection of books about Hawai'i, **Waldenbooks** is the place to go (they also have stores in Kahului, Kīhei, and Lahaina). There is validated parking in the adjacent lot.

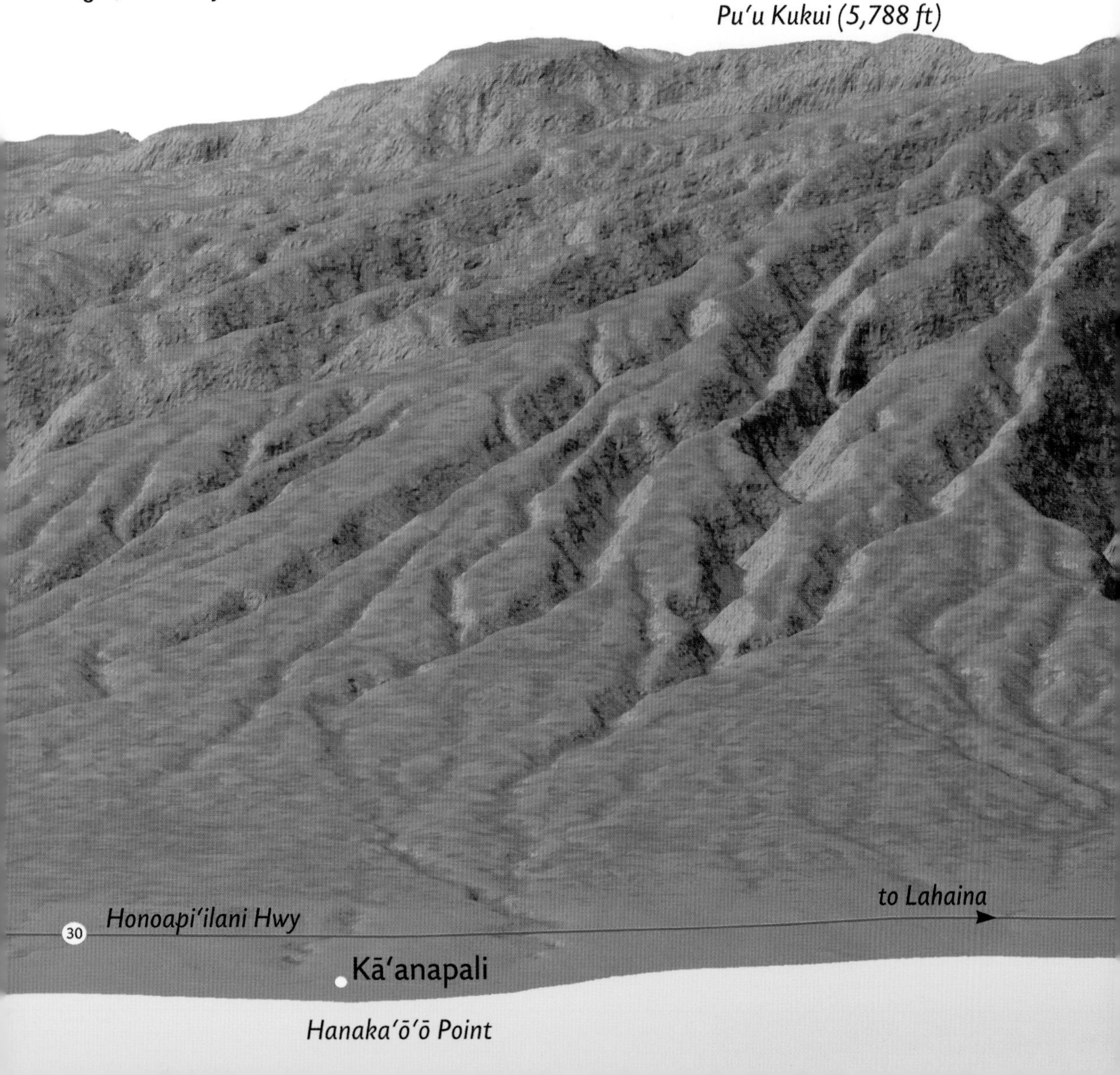

Pu'u Kukui (5,788 ft)

Honoapi'ilani Hwy

to Lahaina

Kā'anapali

Hanaka'ō'ō Point

Every evening at sunset, a native Hawaiian lights a trail of fiery torches as he makes his way to the seaside cliff bordering the Sheraton Maui, known to Hawaiians as Black Rock, or Puʻu Kekaʻa, Hill of Rolling Stones. He then gracefully dives from the 80-foot cliff into the sea and returns to shore, reaffirming the strength and power of Hawaiʻi's ancient *aliʻi*. It was believed that only one with great spiritual strength could escape the spirits of the dead that lurked at Puʻu Kekaʻa and survive such a leap. Kahekili, Maui's last king, fearlessly plunged from the cliff and returned to land, proving that he possessed such spiritual power as well as unbounded physical strength.

As the sun slips behind Puʻu Kekaʻa, you can sit at the Sheraton's Lagoon Bar and watch the brave young Hawaiian reenact King Kahekili's feat, while a chant, specially written for the Sheraton ceremony by cultural advisor Cliff Ahue, is intoned in eloquent Hawaiian. The chant is as follows:

He Mele no Kekaʻa

ʻIke i ke one kea ia Kekaʻa
Kaʻa alanui kīkeʻekeʻe o Māui.
Maʻū ka lepo no kēia ʻāina
Pulupē i ka ua Līlīlehua.
Hū mai ke aloha no ka ʻāina,
ʻĪina kaulana no na aliʻi.
He aliʻi no ʻoe e ʻo Puʻu Kekaʻa.
Tū ʻoe i ke kai, e hoʻi mai,
Mai ke kai ʻAuʻau no Kahuli.
Puana ka inoa no Kekaʻa,
He mele no Kekaʻa.

The Song of Kekaʻa

See the white sands of Kekaʻa
And the jagged pathway of Māui,
    the demigod.
The land is moistened
By the Lililehua rains.
Love swells for this land,
The famous land of chiefs.
Puʻu Kekaʻa, you are a chief.
Standing in the ocean, return to me,
From the ʻAuʻau channel to the peak
    of Kahuli.
So tells the refrain of Kekaʻa,
The song of Kekaʻa.

Opposite top: From aboard the *Trilogy V* sailing catamaran off Kāʻanapali Beach, the island of Lānaʻi can be seen in the distance.

Opposite bottom: Nāpili Bay has one of the nicest beaches on Maui. At the left is Kapalua Beach.

Kapalua

Highway 30 passes Kāʻanapali and heads up to Maui's northwest coast, leading to the **Nāpili Bay** region and the resort area of **Kapalua**, an old favorite of many Maui residents.

There is a cutoff from the main highway down to a secondary road, once the principal highway, that leads past restaurants, condominiums, and private homes. *Makai* of the highway, the shoreline alternates between rocks worn smooth by the tides and small, sandy beaches. Just to the north is Kapalua, 750 acres of meticulous landscaping, golf courses, tennis courts, and pools, all part of a massive, elaborate resort complex with two luxury hotels—the Kapalua Bay Hotel and the Ritz-Carlton, Kapalua—as its focal points.

Kapalua also is famous for its beaches, favorites of local residents, who sometimes drive from as far away as Upcountry just to bask in the sun here. The area also offers a visual bonus: just across a stretch of blue water, the green island of Molokaʻi rises from the sea, giving beachgoers a good view of its coves and deep valleys.

Pristine and lovely, Kapalua has been rated by the famous Dr. Beach as the best beach in the United States.

to Kahakuloa

Honokōhau Bay

Shopping in Kapalua

The **Kapalua Shops**, adjacent to the Kapalua Bay Hotel, include designer boutiques and children's shops. **Hawaiian Quilt Collection**, a small Hawai'i chain, is an excellent place to buy handmade Hawaiian quilts as well as quilt-making kits. Authentic Hawaiian entertainment is offered Tuesday–Friday, including slack key music and a hula show. Call the **Kapalua Discovery Center** (669-3754) for a current schedule.

the **Kapalua** coast

Pu'u Kukui (5,788 ft)

Honoapi'ilani Hwy

30

to Kā'anapali

Kapalua

Nāpili

Oneloa Bay

Nāpili Bay

Though lined by condominium developments, Nāpili Bay has a natural beauty that remains untouched.

The Discovery Center has outstanding exhibits relating to Maui's culture, environment, and history. Note that the shops close at 6 P.M. (5 P.M. on Sundays). The old **Honolua Store**, adjacent to the Ritz-Carlton, opens at 6 A.M. every day (closes 8 P.M.), serving tourists and residents alike with a variety of groceries, plate lunches, and even beachwear. This is a good place to find sweet Kapalua pineapple.

Kapalua Resort, encompassing two hotels—the Ritz-Carlton and the Kapalua Bay Hotel—also includes a shopping center, twelve restaurants, three championship golf courses, twenty tennis courts and a tennis school, an art school, and new condominiums and houses, all developed around what was once a ranch and pineapple plantation—and before that home to thousands of Hawaiians, who farmed and worshiped on these lands. Although pineapple is still grown on the fields above Kapalua, most of the land is now a 1,650-acre planned resort, conceived in the 1970s by Colin C. Cameron, a fifth-generation descendant of the missionary Baldwin family.

The former village blacksmith shop is now the art school, where residents and visitors can paint, draw, and make ceramics. Two churches from the plantation days are still in use, Sacred Hearts Church and Kumulani Chapel. Once a getaway for plantation managers, the Cliff House is now a retreat for guests at the Kapalua Bay Hotel.

When the Ritz-Carlton was being constructed in 1987, it was discovered that the location planned for the hotel was a burial site for ancient Hawaiians. Carbon dating indicates that Hawaiians lived here as early as A.D. 610. Sensitive to the cultural importance of Hawaiian burial grounds, the developers moved the hotel farther inland, leaving the ancestral spirits to watch over the land that borders the sea.

Kapalua Resort continues to adopt policies favorable to preservation of the land and to remain a sanctuary for plants and wildlife. The Kapalua Nature Society coordinates the resort's environmental programs. In 1996 the resort was certified by Audubon International under the Audubon Heritage Program, the first resort in the world to be so recognized for its environmental initiatives. Protected are twenty-three varieties of birds as well as plants found nowhere else on earth.

D. T. Fleming Beach Park, shaded by iron-wood trees, fronts the Ritz-Carlton, Kapalua.

Scenic Drive around the Head

Nearly every roadway on Maui is a scenic drive with awesome mountain and ocean views. The most famous drive is the road to Hāna, but there are others equally as enchanting and with fewer cars.

The road from Kapalua to Wailuku on route 30/340, around the north coast of the island, is one of the most incredibly beautiful drives on Maui, perhaps even surpassing the road to Hāna by virtue of its isolation and varied views. Locals call this drive "coming around the head," referring to Kahakuloa Head, a large hill that can be seen from as far away as the Haleakalā Highway in east Maui, as well as to the head of a person that many people see in West Maui, with the person's torso being the east side of the island when viewed from the air (the person is seen as bending over and contemplating the island of Kahoʻolawe). Plan on taking a couple of hours for this drive; there are no gas stations, and facilities are limited. This is not a drive for the faint of heart. The road is one lane for much of its length, with numerous hairpin curves (beep your horn to warn oncoming drivers of your presence). You're rewarded with magnificent views of the rugged coastline.

Beyond Kapalua, the winding road goes up and down the cliffside past deeply carved bays. At about the 36 mile marker, at **Honokōhau**, there are *kalo* fields. Beyond that, past mile 38, is **Nākālele Point**, where you can pull off

Kahakuloa ("Tall Hill") Head dominates the north coastline of West Maui.

these may or may not be open. Most houses in this colorful town are unpretentious wooden structures. There are two churches, Protestant and Catholic. Kahakuloa is one of the most isolated villages on Maui, and the road to it from the Wailuku side has only recently been paved. Car rental companies used to frown on taking rental cars on that stretch of the road, owing to its rugged, unpaved state, but that condition is now

Above: The blowhole at Nākālele Point is a spectacular sight. A short trail from the overlook area leads down to the blowhole, though when the surf is up it's better seen from the road.

Opposite top: Isolated Kahakuloa Village is home to farmers and fishermen who keep to the old way of life.

Pages 70–71: A rainbow arches over the West Maui Mountains, with sugarcane in the foreground.

and view a powerful blowhole, 200 feet below. State Highway 30 ends where the paving gets rougher, and the county route (340) begins. On down the road, just before mile 16, is a large, famous boulder known as the **Bellstone** on the *mauka* side of the road. When one side of the rock is struck, a clear, bell-like sound rings out on the other side. Don't be too surprised, though, if you don't hear it. Not everyone does.

The road continues to **Kahakuloa**, a small, remote town where the villagers like to keep to themselves. Just before Kahakuloa there's a stunning overlook of the valley and the 636-foot-high **Kahakuloa Head**. A lunch wagon selling snacks and shave ice makes this a tempting place to stop—if the view alone isn't enough to get you out of your car. In the village there are several fruit stands along the road as well as roadside *kalo* terraces. Locals have put up a few stands for food and drink, but

to Wailuku

Hakuhe'e Point

a thing of the past (despite what some tourist publications continue to say).

After you leave Kahakuloa, in a death-defying section of road you'll pass Kahakuloa Head on the left. All along here, look for spinner dolphins in the clear blue waters. A welcome stop after Kahakuloa Head is **Kaukini Gallery** (244-3371), which offers an incredible array of locally made crafts and paintings by Maui artists. A little farther

the **Kahakuloa** coast

Pu'u Kukui (5,788 ft)

Kahekili Hwy 340 Kahakuloa *to Kapalua*

Kahakuloa Head *Kahakuloa Bay*

down the road, past the 10 mile marker, is the studio and gallery of sculptor **Bruce Turnbull** (244-9838), which is open to the public on Tuesdays and Thursdays. Soon after this the road widens, and the trip into Wailuku, 4 miles past the Mendes Ranch, is a dream.

Hiking in the West Maui Mountains

While Haleakalā, in east Maui, translates as "House of the Sun," the West Maui Mountains, dominating Maui's western side, are known in Hawaiian as Halemahina, or "House of the Moon." Puʻu Kukui, at 5,788 feet the highest point in the West Maui Mountains, is accessible only by means of a guided hike that takes place once a year (see page 183). However, the 2.5-mile **Waiheʻe Ridge Trail** (5 miles roundtrip) provides excellent views of waterfalls and rain-soaked swamps in these mountains. The trail starts off Highway 340, about 7 miles before reaching Wailuku. Take the well-marked turnoff leading to a Boy Scout camp for about a mile to the trailhead. The trail climbs the windward slope of West Maui through a brushy guava thicket and wet native scrub forest. Views of Waiheʻe Valley can be seen along the way, and at the peak, at 2,563 feet, are panoramic views of Wailuku to the south and Mount ʻEke (4,480 feet) to the southwest. The summit varies from clear to overcast with showers; this hike is better not taken in rainy weather.

Mā'alaea/Kīhei/Wailea *area*

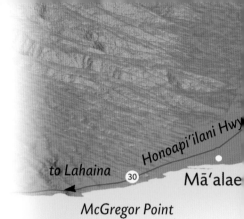

to Lahaina 30

Honoapi'ilani Hwy

Mā'alae

McGregor Point

MAUI'S SO-CALLED SOUTHERN COAST (it's really the western coast of the eastern half of the island) is dry and sunny— a magnet for young beachgoers. Over the years it also has attracted a number of developers who looked at the area's beaches and climate and forecast a need for housing. The result is a string of condominiums leading from near Mā'alaea, a major boat harbor, on through the Kīhei sector and into Wailea, a polished resort area with a number of fine hotels and restaurants. Beyond Wailea lies Mākena, with a network of excellent beaches off the beaten path.

McGregor Point Light guides sailors at Mā'alaea Bay. Cloud-mantled Haleakalā is in the background.

Mā'alaea

To get to Mā'alaea from Kahului Airport, travel on Highway 380 across the isthmus to Highway 30; proceed on 30 and watch for signs for Mā'alaea; the turnoff inter-sects the main highway on the *makai* side. This area is the site of a small boat harbor with a number of charter boats as well as the new Maui Ocean Center (see below), with nice shops and restau-rants in the adjoining shopping center, the new Mā'alaea Harbor Village.

Surfing enthusiasts will find the **Shapers Surf Museum** (877-2111) of interest. Located in the lower level of the new shopping center, facing the harbor, the museum boasts one of the finest

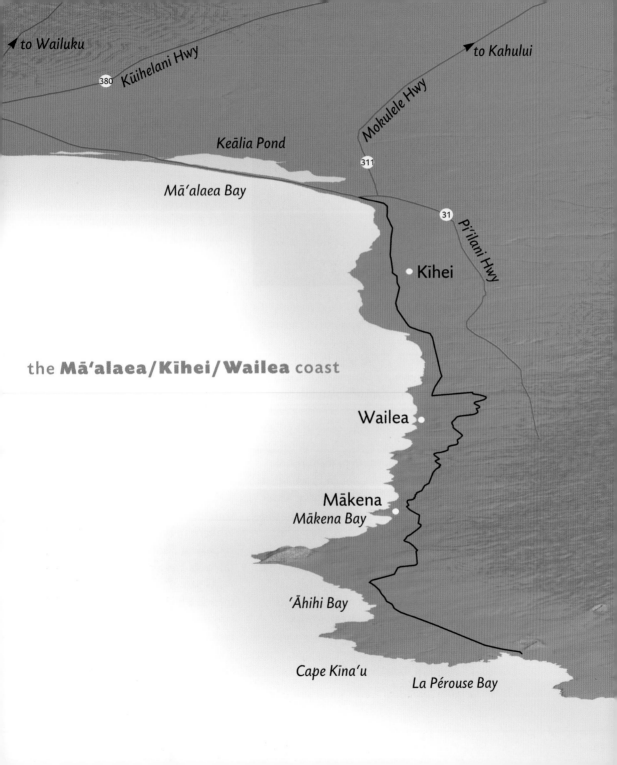

to Wailuku

380 Kūihelani Hwy

Keālia Pond

Māʻalaea Bay

to Kahului

Mokulele Hwy

311

31 Piʻilani Hwy

Kīhei

the **Māʻalaea/Kīhei/Wailea** coast

Wailea

Mākena
Mākena Bay

ʻĀhihi Bay

Cape Kīnaʻu

La Pérouse Bay

Maui Ocean Center

The **Maui Ocean Center** (270-7000), which opened in 1998, is one of Maui's best attractions, captivating young and old alike. Located just above Māʻalaea Harbor, the blue-roofed structure, on the left-hand side of Highway 30 as you're driving from Kahului to Lahaina, can't be missed. The exhibits in the tropical aquarium—the largest in the Western hemisphere—are awesome. In the living reef, colorful fish compete with splendid living coral in hues of orange, purple, red, and green. You'll see an octopus and strange garden eels that live in the depths of the sea. As you walk through a clear acrylic tunnel surrounded all around by sea, sharks will swim over your head and stingrays will glide gracefully by. This is a truly incredible experience, exciting as well as educational. All marine life is kept in as realistic a habitat as possible. There is an excellent exhibit on ancient Hawaiians and the sea, as well as a whale center with life-size models and interactive exhibits. In the touch pool, children can have a hands-on experience with tide-pool creatures.

As part of the Ocean Center complex, there is a huge shop with a splendid selection of items related to the sea, including jewelry, arts and crafts, books, and clothing. There is also a restaurant, Seascape Māʻalaea, with delicious island-style cuisine, as well as a less expensive

Fish-feeding time at the Maui Ocean Center. Large aquariums each house fish from various marine habitats.

collections of surfboards and memorabilia anywhere. There are photos of surfers dating as far back as 1910 and a 12-foot redwood longboard used in the 1920s by the legendary Duke Kahanamoku's brother, Sam Kahanamoku. Informative text labels tell the story of surfing and describe the evolution to the short, lightweight boards of today. If the downstairs door is locked, go up to the surf store above the museum and enter from there.

Māʻalaea is noteworthy for its winds, funneled between Maui's two large mountain ranges. In the 1930s, Maui's first airport was here, no doubt to be on the Lahaina side of the island, but the winds forced its relocation to the other side.

Highway 31 (also marked 310) leads out of Māʻalaea past **Keālia Pond**, a bird sanctuary. There's a parking area between the 1 and 2 mile markers, where there is a short, self-guided walking tour along a boardwalk.

café. The Ocean Center is open daily, 9 A.M. to 5 P.M. Admission is $18, $12.50 for children.

Hiking near Māʻalaea

One of Maui's most frequently recommended hikes, the **Old Lahaina Pali Trail**, starts 3 miles north of Māʻalaea and ends up 3 miles west of the harbor, where your car should be left; you'll have to arrange to be dropped off at the trailhead, reached via an unimproved road adjacent to the junction of Kūihelani Highway (380) and Kīhei Road (31). The parking area at the end of the trail is about one-quarter mile past the Pali Tunnel on Highway 30 going out of Māʻalaea toward Lahaina. This 5.5-mile trail is best hiked in the early morning, as it gets exceedingly hot as the day goes on. Ranging in elevation from 100 to 1,600 feet, the trail offers excellent vistas of Kahoʻolawe and Lānaʻi, and during the winter months whales can be sighted. There are many side trails that lead away from the main trail and then return. This trail is part of a historic, around-the-island trail system on Maui and is maintained by volunteers who participate in the Nā Ala Hele (Trails to Go On) program sponsored by the State Division of Forestry and Wildlife.

Visitors at the Maui Ocean Center inside a clear plastic tunnel, surrounded by fish of all kinds.

Kīheʻi

Upper Kīhei
Uwapo
Uwapo
Kaiwahine
Waimahā
Hoaiike
'Ohukai
'Ohukai
Kīhei Gateway Ctr

Maipoinaʻoelaʻu

Kamaole
Kenolio
Wailana
31

Kalepolepo
Kōʻieʻie Fishpond
Kalepolepo

Kaʻonoʻulu
South Kīhei
Kūlanihākoʻi
Hoʻonani
Nāmauʻu
Waipuʻilani
Kauhaʻa
Long's Ctr
Azeka Place II
'Olowi
Lipoa
Lipoa

Piʻilani Hwy
Piʻilani Ctr

Lipoa
Elleair Maui
Golf Club

Kawililipoa
Halekuʻai
KĪHEI
Welakahao
Halama
Kukui
Mall
Kapuna
South Kīhei
Alahele
Auhana
Wālaka
Kanaloa

Waimahaʻihaʻi

Kalama
Cove Park
Kaluaʻehakoko Point
Young's
Kamaʻole I
Dolphin
Plaza
Rainbow Mall
Kamaʻole Ctr
Kamaʻole II
Keonekai
Kamaʻole III
South Kīhei
Kauhale

Kīhei Small Boat
Launch Ramp
Ponana
Kilohana
Maui Meadows

Piʻilani Hwy
31

Keawakapu
Mapu
Kehola
Kupulau
Kapili
Akolu
Keha
Mōkapu
Okolani
Kumulani
Ulua
Wailea Alanui
WAILEA

Kīhei/
Wailea

Shops at
Wailea
Wailea Iki

Wailea
Wailea Ekolu
Wailea Point
Wailea Blue Course

Polo
Kaukahi
Māena
Wailea Alanui

0 Miles   1 Mile

0 Km   1 Km

Palauea
Hāloa Point
Wailea Emerald
and Gold Courses

Kīhei

At Kīhei, Highway 31 divides between Piʻilani Highway (31), a bypass, and South Kīhei Road, which runs next to the ocean—the route to take if you want to see the sights, which are basically shopping areas and row after row of condominiums. Here, too, are several popular beach parks, including **Maipoinaʻoelaʻu**, at the upper end of Kīhei, across from the **Aston Maui Lu** resort. In the heart of Kīhei are **Kalama** and **Kamaʻole** beach parks. Many people claim this area has the best combination of beaches, weather, and views on Maui—and perhaps in all of Hawaiʻi. With its many shopping centers and shops, Kīhei is a self-contained enclave that caters to a variety of tastes and budgets. From Kīhei's beaches there are excellent views of Haleakalā, the sweep of coastline and the West Maui Mountains off in the distance, as well as good whale-watching vantage points.

Kalama Beach in Kīhei offers a perfect view of the West Maui Mountains.

Opposite: Kamaʻole Beach Park (top) is a favorite spot for picnicking and games, while Kamaʻole I (bottom) offers a sandy shore and good swimming.

Shopping in Kīhei

The **South Maui Shopping Express** (877-7308) operates from 6 A.M. to 10:30 P.M., stopping at major hotels and shopping centers between Māʻalaea and Wailea. Kīhei, with one shopping plaza after another, has an abundance of stores of every kind, catering to locals as well as tourists.

Maui Blooms, at the Kīhei Commercial Center, 300 ʻOhukai Road (874-0875), features Maui's best selection of handcrafted island baskets, protea wreaths and arrangements, and tropical flowers, which can be boxed to carry on the plane or shipped direct. The Kīhei Commercial Center is above Piʻilani Highway (31), close to the entrance to Kīhei (not on the shopping express route).

Aloha Books Café and Gallery, at 2411 South Kīhei Road (874-8070), has a good selection of used books, including collectible Hawaiiana. The small café allows for a tranquil coffee stop. For organic produce, a full line of health foods, and a juice bar with good smoothies, try **Hawaiian Moons Natural Foods** at 2411 South Kīhei Road (875-4356).

Wailea

At the far end of Kīhei is a 1,500-acre complex of fine hotels, restaurants, and shops, with excellent golf courses, tennis courts, and activities such as scuba diving, snorkeling, and windsurfing. This is **Wailea**, Alexander and Baldwin's jewel-like resort set against the arid lava flows of southeast Maui. The resort has grown dramatically over the last decade, with the addition of several new luxury hotels and restaurants.

One of the area's great features is the string of five excellent beaches, one after the other. Maui's beaches lie like a sandy lei around the island, and here in Wailea they seem to sparkle with beauty.

Shopping in Wailea

The Shops at Wailea, a brand-new shopping center at 3750 Wailea Alanui, has everything from the Gap to Tiffany's. While the emphasis is on upscale chains,

Aloha Market in Kīhei is a colorful respite from the shopping centers that line South Kīhei Road.

A bronze sculpture of Kamehameha I by Big Island artist Herb Kāne welcomes visitors to the Grand Wailea Resort.

several smaller Hawai'i retailers of quality goods also have shops here. **Blue Ginger** sells clothing for women, men, and children made from well-designed cotton batik fabrics, as does **Noa Noa**, which also has a selection of Oceanic artifacts; **Crazy Shirts** has distinctive tees; **Honolua Surf Co.** offers beach clothes with a youthful slant; and **Martin & MacArthur** sells quality *koa* furniture.

Ki'i Galleries has the largest art glass collection in Hawai'i, including sparkling jewelry made from Italian glass. For the latest faux tropical look in clothing and household objects, the stylish **Tommy Bahama's Tropical Café and Emporium** is the place to shop—and the open-air café makes a good rest stop. A complimentary shuttle runs to the shops from the Wailea resorts.

Polo Beach, the southernmost of Wailea's five beaches, fronts the Kea Lani Hotel. A wide crescent of golden sand, it offers a perfect spot for watching the setting sun.

A picturesque walkway along the beach begins at the Renaissance Wailea and meanders south for 1.5 miles, past luxury hotels, spectacular condo developments, the new Shops at Wailea, and several public restrooms and showers, ending at Polo Beach Park. Many native Hawaiian plants grow on either side of the pathway, and there's an authentic restoration of a native Hawaiian house site. The sunsets along the coastal walk are spectacular, but even more appealing is to walk the pathway at dawn and watch the rising sun light up first West Maui, then Lāna'i, Molokini, and Kaho'olawe in the distance as the resort area comes to life. Snack bars and restaurants operated by the hotels that border the beachwalk are open to all.

White cranes are commonly seen on Wailea's manicured lawns.

Mākena

Down the road from Wailea, past the Polo Beach resort, is **Mākena**, an area formerly wild and pristine that in recent years has undergone development resulting in the building of the Maui Prince Hotel as well as two championship golf courses and luxurious townhouses and condominiums. Just past the Mākena Surf, Mākena Road goes off to the right for a side trip down to **Mākena Landing** and the picturesque **Keawala'i Congregational Church**, founded in 1832. Sunday services include Hawaiian hymns, and a portion of the sermon is spoken in Hawaiian. Be sure to remove your shoes before you enter the church, as the sign requests at the doorway.

This is an area of superb beaches with untamed beauty but no amenities. Years ago the area was a semipermanent campsite for transients and, as such, attained a certain notoriety. One of the beaches, **Pu'u Ōla'i** (known as Little Beach), still has a reputation as a nude beach and is subject to occasional police visits. **Oneloa** (Big Beach to residents) lies on the other side of the distinctive Pu'u Ōla'i, a 360-foot cinder cone. Big Beach offers not only good swimming but a nice place from which to watch the sun set. In the **'Āhihi-Kīna'u Natural Area Reserve**, unusual marine life abounds

The island of Kaho'olawe can be seen from the beach at the Maui Prince Hotel in Mākena.

Left: Keawala'i Congregational Church at Mākena Landing dates from 1832.

Below: Gray francolins habitate Haleakalā from Upcountry to the shore.

Snorkeling is superb at Āhihi-Kina'u Natural Area Reserve south of Mākena.

in offshore tidal pools. The beaches are rocky, but there are good little coves for snorkeling—in fact, this is one of the best snorkeling sites on the island. Watch for parked cars along the way to indicate good stopping points (never go in the water alone). Towering above, mighty Haleakalā dominates the landscape of lava rock and *kiawe* scrub. The road along here is twisting and narrow, with many blind (one-lane) hills.

South of this natural reserve site is **La Pérouse Bay**, the spot where, in May 1786, the explorer comte de La Pérouse became the first Westerner to set foot on Maui (see page 14). Today the bay named for this Frenchman is reachable by four-wheel-drive vehicle or on foot, as the road over old lava fields is rough. To walk, drive to the very end of the paved road; the roadway turns to lava rock at the La Pérouse monument, where there is a parking area. It's a short walk to the bay and snorkeling area. Well-marked house sites and the ruins of *heiau* dot the rocky lava fields. The sun is fierce, and there is no protection. An ancient path, the **Hoapili Trail**, leads from La Pérouse Bay on south along Maui's rugged coastline. Snorkeling is good here, but currents can be strong, so caution is advised.

According to most historians, this area was the site of Maui's most recent lava flow, which is dated to about 1790. Some seem to base their dating of the flow on La Pérouse's comments, upon first seeing Maui, that the mountains were "clothed in vegetation" and the homes "surrounded by green banana trees," assuming from this that the eruption had to have been after 1786. However, further reading of La Pérouse's journal reveals that the first area he saw was not far from Hāna. The bay where he came ashore was, he said, covered with ancient lava flows, which throws into doubt the 1790 theory.

Hiking the King's Trail

The Hoapili (King's) Trail once encircled the island along the shore. The Maui Prince Hotel in Mākena has preserved sections of the trail on its grounds. The trail can be hiked from La Pérouse Bay, along the shoreline, through barren, jagged lava flows. The climate is hot and arid, and there is little vegetation for cover. Smooth, water-worn stepping-stones (many lost or eroded), laid out to form a path through the lava flows, were originally placed there for kings and

their retinues, who followed the trail to collect taxes from the common folk. This area is the site of many ancient stone walls and house foundations. Good hiking shoes, sunscreen, and plenty of water are a must. Though few will venture this far, after about 15 miles, the trail meets up with Pi'ilani Highway (31) at Manawainui en route to Hāna. From here it's another 6 miles or so to Kaupō, where there is a small store with restrooms. This hike is only for the very adventuresome who have a keen interest in Hawaiian archaeology; otherwise, the landscape is desolate and not of much interest.

You could start hiking the trail at the Manawainui end, where you'd quickly reach ruins of ancient villages, the first being at the start of the trail; the next are nearly 4 miles later. Or you could go from La Pérouse Bay as far as Kanaio Beach and then turn around, for a 2.5-mile roundtrip (the hike most people elect and a fine introduction to the area).

Hikers trek across rough lava fields in the area of La Pérouse Bay.

Pā'ia/Upcountry *area*

MANY PEOPLE PASS THROUGH PĀ'IA, Makawao, and Kula on their way to Hāna or Haleakalā but fail to stop in these fascinating old-style towns. There are many sites of interest in this area, and a day or so could easily be spent exploring the back roads.

Pā'ia

Expert windsurfers from around the world come to Ho'okipa Beach to test their skills.

H. P. Baldwin Park, at mile 6 beyond Kahului on the Hāna Highway (Highway 36) and just before Pā'ia, has a good beach for swimming and surfing (see photo, page 37). The **Rinzai Buddhist Temple** is adjacent to the park. Pā'ia

way of life for many residents. The town is now an important windsurfing hub because it's near **Ho'okipa Beach**, a mecca for the popular sport, attracting windsurfers from all over the world. From the overlook at Ho'okipa you can catch a great view of windsurfers skimming across the water like gaily colored butterflies. Pā'ia's colorful, old-town

was Maui's most important town in the 1930s, at the peak of the sugar era. The sugar mill shut down in 2000, ending a

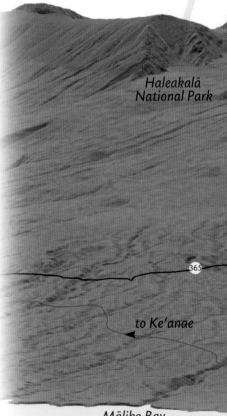

Haleakalā National Park

365

to Ke'anae

Māliko Bay

flavor combines a laid-back lifestyle with an energetic surfing community; some of the residents are aging hippies, while others are entrepreneurial youth. Just on the far edge of town is the **Mantokuji Buddhist Temple**, where a huge gong is rung at dawn and dusk. Neither of the Buddhist temples is open to the public.

The Mantokuji Buddhist Temple is on the *makai* side of the road as you drive out of Pā'ia toward Hāna.

the **Pā'ia** coast

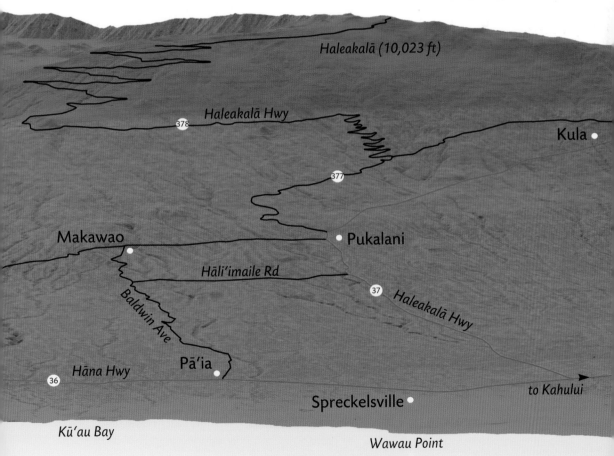

Haleakalā (10,023 ft)

Haleakalā Hwy

378

377

Kula

Makawao

Pukalani

Hāli'imaile Rd

37

Haleakalā Hwy

Baldwin Ave

Hāna Hwy

Pā'ia

36

Spreckelsville

to Kahului

Kū'au Bay

Wawau Point

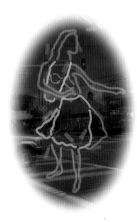

A colorful neon sign welcomes visitors to a Pā'ia shop.

Below: Stephen Burr, *Ha'ikū Taro Farm,* pastel.

Shopping in Pā'ia

The **Maui Crafts Guild** at 43 Hāna Highway (579-9697; www.mauicrafts guild.com) is one of our favorite places to shop on Maui. This artists' coop is in a historic green and white building on the way into Pā'ia, on the *makai* side of the road. Here you'll find some of the best selections anywhere of locally made woodwork, jewelry, baskets, glass items, ceramics, and clothing. The twenty-six artist-members take turns staffing the store. Upstairs is the gallery of woodworker **Arthur Dennis Williams**, who specializes in sculpture and furniture made from local woods. Behind the Guild is the **Aloha Bead Company** (579-9709), which offers beaded jewelry.

Mana Foods, 49 Baldwin Avenue (579-8078), is a very good source for health-oriented products, foods, vitamins,

and organically grown produce. For a cup of coffee in a pleasing café, try **Café des Amis** at 42 Baldwin Avenue (579-6323).

There are a great many boutiques in Pā'ia with nicely designed island-style clothing for men, women, and children. **Moonbow Tropics** at 36 Baldwin Avenue (579-8592) carries a good selection of aloha wear by local designers, including Kahala and Tori Richard. (They also have a shop in the new Mā'alaea Harbor Village.)

Upcountry

Upcountry is a different—and unexpected—world. Cool, green, and dotted with cattle ranches, it reminds many of the American West. The mood is decidedly Western, with horses, cattle, four-wheel-drive vehicles, cowboy hats, rail fences, pine forests, and temperatures that are much cooler than at Maui's lower elevations.

On the slopes of Haleakalā, pheasant and quail can be seen against the green grasses. A wide variety of flowers grows here, including the hardy protea, transplanted from Australia and South Africa and exotic in its many different shapes and colors. The famous Kula onion, known for its mild, sweet flavor, grows here as well. Jacaranda and towering eucalyptus trees line back roads, and from almost anywhere above the 1,500-foot level there are magnificent vistas of the ocean, the West Maui Mountains, and the valley below.

Makawao

Highways 37, 377, and 378 wind through the Upcountry area and lead to Haleakalā. Baldwin Avenue, from Pāʻia, goes up to **Makawao**, which is also reachable by way of Makawao Avenue off Highway 37. This unpretentious cowboy town boasts trendy galleries and shops in storefronts that haven't changed since they were erected more than fifty years ago. Every July 4 weekend, Makawao celebrates its cowboy roots with an annual rodeo and *paniolo* parade. Above Makawao, Olinda Road (Highway 39) leads to the small community of **Olinda**, with rolling green hills, fragrant eucalyptus trees, and expansive views of the West Maui Mountains and the central valley.

Left: Makawao celebrates the Fourth of July with a rodeo and parade.

Below: Lush ranchland in Makawao is backed by mighty Haleakalā.

One mile below the town of Makawao, at 2841 Baldwin Avenue, the historic Kaluanui estate houses the Hui No'eau Visual Arts Center (572-6560), a nonprofit organization. Kaluanui was designed in 1917 by the noted architect Charles W. Dickey, who was responsible for much of Honolulu's Mediterranean-style architecture during the territorial era. The downstairs rooms, with grand high ceilings, are now galleries where changing exhibitions of work by Maui's leading artists take place. A gift shop offers one-of-a-kind creations by fine artists and artisans. There is no admission fee, but donations are welcome (closed Sundays).

Kaluanui was built as the home of Harry and Ethel Baldwin, first family of Maui's sugar and pineapple industries. The remains of one of Maui's earliest sugar mills, run by mule power, are located at the entrance to the ten-acre estate. Ethel Baldwin and her daughter, Frances, founded the Hui No'eau Visual Arts Society in 1934 and attracted artists worldwide to visit Makawao. The family stopped using the estate as a home in the 1950s, and in the 1970s Ethel Baldwin's grandson, the late Colin Cameron (who was the force behind the Kapalua Resort), granted Hui No'eau use of Kaluanui as a visual arts center.

Hui No'eau (which translates as "society of artists") offers classes in painting, drawing, printmaking, ceramics, and other visual arts mediums. The picturesque stables and tack rooms now serve as the ceramics studio, and printmaking and papermaking activities take place in the carriage house. Visitors are welcome in many of the classes.

Upcountry Shopping

If you're doing any cooking while you're on Maui, stop by **Maui Fresh** at 870 Hāliʻimaile Road (573-5129), next to Hāliʻimaile General Store, for the best in local produce. Available in season are asparagus, strawberries, and sweet corn. Tropical produce includes pineapples, bananas, and papayas. They also can do agricultural inspection, so you can take freshly picked pineapples to the mainland with you. Don't miss the jam and salsa selections. Open Monday–Saturday, 10 A.M.–6 P.M.

Ask anyone what to look for in Makawao and they'll tell you not to miss the **Komoda Store and Bakery**, 3674 Baldwin Avenue (572-7261). Legendary for their cream puffs, Komoda's also has great pastries, pies, and cookies. Open Monday through Saturday from 6:30 A.M. until early afternoon, they sell out of favorites early.

Makawao, with its many galleries, is ranked among the top art destinations in the United States. The premier gallery is **Viewpoints** at 3620 Baldwin Avenue (572-5979), which features only local art. **Hot Island Glass** (572-4527), behind Viewpoints, is a working studio and gallery where you can watch fine artisans craft beautiful glass objects. **Ola's**, at 1156 Makawao Avenue (573-1334), has a good selection of contemporary crafts. **Designing Wahine**, 3620 Baldwin Avenue (573-0990)—in the same complex as Viewpoints and Hot Island Glass—has a fabulous line of island-style children's clothes made only from natural fibers and materials and manufactured exclusively for them. Among other interesting boutiques in Makawao is **Collections** at 3677 Baldwin Avenue (572-0781), with stylish women's clothing, nice bath products, and an excellent selection of jewelry, gifts, and greeting cards. **Miracles Bookery** at 3682 Baldwin Avenue (572-2317) has a varied assortment of New Age and self-discovery books, tapes and CDs, videos, incense, cards, and gifts.

Colorful proteas are sold at roadside stands throughout the area. **Proteas of Hawaiʻi** at 210 Mauna Place in Kula (878-2533), across from the University of Hawaiʻi Kula Experimental Farm (see below), will pack and ship flowers for you. **Sunrise Protea Farm** at 416 Haleakalā Crater Road (Highway 378; 876-0200) is a more convenient stop to and from the Haleakalā summit; they also will arrange shipments—and their market sells Maui fruits and vegetables as well as locally made cookies.

Exotic proteas are grown at many Upcountry farms. The hardy flowers will last many weeks.

Kula

Kula's rolling hills are often cloaked with a soft mist.

Right: The eight-sided Church of the Holy Ghost was built by Portuguese settlers in 1897.

Highway 37 leads through Kula to 'Ulupalakua Ranch. The drive is a lovely one, with many places of interest along the way. Not long after the intersection of 37 with 377 (which you'd take if you were going to the summit of Haleakalā), on the *mauka* side of the road (across from mile marker 10), are the **Enchanting Floral Gardens** (878-2531), eight acres of exquisitely landscaped tropical gardens with proteas, orchids, hibiscus, jade vines, and a variety of fruit trees. The gardens are open daily, 9 A.M.–5 P.M.; $5 admission fee.

The **Church of the Holy Ghost** on Lower Kula Road in Kula, the way

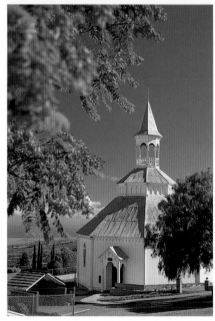

to which is marked by a large sign on Highway 37, is famous for its octagonal shape, which won it a spot on the National Register of Historic Places. This 1897 Catholic church on a hillside above Waiakoa has a large, ornate altar crafted by the Austrian woodcarver Ferdinand Stuflesser and shipped to Maui from Europe; it was brought upcountry by ox cart. The words of the Station of the Cross lining the church's walls are in Portuguese, reflecting the country of origin of Kula's early residents. There is a gift shop with inspirational items as well as the Holy Ghost cookbook ($12), with recipes from members of the Kula community, published to help pay for the 1992 restoration of the church.

From here a short drive takes you to the **University of Hawai'i Kula Experimental Farm** (878-1213). Continue on Lower Kula Road about a half mile to Copp Road (Calasa Garage is on the far corner). Turn left on Copp Road and travel .2 mile to Mauna Place, turn left, and go .4 mile to the University of Hawai'i facility. Here beautiful proteas and a large variety of exquisite roses are grown, along with other tropical and northern hemisphere plants, including *kalo,* cabbage, holly trees, and gladiolas. There's a small parking lot adjacent to the office, where you must sign in and where you can pick up a map of the grounds. Although this facility isn't really set up for hordes of tourists, it's a great out-of-the-way trek both for the plantings and the magnificent views— a sweeping panorama that goes from Kīhei on the left, across to the West Maui Mountains, as far as Pā'ia and the northeastern coastline on the right. The farm is open only Monday–Thursday, 7 A.M. to 3:30 P.M. It is closed Fridays, weekends, and holidays. There is no admission fee; nor are there guides or attendants.

Copp Road winds its way up the mountain, past picturesque farms and homes, until it reaches Highway 377 (Kekaulike Avenue). Turn right here to continue toward 'Ulupalakua. On the left, you'll come to the **Kula Botanical Garden** (878-1715), which features native plants as well as proteas, orchids, and bromeliads. The admission fee is $5 ($1 for children). The site is beautiful, and it is well worth a visit.

For those with an urge to get still farther off the beaten path, there is the 10.5-mile trip on Waipoli Road from Highway 377 up to **Polipoli Springs State Recreation Area**. The road can be driven in a rental car; however, it is bumpy and rutted in

Unique protea blossoms such as this one are cultivated at the University of Hawai'i Kula Experimental Farm.

places, not to mention narrow, making driving conditions hazardous at times, especially if the clouds roll in and impair visibility. With numerous switchbacks, the road climbs about 3,000 feet in the first 6 miles. In wet weather it is advisable to attempt it only in a four-wheel-drive vehicle. Once at the park, you are in the middle of a hardwood forest. If you climb another thousand feet on foot, you can stand atop a volcanic cinder cone and enjoy an astonishing view of the neighboring islands. There is a single cabin in the area that can be reserved through the State Parks office in Wailuku (984-8109). Because of the 6,000-foot elevation of the park, the weather can be quite cool, especially in winter.

Hiking in Polipoli

Below Polipoli, there are a number of connected trails. Redwood, Plum, Haleakalā Ridge, and Polipoli trails form a 3.5-mile loop well worth hiking. Waiohuli Trail, tying up with Boundary Trail, leads to an overlook with a view of Kēōkea, a small Kula community, and on to Maui's Kīhei coastline. Waiakoa Trail (also called the Upper Waiohuli Trail), begins at the Kula Forest Reserve and winds 7 miles up Haleakalā, coming back

Hikers on the Redwood Trail in Polipoli State Park are surrounded by towering trees. Ferns (right) cover the forest floor.

through a series of dramatic switchbacks. The 3-mile Waiakoa Loop Trail, which begins at the game checking station on the Polipoli access road near the top of the switchbacks, passes through native scrub and grass vegetation, with excellent views in all directions. This network of trails offers spectacular views and close-ups of the wide variety of Maui flora. The Department of Land and Natural Resources (873-3506; 54 South High Street, Room 101, Wailuku, Maui 96793) has a free Maui recreation map that details the trails in the Polipoli area.

Kēōkea *and* ʻUlupalakua

Less than one-half mile after Waipoli Road, Highway 377 meets up with Highway 37 (which you left to go to the octagonal church, if you are following our tour). Another 2.7 miles takes you to pristine **Kēōkea Park**, on the left, a good place to picnic, or you can get a homemade pastry and coffee at **Grandma's**

The Henry Fong Store is one of a handful of buildings in quiet Kēōkea.

Top: Looking toward the West Maui Mountains from 'Ulupalakua Ranch.

Above: Pam Andelin, *Upcountry Hale*, oil on canvas.

Coffee House (878-2140), on the *makai* side of the road. Grandma's coffee beans, grown in Kula, are roasted at the back of the store. Local artist **John Wallau** has a studio next door; his colorful paintings go for reasonable prices.

Another 6 miles takes you to the **'Ulupalakua Ranch** and a small visitor center where it is possible to buy wines grown on the ranch. In 1974 the ranch owner, C. Pardee Erdman, and a young winemaker from northern California, Emil Tedeschi, combined their talents to produce Hawai'i's first and only commercial wine. The 2,000-foot elevation and the Carnelian grape have made the wine produced by **Tedeschi Vineyards** (878-6058) a commercial and aesthetic success. Eight wines are produced, including their bestseller, Maui Blanc, a white wine made from the juice of pineapple. The ranch road winds to a tasting room in a cottage that dates from 1874. It was built for Hawai'i's monarch David Kalākaua and his queen, Kapi'olani, who often visited the area—at that time Rose Ranch—up until the king's death in 1891. The wines and other local products, including a small selection of books about Maui, are displayed and sold here. Tours of the grounds and winery operation are offered at no charge (last tour at 2:30 P.M.); open daily except holidays. For Jeep tours of the ranch, see page 186.

Haleakalā

Dominating the Maui scene is spectacular Haleakalā, a volcano 33 miles long and 10,023 feet high, with a circumference of 21 miles and an area of 19 square miles, extending to Maui's southeastern coast. The crater itself is 7.5 miles long, 2.5 miles wide. The national park area surrounding the volcano is 42.6 square miles. One end of the crater gets less than thirty inches of rain a year, while the other gets more than three hundred inches. Hikers and campers in the crater can—and often do—get sunburned and rained on in the same day. Before your visit, check current weather conditions by calling 871-5054.

You will need at least a sweatshirt for cool mornings and evenings—a winter jacket and gloves would not be out of place (many Maui B&Bs keep warm clothing on hand for guests to borrow just for trips to Haleakalā). In the winter, especially, be prepared for wet, windy weather. But you'll also need

Hiking the Sliding Sands Trail in the crater of Haleakalā provides extraordinary vistas that are unlike anyplace else on earth.

sunscreen and a protective hat, as the sun can be unrelenting during the day. Persons with high blood pressure or a heart condition should remember to move slowly in the thin air of upper Haleakalā; such persons are advised not to hike or drive alone. For anyone, the high elevations can bring on fatigue and shortness of breath.

Above: Early morning mist on the lower slopes of Haleakalā.

Right: A view of Haleakalā crater from the summit.

An active volcano, Haleakalā last erupted in the late 18th century; the exact date is not known. Scientists figure that it erupts every several hundred years, which means that we're due for an eruption at least in the next hundred years. Meanwhile, we can rest assured that volcanologists will monitor every underground rumble, and plenty of warning will be given before an eruption occurs.

The most direct route to Haleakalā's summit is to take Highway 37 from Kahului, then eventually veer left onto Highway 377, following the signs. You will come to another left turn, onto Highway 378, for the last 12 miles to the park's entrance. From here, the road makes a series of switchback turns habited island of Kahoʻolawe, and the islet of Molokini. Some hundred miles to the southeast are the tops of the volcanic massifs of Mauna Loa and Mauna Kea on the island of Hawaiʻi.

A quarter of a mile before the entrance to Haleakalā National Park, a paved road leads to the **Hosmer Grove**

Both in and outside the crater, the *nēnē*, a Hawaiian goose that was nearly extinct by the 1940s, is fighting its way back. Hawaiʻi's state bird, the *nēnē* is related to the Canadian goose and probably descends from that bird. Admire the *nēnē* but do not disturb them or disrupt their activities—and do not feed them. There are often tame *nēnē* around park headquarters that are accustomed to visitors snapping photos of them.

in increasingly cooler temperatures on the way to the summit. There is no public transportation to Haleakalā; visitors must use rental cars or travel via an escorted sightseeing excursion to visit the area. There is an admission fee to the park.

The views are spectacular both en route and once there. The road winds through ranchlands, offering with each turn a view of the land below and of the West Maui Mountains (usually peeking through a cloud cover, particularly in the afternoon). In the distance are islands—Molokaʻi and Lānaʻi, the unin-

campground and picnic area, a half-mile from the highway. This area contains a shelter against inclement weather and includes tables and grills. There are tent sites, running water, and parking. There is no charge for camping here, and permits are not required. Stop to enjoy the variety of trees along the trail at Hosmer Grove. Some, planted in 1910 by naturalist Ralph Hosmer in an attempt to revegetate barren land, are from India, Japan, and Australia. He succeeded in his planting project, which unfortunately has made it impossible for native plants to regain a foothold here.

The main **park headquarters**, at the 7,000-foot level and just a mile inside the park entrance, is a good place to start your visit to the area. The headquarters' hours are 7:30 A.M. to 4 P.M. Inside the building is a wealth of information on Haleakalā, including excellent trail maps (free), photographs, a slide presentation, and friendly park rangers who can answer any question about this unique site. Here is where hiking and camping permits are issued.

Four overlooks permit fine views of the crater itself. They are **Leleiwi**, at the 9,000-foot level; **Kalahaku**, 2 miles below the summit; the **National Park Visitor Center** near the summit; and Red Hill, or **Puʻu ʻUlaʻula**, at the very top of the mountain.

At the summit is a cluster of white, somewhat futuristic buildings and domes. This is **Science City**, home of a communications station, University of Hawaiʻi observatories, radar installations, television relay stations, and a satellite tracking station. It is from this area that laser beams have been aimed at satellites as part of the Strategic Defensive Initiative, better known as Star Wars. The site is off-limits to visitors.

A rainbow in Haleakalā crater as seen from Palikū cabin, on the far side of the crater near the Kaupō Gap.

Many people make the effort to witness **sunrise on Haleakalā**—a spectacular sight when it's clear. The name Haleakalā means House of the Sun, and that is surely what it appears to be as the sun rises seemingly from within the crater and spreads its rays across the awesome landscape, breaking over the cinder cones that jut up from the crater floor. To the east, the Big Island forms out of the darkness, then the sun soars well above the horizon, changing the whole spectrum of colors.

The setting sun at Haleakalā is as splendid as the sunrise.

> "**I**t was the sublimest spectacle I ever witnessed, and I think the memory of it will remain with me always."
>
> —*Mark Twain on seeing the sunrise at Haleakalā, 1866*

For those staying at West Maui resorts, however, to view dawn at Haleakalā means rising very early and enduring up to a 3-hour drive. It's a good idea to call Maui's weather/recreation forecast (871-5054) before starting up. That recording also gives the time of sunrise and sunset. In winter it is possible to encounter snow, and occasionally snow forces the temporary closing of the road.

Sunsets are just as rewarding as the sunrise and allow you to sleep in on your vacation. To see the sun drop behind the West Maui Mountains and watch the sky invent new colors is a never-to-be-forgotten experience.

Inside the crater is a desertlike atmosphere. There are lichens, *pili* grass, clover, evening primrose, *'ōhelo, māmane,* tarweed, *'ōhi'a,* and the rare silversword plant. The true grandeur of Haleakalā can be experienced by descending down into the crater, which is large enough to hold the island of Manhattan. You can ride horses or mules into the crater (see page 186), or you can hike any of the 27 miles of trails that allow for trips ranging from less than an hour to as long as three days.

A favorite activity on Haleakalā, drawing hordes of tourists, is riding a bicycle downhill from the summit to Makawao or Pā'ia (see pages 184–85). Bicycles are restricted to paved roads and may not be taken into the crater. A final caveat: when driving your car back down to sea level, use lower gears to avoid brake failure.

Hiking Haleakalā

Hikers should be properly equipped for temperatures ranging between 40 and 65 degrees and for variable weather. Here is a list of what the National Park Service says should be brought on a hike: three quarts of water per person per day; raingear, warm clothing, sturdy shoes or boots, hat, sunscreen, sunglasses, first aid kit, bee sting kit, flashlight, trail map, snacks, a bag for trash, and toilet paper.

For relatively easy outings, hikers can go along **Halemau'u Trail** from the highway for as far as they wish and turn back. The **Sliding Sands Trail** is more difficult but exciting. It is an excellent full-day hike, from the Sliding Sands Trail to the Halemau'u Trail, passing by the Hōlua cabin, providing dramatic views inside the crater and ending with a thrilling climb up majestic basalt cliffs. You'll end up 6 miles away from the Visitor Center where you started, so be sure to arrange for pick-up, or leave your car at the Halemau'u trailhead in the morning and hitch a ride up to the Visitor Center to start your hike. Bring food and water (there's nothing available

to buy at the summit except guidebooks and postcards), and dress in layers for temperatures that might range from close to freezing in the early morning to the 80s as the day progresses.

There are longer hikes, more demanding and more rewarding. One is the hike down Sliding Sands Trail with an overnight stay at the Hōlua cabin campground. Another is a hike to Palikū campground for an overnight stay and a return via the Halemau'u Trail.

There are several points of interest along the way in the crater. One is the **Bottomless Pit** of the Halemau'u Trail, a 10-foot-wide yawning well that, bottomless or not, is clogged with debris 60 to 70 feet down. Be careful approaching the edge.

The **Bubble Cave** is another point of interest and is not far from the Kapalaoa cabin; it is a large, collapsed bubble made by gases from molten lava in an eruption. The lush, green area around the Palikū cabin contrasts sharply with the desertlike crater floor. **Silversword Loop** off Halemau'u Trail has a number of places that may look simply like piles of stone but are the remains of sacred sites constructed by the Hawaiians and should not be disturbed; nor should visitors make piles of stones.

A series of switch-backs leads down Halemau'u Trail to the crater floor.

Another hike, along the **Skyline Trail**, begins at the summit and ends some 5 hours later and nearly 4,000 feet down on the outside of Haleakalā. If you park at the summit, you will have to have someone meet you at the end of the hike. Skyline starts at the lowest point on the Science City Road, passes through an iron gate, and leads across a rugged landscape that has a tremendous view to compensate, then drops down into scrub trees. Halfway down the trail is a marker pointing to the Haleakalā Ridge Trail. A third of a mile in that direction the Polipoli Trail branches off and leads to Polipoli Springs State Recreation Area. This tough but rewarding hike ends in the midst of magnificent hardwood trees.

Tent camping is allowed at two areas in the crater; required permits are free and are issued on a first-come, first-served basis at park headquarters on the day of the trip. Three primitive cabins are available for a small charge; permits are necessary and are issued on the basis of a lottery. See page 231 for details.

Those are the facts of Haleakalā, but like the Hawaiian islands themselves, more than facts are necessary for a real understanding of this incredible mountain. For example, on some late afternoons at Leleiwi overlook, your shadow is thrown against the clouds, frequently encircled by a rainbow. This is the Specter of the Brocken, a phenomenon seen from the summit of high mountains (as on the Brocken, in Germany). The observer and surrounding objects are seen projected on the cloud, seemingly much enlarged owing to overestimation of distance, often encircled by a rainbow. Many consider Haleakalā a magical, mystical spot, enhanced by its magnetic powers (there's no point in trying to use a compass here; it won't work).

An old Hawaiian legend about Haleakalā has almost been lost in time. The Polynesian settlers had in their pantheon of gods four sisters who were goddesses of the snows. The four snow goddesses came from far over the sea and were rivals of Pele, the goddess of fire who lived in the volcanoes. An old tale tells of the fierce battles between Pele and the paramount snow goddess, Poli'ahu, who lived on the snow-covered summit of Mauna Kea. Poli'ahu always won the battles, because at the end of the fiery eruptions caused by Pele, the gentle snow would still fall like a mantle over the summits of the volcanoes. The goddess who lived in Haleakalā was Lilinoe, and on dark, blustery nights in the crater it is easy to believe she still watches over Haleakalā.

Opposite:
A silversword in full bloom. The floor of Haleakalā crater was once covered with these remarkable plants, which bloom from June through October.

"We came upon . . . thousands of silverswords, their cold, frosted silver gleam making the hillside look like winter or moonlight," wrote travel writer Isabella Bird in 1873, describing a descent into Haleakalā crater. The magnificent silversword (*Argyroxiphium sandwicense*), called the ʻāhinahina in Hawaiian, is found few places on earth, among them the desertlike environment of Haleakalā. It can take up to twenty years for a plant to flower, and then it dies. The silversword is a member of the same family as sunflowers, asters, and chrysanthemums. An endangered species, silverswords can be seen in abundance by hikers in Haleakalā's crater, though they are not nearly as plentiful as in Miss Bird's day. At one time they were nearly extinct, but propagation efforts have brought them back. Be careful not to walk too closely to them, as their delicate roots lie close to the surface.

Hāna *area*

EVERY VISITOR TO MAUI, it seems, drives to Hāna. In fact, the annual visitor count to the area is close to a million. To go to Hāna is to turn back the calendar to a place that time has forgotten. Even on Maui, itself a special place, Hāna stands apart, a virtual heaven on earth. Part of its charm lies in its isolation. Although there is a small airstrip served by a commuter airline, access is limited.

Most people make a day trip to Hāna, rushing to get there and visiting only the so-called Seven Sacred Pools, missing many of the wonderful sights coming and going and the numerous other places of interest once there—not to mention the charms of the laid-back lifestyle that Hāna affords.

The Road *to* Hāna

The beautiful Hāna Highway is an experience in itself, with 617 curves along its

Colleen Meechan, *Huelo*, acrylic on canvas.

52 miles ("highway" is a euphemism to be sure). In 2000, President Bill Clinton designated the road Hawai'i's official Millennium Legacy Trail, with a three-day ceremony to mark the historic event. Carved from the hillside in 1927 and generally following the old King's Trail, the road has fifty-four one-lane bridges. Driving is an exhilarating and somewhat challenging experience. Just the effort in getting to Hāna makes it a special place. The drive can take from 2 to 3 hours from Kahului, depending on how often you stop to enjoy the lush scenery. The many scenic lookouts and rushing waterfalls are well worth a leisurely pace. In addition, the small towns along the way offer a glimpse of a Hawaiian lifestyle that is all but lost in other areas of Maui.

Be prepared for a slow drive on the Hāna Highway. The speed limit is 15 much of the way. Where the road is a single lane, watch for signs to yield to oncoming traffic. During heavy rainfalls the road may be closed owing to danger from flash floods and falling rocks. Residents are used to the road and aren't craning to see the spectacular scenery. If there is a line of cars behind you, pull over to let them pass.

There are a number of fruit and flower stands along the road, many of them operating on the honor system. If you plan to make a leisurely trip to Hāna, it might be wise to stop in Pā'ia

The road to Hāna hugs
the rugged coastline.

for a sandwich to bring along, though you can buy cold drinks and smoothies along the way and even get a cup of cappuccino and a freshly made taco in Nāhiku. There are no gas stations until Hāna.

After leaving Pāʻia, the last town of consequence on the Hāna Highway, the road changes from Highway 36 to Highway 360. You'll pass by the villages of **Huelo** (mile 4) and shortly after that a second small town, **Kailua** (mile 6). These quiet, sleepy places add to the aura of peace and contentment along the northeast coast. As the road winds past them, incredibly lush foliage cloaks the roadside. You'll want to drink in the beauty of the streams and waterfalls. Several large stands of bamboo, rainbow eucalyptus, and Norfolk pines—all introduced to Hawaiʻi by early settlers—line the road.

Past mile 9, look for a sign on the right for the **Waikamoi Nature Trail** in the Koʻolau State Forest. This easy loop trail of less than a mile climbs a forested slope to a picnic area, with several look-outs along the way. There are no rest-room facilities. The next place of interest is the **Garden of Eden Arboretum**

Twin Falls are the first of many water-falls along the Hāna Highway. A trail to the falls, which are about half a mile from the highway, begins near the Twin Falls fruit stand.

Opposite top: The rocky shore at Ke'anae Landing.

Opposite bottom: Lanakila Ihi'ihi o Iehova ona Kaua Church, Ke'anae.

(572-9899), past mile 10. This pristine garden, where the opening sequence of *Jurassic Park* was filmed, is well worth the $5 admission fee. Here is one of the most colorful and extensive collections of *ti*, a plant brought to Hawai'i by early settlers from Tahiti. Plants and trees are well labeled, and there are many splen-did views. (Near the waterfall overlook, an artist named Kaj sells quite beautiful beaded jewelry.)

At **Kaumahina State Wayside Park** (mile 13), there are views of Honomanū Bay and Ke'anae Peninsula down below.

The park has restrooms and picnic tables, making it a popular stop. A four-wheel-drive vehicle is advised for the dirt road leading down to the bay at mile 14. **Honomanū Park** has a lovely black sand beach, although there are no amenities and swimming can be treacherous.

A short distance on down the high-way is the **Ke'anae Valley Lookout**, where you can admire views of Wailua in one direction and Ke'anae Valley on up to Ko'olau Gap in the other. Before heading down a narrow paved road (look for the 17 mile marker) to **Ke'anae Landing**, stop at the **Ke'anae Arboretum**, located on the *mauka* side of the road just around the bend from the YMCA's Camp Ke'anae (see page 231). Parking is on the left side of the road, past the arboretum. The gardens feature many native Hawaiian plants as well as timber, food, and ornamental plants from all over the tropics. To reach the gardens, walk .1 mile down a paved pathway. Most of the walkway in the park is paved, though a section extends down a dirt road. This is not a great garden—state maintenance seems to be minimal—but it is free. At one time sixty varieties of *kalo* were cultivated here, but today those fields are over-taken by jungle. Take note that this area is home to hordes of hungry mosquitoes. There are no restrooms or picnic tables.

Down on the peninsula, modern *kalo* farms look much like their older counterparts. Many of the area's residents are Hawaiians who pridefully hold onto the old ways. A notable feature of Ke'anae, aside from its peaceful setting and *hala*-lined shore, is the **Lanakila Ihi'ihi o Iehova ona Kaua Church**, dating to 1860. It is constructed from rocks and coral from the surrounding shore area. For cement, coral was melted in an *imu*, which can still be seen at the entrance to the church. The roof of the

the **Ke'anae** coast

Waterfalls along the Hāna Highway create clear freshwater pools for a cooling dip.

Below: Kalo grows in abundance on the Ke'anae Peninsula, an easy side trip off the main road to Hāna.

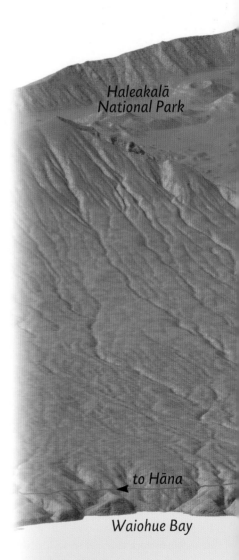

Haleakalā
National Park

to Hāna

Waiohue Bay

church has been poorly restored, but it is still an architecturally interesting structure. There is a fruit stand in Ke'anae where fresh-fruit smoothies, taro chips, and banana bread are sold.

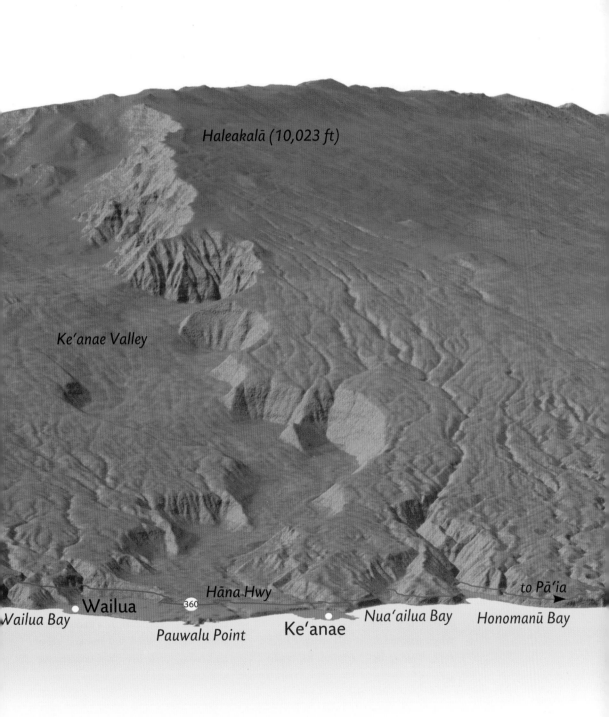

Haleakalā (10,023 ft)

Ke'anae Valley

Hāna Hwy

Wailua

360

to Pā'ia

Wailua Bay

Pauwalu Point

Ke'anae

Nua'ailua Bay

Honomanū Bay

The next stop is the village of **Wailua**, remarkable for its well-known **Coral Miracle Church**. Take the narrow paved road *makai*, just past mile 18, go past a *kalo* field on the left, and look for the white church on the same side of the road, beyond and behind an old shingled church. The real name for the Coral Miracle Church is **Our Lady of Fatima Shrine**. (Many guidebooks refer to it as Saint Gabriel's Church, an older name.) You'll have to park on the road and walk to the church, entering where there is a white cross. The reason it is

Our Lady of Fatima Shrine in Wailua is known as the Coral Miracle Church.

known as the Coral Miracle Church is that when parishioners set out to build a church in 1860, they found sand and coral washed ashore, which they used as building materials. The church's white-painted walls and stenciled decorations are quite charming. Especially

noteworthy are old wall paintings on either side of the altar.

Past Wailua is **Nāhiku**, a rainswept area 3 miles down from the highway, once the location of a rubber plantation and today the occasional residence of George Harrison of the Beatles fame, who owns a home in this rainforest paradise. The turnoff is identifiable only by a narrow paved road leading *makai*. At the turn of the century, Nāhiku was the only place in America where rubber was grown commercially. Today there are still a few rubber trees in evidence. Two good swimming holes are located here, one reached from the landing at the end of the road, one via a path on the right after the village's two churches.

Back on the main road and continuing toward Hāna, watch on the *makai* side of the road for **Nāhiku Ti Gallery and Café** (248-4887), open daily. Owned by artist Lana Stuart, the gallery has an excellent assortment of locally made gifts at fair prices. Check out the great umbrellas (not made locally but a unique find). Lana doesn't take credit cards, but she'll ship C.O.D. if you don't have enough cash or a check (not a bad deal, since you can then avoid the state sales tax). The café serves a variety of coffee drinks, excellent (but pricey) fresh-fruit smoothies, and an assortment of pastries. Next door is a makeshift stand selling grilled and smoked kabobs and tacos, made from *'ahi*, chicken, or

beef. Next to that is a fruit stand with coconuts and coconut candy. An artist named J.T. has been at the fruit stand for six years, every day but Thursday (when he's at the Hāna craft fair), making and selling beautifully crafted baskets, which he sells for a song.

From here, it's a 5-mile drive to Hāna with fewer hairpin turns. The remaining sights on the way are better seen when you're rested and have time for exploration, but if you're not staying in Hāna and won't be able to come back, we suggest that you not forgo the following.

At about mile 31, look for a turnoff going *makai*, 'Ula'ino Road, which leads 1.5 miles down to **Kahanu Garden** (248-8912), a National Tropical Botanical Garden devoted to plants that are culturally important to the Hawaiian and Polynesian people. On the grounds is the awesome **Pi'ilanihale Heiau**, said to be the largest in all the islands, its huge walls, more than 50 feet in height, still intact. The *heiau*, the size of two football fields, was until recently covered with jungle growth. The owners of the property have done an amazing job of restoration. Open only from 10 A.M. to 2 P.M., Monday through Friday, the garden can be explored on one's own ($5) or on a guided tour ($10), for which reservations are required.

Continuing on 'Ula'ino Road for another 1.5 miles, park at the end of the road, the site of the abandoned village of 'Ula'ino, and walk on the beach to beautiful Heleleike'ōhā Falls, where there is a nice oceanside pool, called **Blue Pool** by locals, for swimming. Note that 'Ula'ino Road is unpaved most of the way, and you'll have to drive through two streams, one before Kahanu Garden and the other before Blue Pool. Unless there have been heavy rains, the road is usually passable in a regular car. If it's not, leave your car near Kahanu Garden

Wailua is a sleepy farming community whose main crop is *kalo*.

Below: Francis Lono Jr. is the caretaker of Pi'ilanihale Heiau.

and hike to Blue Pool, where you can take a refreshing dip.

Returning to the main road, you are less than a mile away from Hāna's airport; the turnoff is clearly marked. Just past the airport turnoff is a side road that leads down to **Wai'ānapanapa State Park**, a dramatic seacoast area of great natural beauty. Trails lead through the Wai'ānapanapa and Waimao caves, as well as to **Ohala Heiau**, a .7-mile trek along the old King's Trail, a 16th-century construction project spearheaded by the great chief Pi'ilani. It's possible to take the trail all the way into Hāna. The 3-mile hike on a path that is well defined but rugged takes about 2 hours; good hiking shoes are recommended. The cinder and rock trail along a spectacular coast is partly shaded by *hala* trees. The occasional large, smooth steppingstones you'll see are remnants of the original King's Trail. Cabins are available in the park for limited stays, and tent camping is permitted (see page 231). For those who like camping out, Wai'ānapanapa is an ideal spot in an incomparable setting.

Along the shoreline beyond the caves, a natural blowhole and a high arch distinguish the point. Nearby **Pa'iloa** black sand beach fringes the small bay, where swimming is good when the water is calm but otherwise treacherous (see Beaches). It's a picture-perfect beach, though, and popular with locals as well as visitors.

A group hiking near Pa'iloa Beach in Wai'ānapanapa State Park.

Right: Pa'iloa Beach is famous for its sparkling black sand.

Opposite: Ohala Heiau is an ancient place of worship on the old King's Trail, less than a mile from the parking lot at Wai'āna-panapa State Park.

Like many Hawaiian areas, Wai'ānapanapa is the source of both legend and fact, the two occasionally melding. Wai'ānapanapa Cave is partially filled with water, which turns red in the spring. Folklore has it that a jealous husband, the chief Ka'akea, followed his wife, the princess Popoalaea, to the cave where she had gone to hide for fear of her life. Ka'akea killed Popoalaea, dashing out her brains upon the rocks and leaving the waters red with her blood. Presumably the waters turn red each year on the night of Kū, the god of justice in one of his guises.

Others attribute the color of the water to tiny red shrimp that spawn in the cave. Some people on Maui who find spiritual power in certain sites claim that Wai'ānapanapa is a place of great spirituality.

Hāna

In Hāna town the pace is easy and the sights are heartwarming. The town's population is mostly Hawaiian, with a sprinkling of celebrities who have found the town's quiet ways to their liking. The homes and few shops huddle in the arm of **Ka'uiki Head**, a volcanic outcropping.

Hāna was the birthplace of Ka'ahumanu, who became a favorite (and strong-willed) wife of Kamehameha I, whose armies crushed the Maui armies in a battle that raged near Ka'uiki Head. Hāna evolved into a plantation town, but sugar began to diminish as an area industry in the 1940s, and many people left Hāna for employment elsewhere. Then San Francisco industrialist Paul Fagan bought 14,000 acres and converted them into a cattle ranch. He also built the lovely **Hotel Hāna-Maui** (see page 215), which opened in 1946 as the Ka'uiki Inn, with ten rooms for well-heeled guests. In its first ten years, the hotel grew to fifty guestrooms and

Left: A rainbow over Ka'uki Head.

Kīpahulu Valley

Waiho'i Valley

◄ to Kīpahulu

Hāmoa 'Ālau Islet

the **Hāna** coast

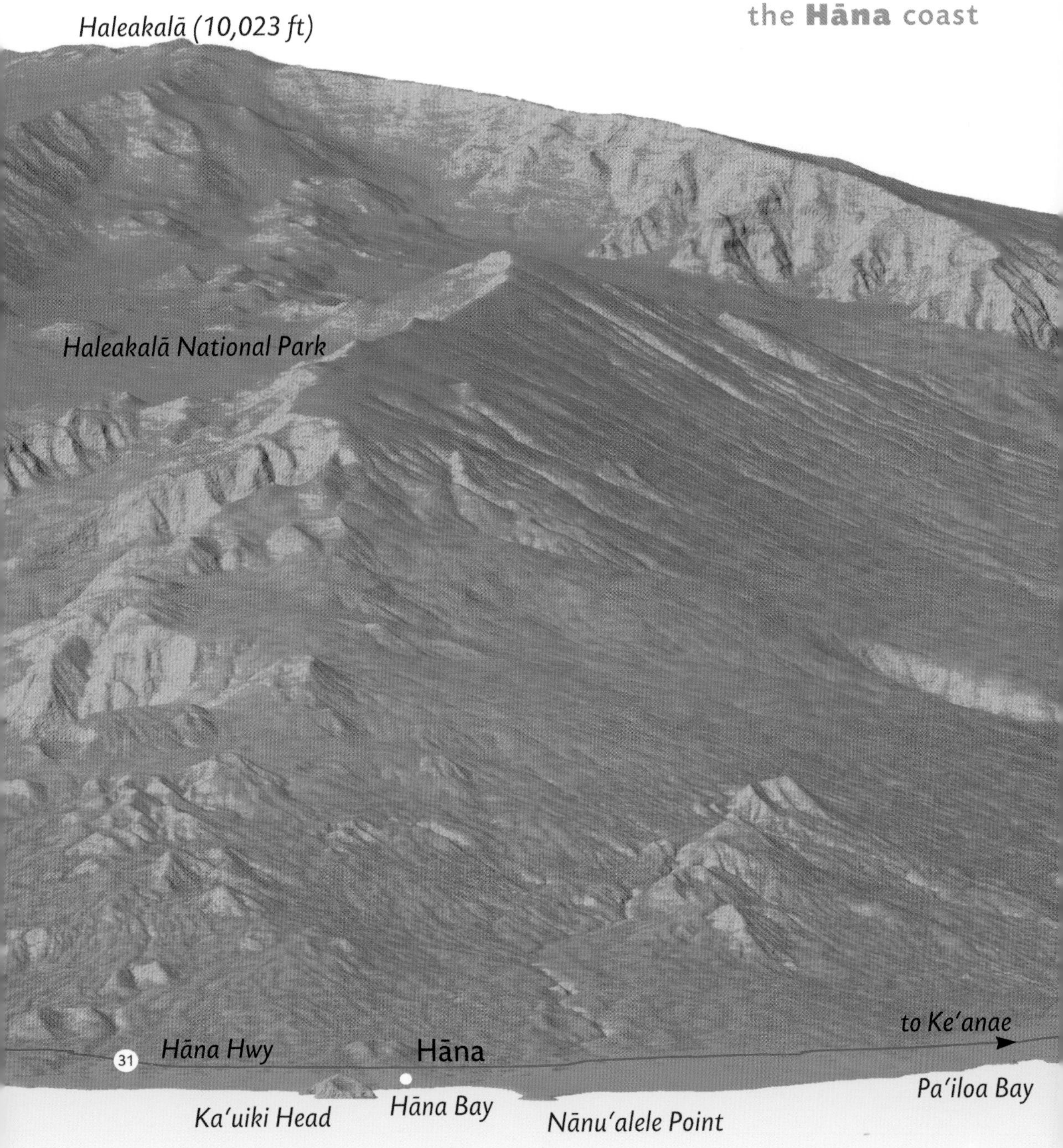
Haleakalā (10,023 ft)
Haleakalā National Park
31
Hāna Hwy
Hāna
to Ke'anae
Ka'uiki Head
Hāna Bay
Nānu'alele Point
Pa'iloa Bay

Ed Lane, *Hāna Bay Fisherman*, oil on linen.

Opposite top: The tranquil pool at the beautiful Hotel Hāna-Maui is a reminder of a more gracious era.

Opposite bottom: Hasegawa General Store in downtown Hāna.

colorful and sometimes turbulent past. The museum is housed in the **Hāna Cultural Center** (248-8622), open daily. Admission is free; however, a donation is suggested. The small gift counter has a good selection of locally made crafts. If you're looking for an authentic home-made Hawaiian quilt, this is the place to go (price: $1,200). Next door to the Cultural Center is Hāna's original court-house, built in 1871 and refurbished in 1989 to look much as it did in the 19th century. The courthouse is still used monthly for county court. Also on Cultural Center grounds are examples of traditional grass *hale*, including a meeting house, a sleeping house, a cook-house, and a canoe house. Six varieties of *kalo* are grown in the *hale* complex.

There is a park with public tennis courts near the center of Hāna, and down along the bay an old pier affords a good look back at Hāna. From the pier, a trail goes off to the right and onto Kaʻuiki Head (not an easy walk) and to a site where a plaque marks Kaʻahumanu's birthplace. **Hāna Beach Park** (see Beaches), a popular swimming and pic-nicking spot for locals, is not very pretty.

Hasegawa General Store, a long-time Hāna landmark, burned down in the summer of 1990 but has opened in a new location just across the street from the Chevron station, in a weathered green building that was formerly the Old Hāna Theater. It still brims with

received over 30,000 guests. On a *puʻu* rising above the town is a large cross, memorial to Fagan. The panoramic view of Hāna from the cross is spectacular.

Stop and relax in this quiet town. This is the place where, for years, when you telephoned the police department, you got a recorded message: "If this is an emergency, leave your name and number and we'll call you back." This is also the town where Sunday services at **Wānalua Church** are conducted in both Hawaiian and English.

Hale Waiwai o Hāna (248-8622), a museum on Uakea Road, which goes down to Hāna Bay, chronicles Hāna's

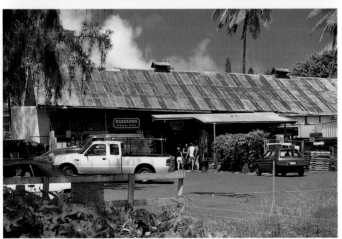

groceries, staple items, and souvenirs. Hasegawa's was celebrated some years ago in a song performed by Paul Weston's orchestra that was a national hit. The **Hāna Ranch Store** is the other market in town, offering food and sundries as well as souvenirs and postcards. If you want to see what's going on in town, take a look at the community bulletin boards just outside the entrances to these stores, with notices advertising everything from vacation rentals to massage therapists. There is a branch of the **Bank of Hawai'i** in town (248-8015), open from 3 to 4:30 weekdays.

The Hotel Hāna-Maui houses the **Hāna Coast Gallery** (248-8636), where there is a fine selection of paintings, sculpture, and woodwork by Hawai'i artists. Every Thursday, from 9:30 A.M. to 3:30 P.M., the **Hāna Farmers and Crafters Market** takes place at the Hasegawa Service Station.

Hāna is not particularly noted for its dining, and choices are limited. The **Hāna Ranch Restaurant** (248-8255), open daily for breakfast and lunch and several nights a week for dinner, serves up fair food at unfair prices (the last we heard, it will be closed for an extended period of time for renovations and will reopen with an upgraded menu). Also expensive is the **Dining Room at the Hotel Hāna-Maui**, but the food is quite good and the ambiance can't be beaten. Breakfast, lunch, and dinner are served; reservations are required for dinner (248-8211). The **Paniolo Bar** at the hotel serves *pūpū* in the evenings that can suffice for dinner if you're a light eater. **Tutu's** (248-8224), a takeout counter by the pier, offers plate-lunch-type fare.

Sunrise at 'Ālau Islet, a seabird sanctuary south of Hāna, off Kōki Beach Park.

There are three adventure activities of note in the Hāna area. Naturalist Kevin Coates will take you on an exciting kayak tour of magical sites along Hāna's coastline (see page 177). To soar above the coastline, you can go hang gliding in a powered two-person trike (see pages 176–77). And to explore the underground world, you can tour 30,000-year-old Ka'elekū Caverns, led by a lava-tube specialist (see page 187). In addition, hiking excursions offered by the Hotel Hāna-Maui are open to the public. For horseback riding in the area, see page 186.

Beyond Hāna

Past Hāna town, the sense of isolation continues. The road follows the coastline, marked by waterfalls and small bridges over rushing streams. This is Highway 31, which leads into Kīpahulu, a part of Haleakalā National Park.

En route, after mile 51, you'll pass Haneoʻo Road, the turnoff to **Kōkī Beach Park**. This beach is an idyllic setting, isolated and picturesque. An ancient fishpond hugs the shore, and in the distance is small ʻĀlau Islet. However, strong currents make swimming here extremely dangerous. Farther along Haneoʻo Road is **Hāmoa Beach** (see Beaches), a lovely white sand beach,

Lovely Hāmoa Beach is used by guests at the Hotel Hāna-Maui, but like all Hawaiʻi beaches it is open to everyone.

part of which belongs to the Hotel Hāna-Maui. The beach has an outdoor shower and a restroom designated for public use. The other facilities are for hotel guests only. Haneoʻo Road makes a loop and comes out back on the highway.

At mile 48, there's a great freshwater swimming pool just off the road. Park near the bridge and follow the trail toward the ocean. You'll come to Waioka

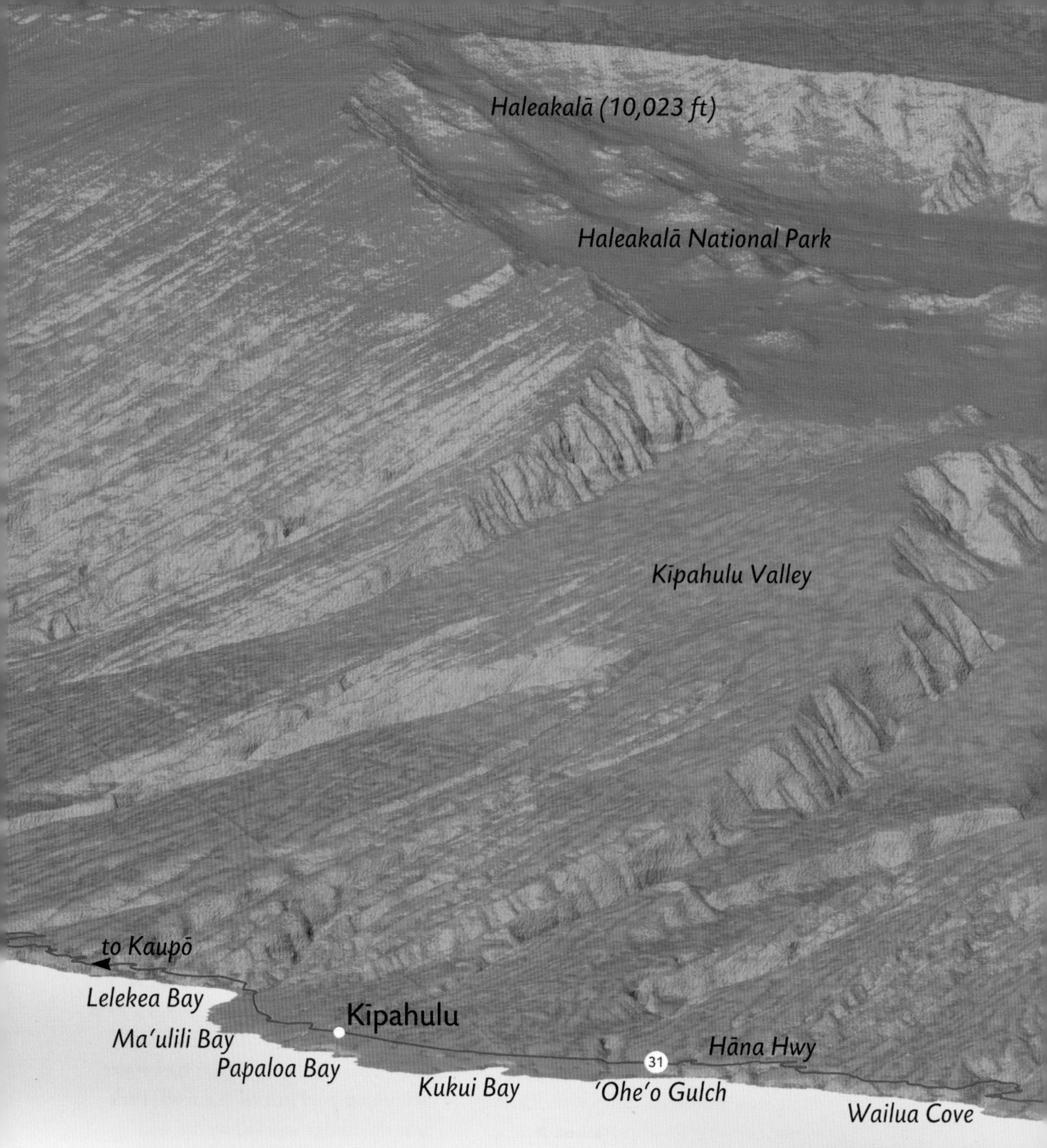

Haleakalā (10,023 ft)

Haleakalā National Park

Kīpahulu Valley

to Kaupō

Lelekea Bay

Maʻulili Bay

Papaloa Bay

Kīpahulu

Kukui Bay

Hāna Hwy

31

ʻOheʻo Gulch

Wailua Cove

the **Kīpahulu** coast

Pond, known locally as **Venus Pool**, a beautiful spot to spend some time swimming and picnicking.

Wailua and **Kanahuali'i Falls** crash down steep lava cliffs about 7 miles outside Hāna (mile 45). A trail leads down to a rocky beach where a settlement was wiped out on the morning of April 1, 1946, by a tsunami generated by an earthquake in Alaska. Above the road is a concrete cross honoring one Helio, a Hawaiian Catholic who lived during the 1840s and converted hundreds of people.

A favorite spot inside the national park is **'Ohe'o Gulch**, where twenty-four pools topple one into another and finally into the sea. This is also known, erroneously, as **Seven Sacred Pools**. A path on the left bank of the Pīpīwai Stream leads down to fine swimming and picnicking areas. On the other side and some distance above are *kalo* farms maintained by the Hāna Cultural Center. There are free tours of this area conducted by National Park rangers; call 248-7375 for schedules and information or stop by the Kīpahulu Visitor Center.

Wailua Falls, outside Hāna, plummet 95 feet to fill a pool below.

Hā'ō'ū   *to Hāna* ▶

Keawa Bay

Waimoku Falls Trail cuts through a magnificent stand of bamboo with a boardwalk to traverse muddy areas.

Below: Palapala Hoʻomau Church in Kipahulu is the site of Charles Lindbergh's simple grave.

A good short hike is up **Waimoku Falls Trail** to **Makahiku Falls**, a half-mile walk along Pīpīwai Stream, and then another 1.5 miles to 400-foot **Waimoku Falls**. The easily hiked trail winds up through a forest of non-native plants such as bamboo, mango, and guava. You can swim in the pool formed by Waimoku Falls, though the possibility of falling rocks discourages many from getting too close to the waterfall. Swimming in any of the pools in Pīpīwai Stream that you pass by on this hike can be a glorious experience. But be aware that in a flash flood, water can rise 4 feet in 10 minutes; head for higher ground if it starts to rain.

At Kīpahulu Ranch, look for the roadway on the *makai* side of the road (just past mile 41) that leads into the churchyard of **Palapala Hoʻomau Church**, where famed aviator Charles A. Lindbergh is buried. Lindbergh spent much of his later years in Hāna and helped restore the church. A year before his death in 1974 he picked this as his burial site.

Scenic Drive *to or from* **Hāna**

The "other" road to Hāna (Highway 31), coming around the southeast side of the island, is a spectacular route—37 miles from Hāna to ʻUlupalakua Ranch. Not for the faint of heart (like the drive around the head; see pages 67–70), this route takes you away from what may sometimes seem like bumper-to-bumper tourists on the Hāna Highway. The road is called the Piʻilani Highway, built by Piʻilani, a king of Maui in the 16th century. Archaeologists have discovered that this side of Maui was once occupied by

thousands of Hawaiians, whose villages of thatched huts would have dotted the landscape. Today few people live here, beyond the power grid, where solar energy is the only source of electricity.

Maintained by the county, this road is unpaved for the 6 miles between Kīpahulu and Kaupō. In rainy weather, areas can become washed out. But otherwise, the county does an excellent job of maintaining the road. You can take this road either going to or leaving

Hāna; we prefer the latter since we're chicken and would rather drive on the *mauka* side of the road, with the *makai* side perilously close to ocean cliffs with no guardrails. There are many one-lane blind curves, at which it is essential that you toot your horn to warn oncoming traffic of your approach.

Before the 35 mile marker, there is a roadway down to **Huialoha Church**, built in 1859 and since restored. The black sand beach is not recommended

Huialoha Church in Kaupō is a favorite spot for local weddings.

123

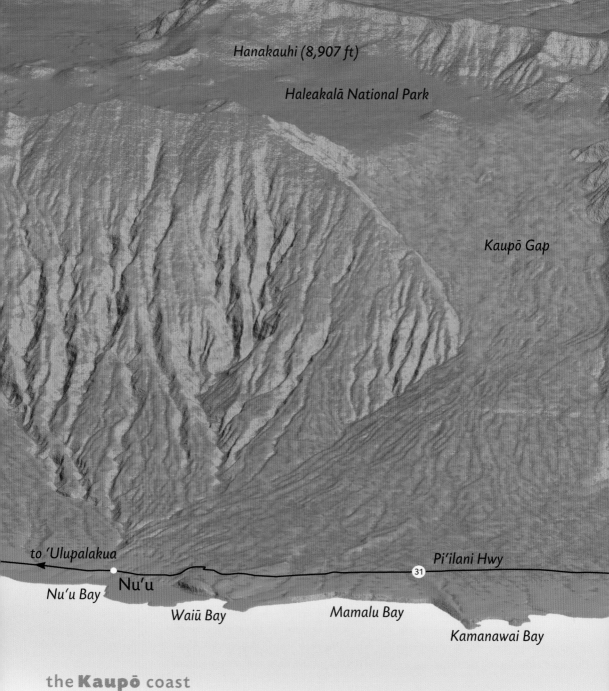

Hanakauhi (8,907 ft)

Haleakalā National Park

Kaupō Gap

to 'Ulupalakua

Pi'ilani Hwy

31

Nu'u Bay

Nu'u

Waiū Bay

Mamalu Bay

Kamanawai Bay

the **Kaupō** coast

for swimming owing to strong currents. At times there are Hawaiian monk seals on the beach. On a hill above the road are the remains of a *heiau;* another larger one, the 16th-century Loʻaloʻa Heiau, lies at the head of the Kaupō Gap, behind the small school.

The **Kaupō Store** (248-8054), in the heart of tiny Kaupō, has been a fixture since 1925. It was built by a Chinese man named Nick Soon, who was a photographer. His photos of town events and people from the 1920s, '30s, and '40s are in a scrapbook at the store that the present owner, Mannie, will be happy to show you. One photo shows the Model T Ford that Mr. Soon had shipped to him in parts, which he then assembled. Mannie has run the store for twenty years, but Mr. Soon's cameras still line the shelves. Mannie won't sell them, preferring to keep the store as

Sign for the Kaupō Store.

Below: The drive on Piʻilani Highway offers views of the back side of Haleakalā crater.

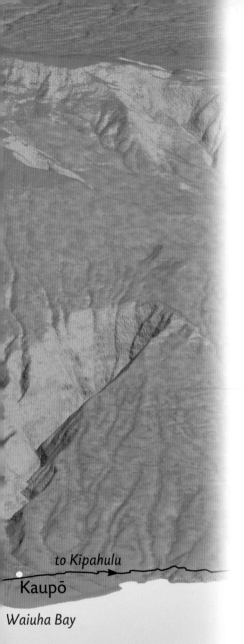

to Kīpahulu

Kaupō

Waiuha Bay

The rugged back side of Haleakalā may once have been home to more than three thousand Hawaiians, according to archaeologists working at a dig at Kahikinui. The name Kahikinui itself means "Large Tahiti." The dig, led by an archaeologist from the University of California at Berkeley, has been going on for nearly a decade and is the biggest archaeological project in Hawai'i. The team has uncovered 2,500 ancient sites, including thirty *heiau*, one of them a large platform that may have been dedicated to the hula. It is visible from afar, and the drums would have been heard for miles. Land that is now barren, devastated by cattle and goats, was once verdant forest land. By the 1830s, only one hundred people still lived in the district.

Remote southeastern Maui, looking toward Kaupō Gap on Haleakalā.

a museum of sorts. (Asked if he would sell some of the vintage pieces, Mannie says, "I have a price—no price.") There are restrooms at the Kaupō Store and a good supply of sodas, ice cream, and other snacks.

Past the Kaupō Store there are two roadside stands, **Auntie Jane's Café** and a hot dog stand run by **Auntie Margaret**. Either of these places might be open for a cold drink and snack. If you look to the right up Kaupō Gap, you'll see the rim of Haleakalā Crater. And if you look across the ocean, on a clear day you'll see the island of Hawai'i across the 'Alenuihāhā Channel.

Although the road along this coastline is bumpy, narrow, and difficult to navigate at times, the journey is exciting, and along the way are great views of unrivaled beauty. Past the old Nu'u Landing (mile 31) and at the end of a dry creekbed, there are caves and petroglyphs. Soon after, the road turns inland. In the distance you will see Molokini islet and beyond it the island of Kaho'olawe.

Finally, at mile 23 (still more than 30 miles from Kahului) the roadway becomes well paved. This beautiful country road winds through ranchland. To the left are views of La Pérouse Bay, Mākena, Wailea, and Kīhei. At 'Ulupalakua, the Upcountry area begins. From this ranch region the road winds down through Kula, and you are suddenly a world away from remote Hāna.

Kahului and Wailuku

to Lahaina

to Kīhei

380 Kūihelani Hwy

311 Mo

to Haleakalā

Kahului/Wailuku *area*

CENTRAL MAUI WAS FORMED BY gradual erosion of lava flows from Haleakalā and the West Maui Mountains over a million years ago. This broad isthmus is the site of thousands of acres of sugarcane. Within the area are two of Maui's major towns and its commercial heart. Kahului, where the main airport is located, is also a deepwater port. Three miles toward the mountains is Wailuku, Maui's capital.

Kahului

Kahului is Maui's supply center—it contains the shops and stores where staples are sold, including big box outlets Costco and K-Mart. When Maui residents say they are "going to town" for gas, groceries, clothing, furniture, or building materials, they are likely talking about Kahului. Much of what they buy is contained in shopping malls that line Dairy Road and Ka'ahumanu Avenue, named for the favorite wife of Kamehameha I.

There are several places of interest as you head in the direction of Wailuku from the airport. The first is adjacent to the airport itself—**Kanahā Beach Park**, reachable via Alahao Street just off the baseyard road to the Department of Water

Kanahā Beach Park

Pu'u Kukui (5,788 ft)

'Īao Valley

Main St

30 *Honoapi'ilani Hwy* 330 *Kahekili Hwy*

to Waiheʻe ▶

32 ● **Wailuku**

340

Kahului ● *Kahului Bay*

Hobron Point

Kahului Airport

Papaʻula Point

Haleakalā Hwy 36 *Hāna Hwy* *to Hāna* ▶

A Hawaiian stilt (*ae'o*) at Kanahā Pond.

Below: The SS *Independence*, whose home port is Kahului, has 23,000 square feet of open deck.

Supply. There are restrooms, large shade trees, and a view across Kahului Harbor. Generally uncrowded, the park is overlooked by most visitors. Between the airport and town is **Kanahā Pond**, a protected wildlife refuge and home of the migratory Hawaiian stilt, the *ae'o*. Kanahā Pond, formerly a royal fishpond, is one of the few remaining places in Hawai'i where the stilt can breed and feed unmolested.

The harbor near the edge of town has become important to Maui as a place where goods are received. To the Japanese fishermen who fish these waters, it is important as a fueling base for their boats. Here also is the state's first bulk sugar plant. American Hawai'i Cruises, which has docked at the harbor for years, has recently made Kahului the home port for the **SS *Independence***, an ocean liner that calls at five ports in tours around the Hawaiian islands. It sails every Sunday at 2 P.M. (see page 209).

Take Beach Road to the **Maui Arts and Cultural Center** (242-2787), a modern structure on the *mauka* side of the road. Here in a beautiful setting across from the ocean is an architecturally striking complex of two theaters, dance classrooms, an outdoor amphitheater, and the **Schaefer International Gallery** (244-8272). The gallery, Maui's only museum-quality exhibition space, hosts a wide range of art exhibitions throughout the year, including the popular Art Maui show each spring, a juried exhibition of works by the island's foremost artists.

Continuing on Beach Road takes you to **Haleki'i**, a partially restored *heiau* just outside Kahului. It can be reached by turning off Waiehu Beach Road onto Kūhiō Place, just past a bridge over 'Iao Stream. Haleki'i was in use during the reign of Maui's famous King Kahekili in the late 1700s. An onsite diagram explains the layout of the walls and terraces. A path leads from the site toward the mountains and ends in a second place of worship about a hundred yards away. This latter site, **Pihana**, dates from 1779 and was a sacrificial temple. From the Haleki'i site there is an especially good panoramic view of Kahului Harbor.

Shopping in Kahului

Kahului's many shopping centers offer a variety of stores, from local surf shops

to chain stores like Old Navy and Borders. Maui's first shopping center, Kahului Shopping Center on Kaʻahumanu Avenue (Highway 32), opened in the 1940s. Take a stroll through **Ah Fook's Super Market**, an old-time Maui grocer, and you'll feel like you've stepped into another world.

A bit down the road is the **Queen Kaʻahumanu Center**, whose anchor stores include Sears and Liberty House. A local department store chain founded in Honolulu in 1849, **Liberty House** is a great source for made-in-Hawaiʻi fashions and gifts. You'll find many other shops of interest at Queen Kaʻahumanu Center, though the recent poor economy has left some storefronts empty.

If you're looking for coffee, a good bet is the **Coffee Store** in Queen Kaʻahumanu Center (871-6860). They also have outlets at Azeka Place II in Kīhei (875-4244); Nāpili Plaza in Lahaina (669-4170); and Māʻalaea Triangle in Māʻalaea Harbor (242-2779). Their freshly roasted local coffees make great gifts for those back home. Prices are reasonable for delicious Kona, Maui, Kauaʻi, and Molokaʻi coffees. Also, they'll ship coffee to you once you're home; call 800-327-9661 (or check out www.mauicoffee.com).

Down to Earth at 305 Dairy Road (877-2661) is an excellent natural foods and organic produce market, with locally baked products and a fine selection of locally grown fruits and vegetables. A small café with eating area sells sandwiches, salads, and smoothies. They have another store in Makawao at 1169 Makawao Avenue (572-1488). **Maui Natural Foods** in the Maui Mall (877-3018), on Kaʻahumanu Avenue

near the intersection with the Hāna Highway (Highway 36), is another source for vitamins, herbs, skin care products, organic foods, and teas.

If you want to read more about Hawaiʻi while you're here or take some books home with you, **Borders** (the big mainland chain) at 270 Dairy Road (877-6160) has an exceedingly large selection of books from local publishers. They're open until 10 P.M.; Fridays and Saturdays until 11 P.M.

The Maui Arts and Cultural Center in Kahului brings noted performers to Maui and houses the Schaefer International Gallery, which hosts art exhibitions throughout the year.

The tower and bell of Ka'ahumanu Church were added to the 1876 structure in 1884, with a "fine tower clock from the U.S. costing $1,000."

Below: Wailuku's streets are lined with old wooden structures.

Wailuku

Wailuku, Maui's county seat since 1905, is a funky, old-fashioned town with twisting streets and old wooden structures as well as unique shops and a few noteworthy restaurants. It is easy to explore on foot. The same Ka'ahumanu Avenue that runs through the center of Kahului melds directly into Wailuku's Main Street. That goes on to become 'Īao Valley Road, leading directly into 'Īao Valley. If you park near the town's only "high rise," the nine-story **Kalana o Maui** (County Office Building), you can see most things of interest just by strolling around (follow signs for public parking). The town has published an informative brochure about its historic sites, complete with a map. Titled "Discover Wailuku," it is available in many public places.

Across High Street from the County Office Building area is the **Wailuku Public Library**, designed by architect Charles W. Dickey in 1928 and home to a fine Hawaiiana collection. Next to the library is the old **Territorial Building**, a Dickey design from 1930. And next to that is **Ka'ahumanu Church**, a Congregational church built in 1876, now a Wailuku landmark. The church was the fourth built by Maui's first Christian congregation. It replaced an earlier building dating from 1842, which itself had replaced a grass-thatched structure and before that a simple shed where Queen Ka'ahumanu attended services in 1832. An interesting way to sample the flavor of Maui is to attend the church service held at 9 A.M. on Sundays. While the service is in English, the invocation and hymns are in Hawaiian.

If you walk down East Main Street for two blocks from High Street (passing Church Street), you'll come to Market Street, the center of Wailuku's commercial activities (see Shopping, page 135). The most interesting structure here is the **'Īao Theater**, dating from 1928 and now used by a community theater group. The facade of the art deco

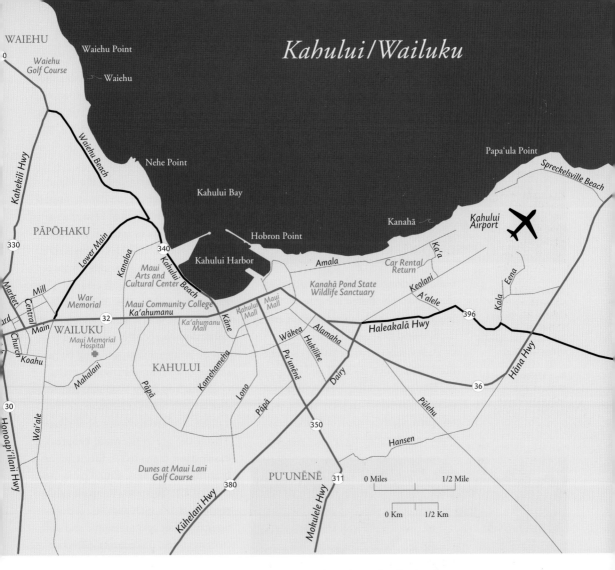

Kahului/Wailuku

WAIEHU

0

Waiehu Point

Waiehu Golf Course

Waiehu

Nehe Point

Kahului Bay

Papaʻula Point

Spreckelsville Beach

Kahului Airport

Kahebili Hwy

Waiehu Beach

PĀPŌHAKU

Kahului Harbor

Hobron Point

Kanahā

Kaʻa

330

340

Kahului Beach

Amala

Car Rental Return

Keolani

Kala

Eena

Kanaloa

Maui Arts and Cultural Center

Kahului Harbor

Kanahā Pond State Wildlife Sanctuary

Aʻalele

Lower Main

Mill

War Memorial

Maui Community College

Kaʻahumanu

Kahului Mall

Maui Mall

396

Market

Central

32

WAILUKU

Ka'ahumanu Mall

Kāne

Wākea

Hukilike

Alamaha

Haleakalā Hwy

Hāna Hwy

Main

Maui Memorial Hospital

KAHULUI

Kamehameha

Puʻunēnē

Dairy

36

Church

Koahu

Mahalani

Pāpā

Lono

Pāpā

Pāilehu

30

Waiʻale

350

Hansen

Honoapiʻilani Hwy

Dunes at Maui Lani Golf Course

PUʻUNĒNĒ

311

0 Miles   1/2 Mile

380

Kūihelani Hwy

Mokulele Hwy

0 Km   1/2 Km

building has been restored, but work is ongoing inside.

Walking in the other direction, on West Main Street, leads to the **Bailey House Museum** (244-3326). The main building was constructed by missionaries in 1833 to house the Wailuku Female Seminary, a boarding school whose aim was to educate girls to be "good Christian wives." The missionary Edward Bailey came from Boston in 1837 to lead the school and supervised the building of the kitchen-dining room in 1838. He and his wife, Caroline, lived in the main

The Wailuku Court-
house, built in 1907,
is still in use. Behind
it rises the nine-story
Kalana o Maui (County
Office Building).

Below: Bailey House
Museum was
built in 1833 as a
missionary school.

out of my make-up," he said). He did,
however, enjoy some success as a
painter. His depictions of Maui, in the
style of the Hudson River School, hang
in the museum. They offer a rare view
of 19th-century Maui.

The complex is run by the Maui
Historical Society. On view are important and rare traditional Hawaiian artifacts, from *kapa* to tools to furniture.
In back of the building is a canoe shed
with a hand-hewn *koa* canoe made on
Hawai'i in the early 19th century. The
Bailey House Museum is open daily
from 10 A.M. to 4 P.M. There is a small
admission charge, and conducted tours
can be arranged. The gift shop has a
choice collection of Hawaiian crafts.

building along with the girls attending
the school. The home is made of
twenty-inch-thick lava rock walls and
sandalwood beams carved by hand.

Bailey was the principal of the school
until 1849, when it closed and he bought
the land and buildings. He and his sons
raised sugar commercially, but he was
not particularly successful in business
("the taste for making money was left

A side trip from Wailuku, continuing
down High Street (Highway 30) for
3 miles, leads to the town of Waikapū.
This is the site of the **Maui Tropical
Plantation** (244-7643), fifty acres of
beautifully kept agricultural park. Open
daily, 9 A.M. to 5 P.M., the park exhibits
tropical plants such as ferns, orchids,
bougainvillea, and pineapple and such
trees as coffee, macadamia, papaya,
avocado, and starfruit. A 40-minute
"Tropical Express" narrated tram ride
through the park (walkers not permitted) runs from 10 A.M. to 4 P.M., departing every 30 minutes ($8.50; children
$3.50). Exhibits detail the history of
macadamia nut farming, irrigation,
coffee, and sugar in Hawai'i.

Shopping in Wailuku

First, don't even think about coming to Wailuku on a Sunday except perhaps to eat. Everything save a few restaurants will be closed. However, on any other day there are a variety of small shops to explore up and down Market Street.

As you walk by 21 North Market you can't help but notice the sweet smell of freshly cooked popcorn at the **Maui Popcorn Factory** (242-9888). Tourists favor the macadamia nut popcorn, while locals go for the Volcano mix: popcorn with *mochi* (rice) crunch and *furikake*

(seaweed). Stop at **Sig Zane Designs** at 53 North Market (249-8997), where native Hawaiian Zane sells dresses, aloha shirts, and tee shirts made from fabrics of his own design. Zane bases his strong graphics on native plants. The 100-percent-cotton fabric is also sold by the yard. There are several good antique stores on Market Street, including **Brown-Kobayashi** at no. 160 (242-0804), which specializes in fine Asian, European, and Hawaiian furniture and art objects. Their prices are half those of San Francisco or New York, and they don't charge for packing. Among the selections are Japanese *tansu* (chests), Chinese tomb figures, and old *koa* and *milo* bowls from Hawai'i.

If you'll be cooking, there's no better place for fresh fish than **Wakamatsu Fish Market** at 145 North Market (244-4111). **Ooka's Supermarket** at 1870 Main Street (244-3931), on the right as you enter town coming from Kahului, is where the locals shop. It's a great place to walk the aisles and see food representing Hawai'i's rich ethnic heritage, especially Portuguese, Filipino, and Japanese. Check out the *ono* pastries like butter and sweet potato *mochi* and chocolate *haupia* cream pie. Fresh Upcountry flowers and leis are reasonably priced.

Left: The pristine gardens of Maui Tropical Plantation.

Below: Plants native to Hawai'i, such as this white hibiscus, are found on the grounds of the Bailey House Museum.

pu'unēnē

When sugarcane is ready to harvest, the field is first burned to reduce the amount of so-called trash—the leaves and dead cane. The juice-filled stalks do not burn during the fire. The sight of dark smoke rising from the fields startles some visitors, especially a view of the fires at night, but the practice is widely accepted and used. The debris of the burning cane, black flakes sometimes referred to as "Hawaiian snow," occasionally drifts over a town or residential area, forcing residents to close their windows until it passes.

Pu'unēnē

Pu'unēnē Sugar Mill is the last remaining sugarcane processing plant on Maui.

Below:
Lowell Mapes, *Cane Shack*, oil on canvas.

Opposite: Burning cane before harvest.

An interesting side trip, just 10 minutes from the Kahului airport, is the Pu'u-nēnē Sugar Mill, reachable by traveling a mile or so on Dairy Road (380) to the turnoff for Kīhei (350). Follow this road for one-half mile to the sugar mill, the only one still operating on Maui, and the **Alexander & Baldwin Sugar Museum** (871-8058). This little museum is well worth the stop for anyone with even the slightest interest in sugar. Ever wonder why sugarcane fields are burned at harvest time? We found out why here. The museum is located in a historic sugar plantation residence, next to the Pu'unēnē Sugar Mill. Exhibits tell about Maui's sugar industry and plantation life, with artifacts dating back to 1878, large photo murals, scale models, and a video. The museum is open Monday–Saturday, 9:30 A.M.– 4:30 P.M.; admission is $4; children $2.

Kepaniwai Heritage Gardens

Leaving Wailuku on Main Street and heading past the Bailey House Museum, the road winds on into 'Iao Valley, a 3-mile drive alongside 'Iao Stream. Two miles along the road is a well-maintained Maui County park known as **Kepaniwai Heritage Gardens**, the grounds of which hold buildings constructed to reflect the multiethnic heritage of Hawai'i. There are a Japanese teahouse and *koi* pond, a Chinese countryside gazebo, a Hawaiian thatched house, a New England saltbox-style house, a Portuguese villa, and a Filipino ranchhouse made of bamboo. All are linked by water gardens, with plantings reflecting the various countries they represent. Most folks on the way to 'Iao whiz by this fascinating and tranquil park, which is well worth a stop. The gardens are open daily, 7 A.M. to 7 P.M., and there is no charge.

'Iao Valley

Lush **'Iao Valley**, at the end of Highway 32, is called Maui's Valley of the Kings. 'Iao is a multifaceted Hawaiian word bound up in the concept of light and supremacy, reflecting the grandeur of the area, which Mark Twain called "the Yosemite of the Pacific." Though far

The quiet area around Kepaniwai Heritage Gardens was not so peaceful in 1790, when the forces of Kamehameha I clashed in a bloody battle with the warriors of Maui. The Maui army, led by Kalanikupule, the son of Maui King Kahekili, was no match for Kamehameha, who brought with him from the island of Hawai'i two English friends, John Young and Isaac Davis, so that they might man a cannon that had been retrieved from a British ship. Kamehameha's army defeated the Mauians in a battle that gave the place its name—Kepaniwai, or Damming of the Waters—after 'Iao Stream was blocked by the bodies of the defeated Maui fighters.

smaller than Yosemite, ʻĪao has been a sacred spot for Hawaiians since ancient times. Near the center of the valley is the famous **ʻĪao Needle**, a 1,200-foot pillar of stone that forms a dramatic sight from several vantage points in ʻĪao Valley State Park. A paved pathway leads up to the top of a ridge for a view of the needle, and another, less heavily traveled trail, goes down to ʻĪao Stream through a variety of exotic foliage, with views of the needle along the way. Look for *kukui* trees, identifiable by their green nuts. Neither of the walks is long or difficult. A trail leading off from the upper viewing area is on private land and should not be used.

Another attraction in the valley is **Pali ʻEleʻele** (Dark Gorge). Before reaching the park area there is a sweeping curve in the road where visitors often stop to gaze at boulders on a distant ridge. The boulders are said to form a likeness of the late President John F. Kennedy. This phenomenon, like beauty, is in the eye of the beholder. Some people see the resemblance; others can stand looking at the boulders for a long time and never discern the profile hidden among the dark boulders.

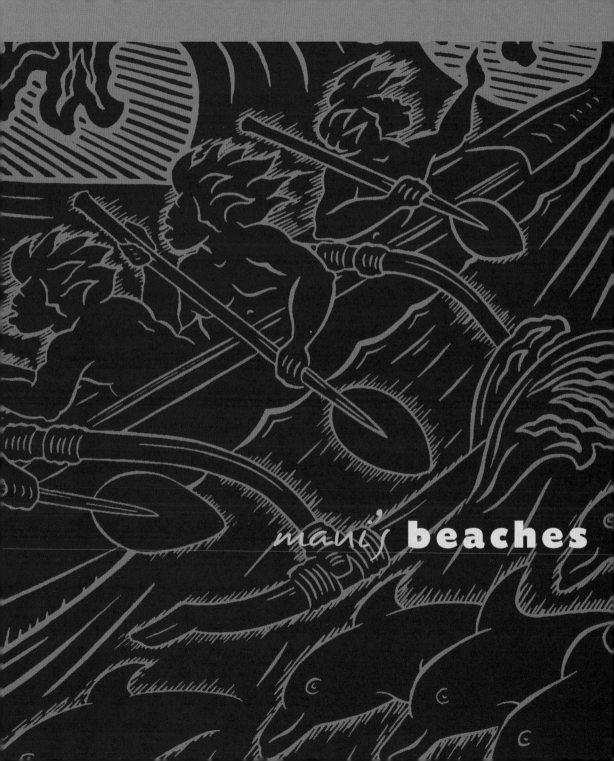

maui's **beaches**

*M*aui's beaches silently hold tales of the island's past. Black Rock on Kāʻanapali Beach is where Kahekili, Maui's last king, plunged into the sea to prove his bravery. The beach at the bay that now bears his name is where the first European set foot on Maui, in 1786. La Pérouse remarked on "a shore made hideous by an ancient lava flow." The beach at Lahaina is where the great Kamehameha I rendezvoused with his forces before sailing on in waves of conquest that eventually brought all the islands under his control.

Maui has more swimmable beaches than any of the other Hawaiian islands. Its splendid shores delight the eye, with waves curling up on curving stretches of golden sand or rocks worn smooth by crashing waves. All of Hawaiʻi's beaches are public and accessible to everyone.

Many consider Wailea's white sand beaches the most beautiful on Maui.

Pages 140–41: Detail from *Pāhāhā Nalu,* a linocut by Dietrich Varez.

Warnings

The sea must be approached with respect and caution. Few of Maui's beaches have lifeguards; all warning signs should be heeded.

Especially dangerous are shorebreaks, where incoming ocean swells cross abruptly from a deep to a shallow bottom and the waves break with enormous downward force. Though they are dangerous for swimmers, these beaches are popular, as they provide excellent conditions for body surfing. It is well, though, to know how to deal with the waves. Neck and back injuries can be sustained, and turning your back on or trying to jump over or through a large incoming wave invites trouble. The force of the waves can pound you against the bottom. The trick is to take a deep breath and dive *under* the wave.

If you get caught in a rip current, a strong sideward flow of water, the best course of action is to flow along with it until its force diminishes. Don't exhaust yourself trying to swim against the current. It's easier and safer to walk back along the beach to the place where you started than to fight the water. Some rip currents flow straight out to sea through channels in the reef. If you are caught in one of these, swim to the side of it and get out as quickly as you can.

Never venture out to the edge of rock ledges where surf is breaking. Freak waves can wash over the rocks without warning; many unsuspecting people have been knocked unconscious or swept away by such waves.

Shark attacks are rare in Hawai'i, but they do occur, almost always at sunrise or sunset, or when waters are murky.

Ratings

We have rated Maui's beaches according to our interpretation of the following criteria: water safety, bottom configuration (sand, rock, coral), cleanliness/maintenance of beach area, and type and quality of facilities (restrooms, showers, picnic tables, barbecue pits, parking). This is naturally arbitrary, and not everyone will agree with the ratings.

Maui is blessed with a variety of beaches. Some, such as Nāpili, Fleming's, or Oneloa, afford great views. Others, such as the beaches at Mākena, are far enough off the beaten track to remain relatively uncrowded. Hāmoa Beach, at Hāna, is a little jewel of a beach that may match every person's dream of a tropical paradise, while the stretch of sand at Kāʻanapali is long, wide, and unblemished.

Our ratings are: Superb, Excellent, Good, and Fair. The descriptions of beaches are arranged beginning with the beaches in West Maui and moving in a counter-clockwise direction around the island.

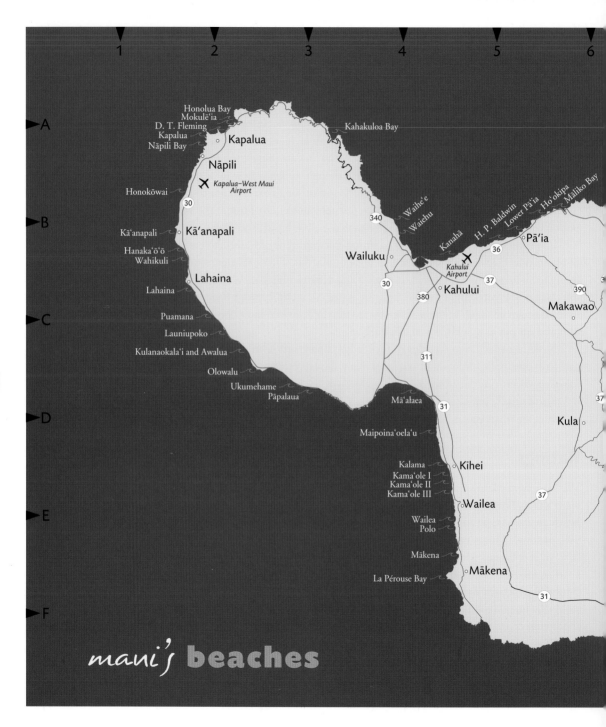

1   2   3   4   5   6

A
B
C
D
E
F

Honolua Bay
Mokuleʻia
D. T. Fleming
Kapalua
Nāpili Bay
Kapalua
Kahakuloa Bay

Nāpili

Kapalua–West Maui Airport

Honokōwai

30

Kāʻanapali
Kāʻanapali

Hanakaʻōʻō
Wahikuli

Lahaina
Lahaina

Puamana

Launiupoko

Kulanaokalaʻi and Awalua

Olowalu

Ukumehame
Pāpalaua

Waiheʻe
Waiehu
340
Kanahā

H. P. Baldwin
Lower Paʻia
Hoʻokipa
Māliko Bay
Pāʻia

Wailuku
36

Kahului Airport
30
380
Kahului
37

390

Makawao

311

Māʻalaea
31

37

Kula

Maipoinaʻoelaʻu

Kalama
Kamaʻole I
Kamaʻole II
Kamaʻole III

Kīhei

Wailea
37

Wailea
Polo

Mākena
Mākena

La Pérouse Bay
31

maui's beaches

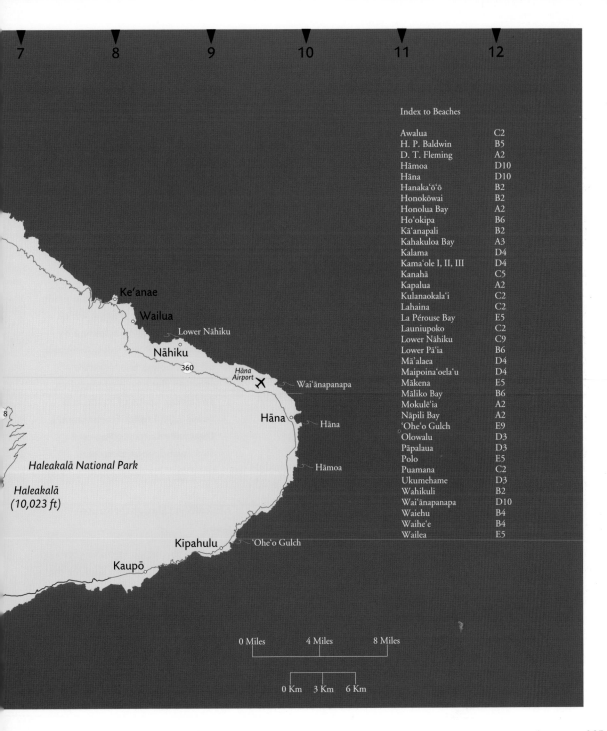

7 8 9 10 11 12

Ke'anae

Wailua

Lower Nāhiku

Nāhiku

360

Hāna Airport

Wai'ānapanapa

Hāna — Hāna

Haleakalā National Park

— Hāmoa

Haleakalā
(10,023 ft)

8

Kipahulu — 'Ohe'o Gulch

Kaupō

0 Miles   4 Miles   8 Miles

0 Km   3 Km   6 Km

Kahakuloa/Kapalua/ Kāʻanapali/Lahaina *area*

Kahakuloa Bay to Honolua Bay

Fair (but **Superb** for its scenic/historic significance)

Kapalua Beach, at right, fronting the Kapalua Bay Hotel, is a perfect crescent of golden sand.

Below: The rugged north coast near Kahakuloa.

The lovely shoreline along this northwest end of Maui holds an important spot in the hearts of Hawaiians. This is where the Polynesian voyaging canoe *Hōkūleʻa* left for its epic journey across the Pacific. Drive along the coastline and admire the dramatic sea cliffs. Water enthusiasts, however, would be wise to go elsewhere. The ocean is difficult to reach and is certainly too hazardous to go into unless you are a strong swimmer. Maui surfers go to several spots along this coast to perfect their skills, but visitors likely would be happier at areas with easier access and fewer hazards.

On May 1, 1976, the Polynesian voyaging canoe *Hōkūleʻa*, a replica of an old Polynesian seagoing, double-hulled canoe, left from Honolua Bay to sail in the wake of the ancient voyagers. The purpose was to prove that the ancient Polynesians had been able to navigate without instruments—utilizing the stars, ocean currents, and other natural phenomena as their guides— and that there was strong justification for Polynesian pride in their ocean journeys, which eclipsed anything achieved by Europeans of the time. A month after it sailed, the *Hōkūleʻa* reached the island of Mataiwa, 168 miles north of Tahiti and some 2,500 miles from Hawaiʻi, then sailed on into Papeete to a tumultuous welcome.

Mokulēʻia (Slaughterhouse)
Good

Access to this beach (2 miles north of Kapalua) is marked by a sign for the Mokulēʻia-Honolua Marine Reserve, where cars are usually parked along the road. A steep dirt and rock trail leads down from the road to the rocky beach below. The bay is an excellent spot for snorkeling and swimming during the

Kahakuloa
Kapalua
Kā'anapali
Lahaina *area*
(continued)

summer months when calm conditions prevail. Winter's big waves make this beach a favorite with bodysurfers, but ocean conditions make it too hazardous for other water sports. No offshore fishing is allowed, since this is designated as a Marine Life Conservation District. Locals call this beach "Slaughterhouse" after a slaughterhouse built by Honolua Ranch on the site, which was torn down in the 1960s.

D. T. Fleming Beach Park Superb

Most water sports are possible at this scenic beach, but caution is advised. The ocean can be hazardous in some conditions, and an eye should be kept on the incoming swells. Bodysurfing and body boarding are popular activities here. There is occasional confusion about the name of this beach park—some people incorrectly refer to the beach at Kapalua as Fleming's Beach. The park honors community leader David Thomas Fleming (1881–1955), who was born in Scotland but adopted Maui as his home and was involved in many aspects of community life here. As manager of the Honolua Ranch, he converted ranchlands to lucrative pineapple fields, forming the Maui Land and Pineapple Company, which continues to harvest and market pineapples in West Maui. The park includes paved parking, showers, restrooms, and public access. There is a lifeguard stationed at the beach.

Kapalua Superb

Perhaps the most stunningly beautiful of all Maui beaches, Kapalua Beach has been a Maui favorite for years. A public right-of-way leading to a small parking area is located past the Nāpili Kai Beach Club. Formerly known as Fleming's Beach, this curving, white sand beach is sheltered by two rocky lava arms and a coral reef. Its clear, calm waters are ideal for safe snorkeling and swimming. There's an excellent view of Moloka'i. Palm trees provide shady areas for relaxing out of the sun. Facilities include public showers and restrooms. This is definitely one of the top beaches in the islands, as attested by its designation in 2000 as the best beach in the United States by Dr. Stephen Leatherman, the famous Dr. Beach.

Nāpili Bay Excellent

A long, curving beach rims this beautiful bay, sheltered by rocky outcroppings. The picturesque, palm-fringed beach affords a splendid view of Moloka'i, which looms large and seemingly close. The swimming is generally excellent except during high waves. Winter months can bring higher surf and good conditions for board surfing. There are two public rights-of-way to the beach, one just past the Nāpili Shores, the other at the Nāpili Sunset on Hui Street. Parking is along the street. There are no public facilities.

Honokōwai Beach Park Excellent

Located off the Lower Honoapiʻilani Highway, this narrow white sand beach features a nice spot for children to play in the water. Past the rocks on the beach lies a good area for snorkeling, but it is only fair for swimming. The park includes an off-street parking area, restrooms, barbecues, picnic tables, and showers.

Kāʻanapali and Hanakaʻōʻō Superb

The wide, clean, curving beaches of Kāʻanapali are among the most photographed in the world. Nearby, Hanakaʻōʻō, called Sand Box Beach or Canoe Beach by residents, is narrow at the south end but broadens as it rounds to the attractive area around Hanakaʻōʻō Point. Both beaches offer excellent conditions for water lovers. Swimmers, snorkelers, and surfers enjoy Hanakaʻōʻō, and Kāʻanapali is good for swimming and beginner windsurfing. Black Rock, near the Sheraton Maui, is famous for spectacular snorkeling. Beginner scuba divers practice here.

Sugarcane once covered most of Kāʻanapali, and near the Black Rock area was a boat landing for shipping the cane. Following the decline of the sugar industry, the Kāʻanapali Resort has since made the beach, and Maui, famous.

No fringing reef protects this area, but inshore waters usually are calm. Nevertheless, an infrequent storm can cause high waves along the beach. Public access to Hanakaʻōʻō goes through private property, so many visitors come up the beach from Kāʻanapali. A county lifeguard is usually on duty at Hanakaʻōʻō, and there are showers and restrooms. Access to Kāʻanapali is via a public right-of-way at the north end of the beach.

Wahikuli State Wayside Park Excellent

Breathtaking views and excellent swimming and snorkeling make this one of West Maui's most attractive beach parks. The park's lovely sandy beach and its convenient access regularly draw a crowd. There are good facilities, including restrooms, showers, pavilions, grills, and picnic tables.

Lahaina Good

Snorkeling, scuba diving, and surfing are popular at this beach, which begins at the end of the boat harbor and continues along Front Street. A shallow and very rocky bottom between the reef and the beach discourages most swimmers.

Honokōwai
Kapalua–West Maui Airport
30
Kāʻanapali
Kāʻanapali
Hanakaʻōʻō
Wahikuli
Lahaina
Lahaina

Background: D. T. Fleming Beach Park

**Kahakuloa
Kapalua
Kā'anapali
Lahaina** *area*
(continued)

Puamana Park and Launiupoko State Wayside Park Excellent

These convenient parks, located near mile markers 19 and 18 respectively, have a pleasant atmosphere and large trees, perfect for a relaxing beachside picnic. Both beaches have pockets of sand and rock. A word of warning: sharks have been sighted in the shallow waters off Launiupoko, so swimming is discouraged. The parks include paved parking lots, barbecue grills, showers, restrooms, and picnic tables.

Kulanaokala'i and Awalua Good

The picturesque view of other islands from these beaches and the easy swimming offshore make this a popular area with visitors. A low spit of sand called Cut Mountain divides the beaches. These are unimproved yet attractive beaches, with easy access but without amenities. The Hawaiian word *kulanaokala'i* translates beautifully: "to stand firmly in the calmness of the sea." Located near mile 16.

Olowalu Fair

This excellent spot for snorkeling also holds an important place in Maui's history as the site of a famous massacre (see page 44). Today, visitors can combine a walk among petroglyphs

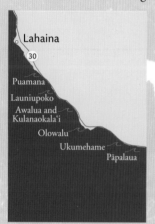

Lahaina
30
Puamana
Launiupoko
Awalua and
Kulanaokala'i
Olowalu
Ukumehame
Pāpalaua

Background:
Petroglyphs at
Luahiwa, Lāna'i
(see page 285).

Olowalu is the site of ancient petroglyphs. From the paved road behind the small strip mall with the restaurant Chez Paul, turn *mauka* at the water tower onto a bumpy dirt road lined with telephone poles. The land here belongs to an out-of-business sugar company. The petroglyphs—drawings incised in stone—are about one-half mile down this road, on the right. There is a walkway with a metal railing to assist in walking up to the petroglyphs. An old wooden stairway is broken down, so you'll have to scramble a bit to get up to the walkway.

No one knows why the ancient Hawaiians carved petroglyphs or what the meanings of these enigmatic drawings were. The most common images are human figures, dots, and circles. Sailing canoes and animals, such as horses and dogs, are also frequently found. Images of human figures with triangular bodies, dogs, and sails can be seen at Olowalu. Unfortunately, the site has been defaced by vandals.

and the remains of a *heiau* with snorkeling. The swimming is only fair because of the shallow offshore reef. It's wise not to venture beyond the reef, as sharks have been known to frequent this area. There are no amenities, and parking is roadside. Located near mile 14.

Ukumehame Beach Park   Good

This narrow roadside park, located near mile 12, is a popular spot among local fishermen as well as a good place to swim. Near the shore the ocean is shallow, and the bottom has patches of sand and rock. As at Olowalu, it's advisable not to venture too far out because of the occasional sharks that swim in these waters. The area can get windy. There is public access with a small paved parking area.

Pāpalaua State Wayside Park   Good

A long, narrow beach fronts this roadside park and provides a wonderful vantage point for viewing the island of Kahoʻolawe. The offshore ocean bottom is rocky and shallow. The beach has public access, barbecue grills, picnic tables, and portable potties. This is a good swimming and picnic site, though sharks in the deeper waters should keep you close to shore. Look for a sign for the park at mile 11.

Sunset and a new moon from Launiupoko State Wayside Park.

Mā'alaea
Kīhei
Wailea
area

Mā'alaea Good

To the east of this beach is a bird sanctuary and to the west a boat harbor, a newly developed shopping center, and the Maui Ocean Center. Not an especially good swimming beach, Mā'alaea offers at least two good surfing areas.

At times a strong wind makes this area uncomfortable for picnickers but attractive to windsurfers. Maps may show a variety of names for this beach, but they are simply old shoreline names. Fitness buffs know it as a place where they can jog on hard-packed sand, but again, the strong winds can act as a deterrent. There are no public facilities, but there is public access located past the Makani a Kai condominiums, on Hauoli Street.

Maipoina'oela'u Beach Park Superb

The name in Hawaiian means "do not forget me," and the park is dedicated to "all those who sacrificed their lives to preserve our freedom for all humanity." Consequently, the park is known as Veterans Park or Memorial Park. The beach, located just north of the Aston Maui Lu Resort, is a continuation of the long ribbon of sand that extends along the southwest coast. There is a fine, sandy bottom offshore with only a sprinkling of rocks. This beach is Maui's

second most popular windsurfing spot—the first is Ho'okipa on the north shore. Facilities include a small paved parking lot, showers, picnic tables, and restrooms.

Kalama Beach Park Excellent

This park is as much a playground for the athletically inclined as a haven for water lovers. The park is huge (thirty-six acres), with a dozen pavilions, along with restrooms, showers, picnic tables, grills, tennis courts, a soccer field, volleyball courts, a new in-line skating rink, and more. Offshore, the bottom is rocky, with pockets of sand, but off to the right is a long stretch of sandy beach. There is a county lifeguard on duty.

Kama'ole Beach Parks Superb

These three separate beach parks—Kama'ole I, II, and III—are simply unbeatable for good swimming, sandy beaches, brilliant views, and a fine climate. Interspersed rocky areas provide good snorkeling. These are among the best beaches in Hawai'i. The only time swimming is not safe is during the occasional winter storms that come up from the south-southwest, known as Kona storms. Facilities are excellent, with paved parking, grills, picnic tables, showers, and restrooms. Lifeguards are sometimes on duty.

Legend has it that it was at the site where the Aston Maui Lu now stands that the British sea captain George Vancouver and his men set foot on Maui on March 6, 1792. A year later, Vancouver brought gifts of cattle to Maui's king, Kahekili, and thus Maui's cattle industry was born. Vancouver's explorations in search of a northwest passage brought him to America's northwest coast, where Canada's Vancouver Island is named after him. In homage to the link between Canada and Maui, Gordon Gibson, a Canadian and the original owner of the Maui Lu, erected a monument in tribute to Captain Vancouver on the beach across from the hotel. Included as part of the monument are two totem poles, incongruous elements on a palm-studded shore.

**Mā'alaea
Kīhei
Wailea** *area*
(continued)

Ulua beach (right)
fronts Wailea Elua
Village, a luxury
condominium com-
plex, and Polo Beach
(below) is overlooked
by the spectacular
Kea Lani Hotel and
the Maui Polo Beach
Club, another upscale
condo development.

Wailea Superb

Conjure up the ideal shore, one with
wide, white sand beaches that gracefully
curve, sheltered coves, and offshore
views of other islands, and you'll be
close to the image of Wailea. The broad
expanse of sand and unbeatable climate
make this an attractive spot for sun
worshipers and water lovers. There is
marked public access to the four
beaches: Keawakapu, Mōkapu, Ulua,
and Wailea. Mōkapu and Ulua are
great snorkeling spots for beginners.
Underwater visibility at Wailea's beaches
averages 80 to 100 feet—50 feet close
to shore; water temperature is about
80 degrees. Public facilities consist of
showers at Keawakapu and restrooms
and showers at Mōkapu, Ulua, and
Wailea. These beaches lie in front of
some of Maui's most deluxe resorts,
with lush landscaping enhancing the
picturesque setting.

Polo Excellent

Long and wide, Polo Beach is located
past the Kea Lani Hotel and next to
the Polo Beach condominium complex.
Swimmers and snorkelers should watch
for storms or high surf, which can
cause strong currents and a dangerous
backwash. The beach has a small park
and a paved parking area, showers,
and restrooms.

Mā'alaea
Kihei
Wailea *area*
(continued)

Captain Jean-François de Galaup, comte de La Pérouse, came ashore on Maui south of Mākena on May 30, 1786. The reports he sent back to France indicate that the first land he saw after traversing the channel between Hawai'i and Maui had water cascading from the tops of lush mountains. He wrote of banana trees surrounding the homes, with "dwellings so numerous that a single village extends for three or four leagues." Unable to land because of rough seas, La Pérouse continued on to the first sheltered area he could find, "a shore made hideous by an ancient lava flow," where he set anchor and went ashore. The Hawaiians presented him with a pig, in exchange for which he gave them medals, hatchets, and pieces of iron. During their time on land, La Pérouse and his men were taken to see four small villages of ten or twelve houses each. He described the houses in a letter:

"These are made of grass and are covered with the same material. They have the same shape as the thatched cottages found in certain parts of France. The roofs are pitched on two sides, and the door, which is located on the gable end, is only 3 feet high, so that it is necessary to stoop when entering. The furnishings consist of mats, which like our carpets make a very neat flooring on which the islanders sleep. The only cooking utensils they have are gourds painted in various colors. Their cloth is made from the paper mulberry tree . . . painted in a great variety of colors."

La Pérouse was one of France's finest navigators and explorers. His lively accounts of his discoveries in the Pacific were read eagerly by the people back home, who were fascinated by the exoticism of such places as Samoa and the Easter Islands. The voyage that brought him to Hawai'i was to be his last. After he left Maui, he traveled north to Alaska and California, then southwest to Macao and the Philippines. He cruised the coasts of Japan and Russia before turning southward to head for the Samoan and Tongan islands His last letters home were sent from the port of Botany Bay, Australia, on January 21, 1788. After leaving Australia, his vessel and all hands disappeared. It is likely they were shipwrecked at an island near Fiji named Vanikoro, where many of the men were killed by natives. There a few of the men lived on and became integrated with the local society. The fate of La Pérouse has never been discovered.

Mākena Superb

The sweeping beaches at Mākena are beautiful stretches of sand with plenty of room and panoramic views of Molokini and Kahoʻolawe, lying offshore more or less adjacent to each other. The beaches of Poʻolenalena, Maluʻaka, Oneuli, Puʻu Ōlaʻi, and Oneloa (commonly called Big Beach) have good swimming and snorkeling. Board surfing at Puʻu Ōlaʻi and Oneloa is popular, as is bodysurfing at all but Oneuli. Puʻu Ōlaʻi is a pretty, secluded spot known locally as Little Beach. It can be reached by hiking up and over Puʻu Ōlaʻi, a rocky cinder cone at the western end of Big Beach. Although officially illegal, nude bathing is part of this beach's popularity. The beaches are reached via the same road that leads through Wailea and Kīhei. It is best to visit these beaches early in the morning, as it is not unusual for the skies to cloud over by around 11 A.M.

La Pérouse Bay Good

Fishermen more than swimmers come to this public beach, where the first non-Hawaiian, the sea captain Jean de La Pérouse, set foot on Maui. Here at the bay named for the French explorer, a series of small beaches lie between rocky outcroppings, and there are many tide pools. Waters can become rough during storms or high surf. There is public access, but there are no facilities

at this rocky beach. Snorkeling is good on the right side of the bay. You have to enter the water where there is public access and swim over to the right, where the shoreline area has been fenced off by residents.

Beyond La Pérouse Bay, the coastline is rugged and dramatic. In general, the beaches of this area are small, remote, and lacking in both facilities and easy public access. Continuing past the pavement is unwise without a four-wheel-drive vehicle. Visitors who are able to make their way down to these areas would do well to admire them without getting into the water. Additionally, there are many scenic shoreline areas before reaching the Nuʻu Landing, including many small inlets that are visible as the road winds down toward the coast from ʻUlupalakua to the dark sand beach of Huakini Bay.

Oneloa, which translates as "long sand," is commonly known as Big Beach.

Below:
La Pérouse Bay.

Hāna *area*

'Ohe'o (Seven Sacred Pools) Fair
(but Superb for its natural beauty)

One of the twenty-four pools at 'Ohe'o Gulch.

The beach itself is dangerous, but the many beautiful pools below the highway are stunning. The popular name notwithstanding, there are more than seven pools—actually twenty-four in all—and the place isn't considered to be sacred. Swimmers should beware of flash flooding during heavy rainfall. The bridge over Pīpīwai Stream allows views up and down Kīpahulu Valley. Hiking and camping in the area are possible, but remember: no ocean swimming here because of strong currents and the prevalence of sharks. The area has many legends and for years was erroneously called sacred; it is a favorite stopping place for visitors.

Hāmoa Superb

The jewel-like setting is an idyllic tropical paradise, with its high cliffs and sheer beauty. The good running surf makes this a popular swimming and bodysurfing beach. Breaking surf comes straight in to the beach and often creates strong currents near the shore. At times there is a lifeguard provided by the Hotel Hāna-Maui, whose guests frequent the beach. There is public access via a stairway descending from the road. The Hotel Hāna-Maui owns the private restroom facilities and covered picnic pavilion situated at the back of the beach; one restroom is designated for public use. A beachside rinsing shower may also be used by nonguests.

Hāna Beach Park Good

A favorite of residents, this large, pleasant beach park features good swimming and snorkeling but some fearsome currents out past the sheltered bay. Nevertheless, the bay area is safe and generally calm, with shorebreaks and gentle winds. The sand is brown and clean. The Ka'uiki Lighthouse stands on a small island just off the beach. The park includes paved parking, a pavilion, picnic tables, restrooms and showers, and a boat ramp.

Wai'ānapanapa State Park Superb

This large, scenic, and historic park is a
good spot for picnicking and for swimming when the water is calm and if you
are a strong swimmer. Wai'ānapanapa
must be approached with some caution
because of strong rip currents and a
beach unprotected by a reef. Farther
along at Pa'iloa, sunbathers and explorers
will enjoy the black sand beach. It is
easy to spend long hours in this area
because of the ancient legends associated
with it (see page 113), and visitors should
plan to bring a lunch and stay awhile.
The park has excellent facilities, from
paved parking to restrooms and picnic
areas. Cabins and tent camping are
available (see page 231).

Lower Nāhiku to Māliko Bay Fair

The coves and inlets along this fascinating but rugged coastline are not good
for swimming or other water sports.
Board surfing and snorkeling are possible, but public access is difficult to find.
There are places where the water is
murky from stream runoff, and still
other places where the calm ocean suggests fishing or just strolling along the
shoreline, not swimming. In at least one
spot, the county of Maui has posted
"keep out" signs because rental cars
frequently get stuck. Still, the coastline
itself is engaging.

**Below: The colors
of nature are every-
where evident at jet-
black Pa'iloa Beach.**

**Background:
Hāmoa Beach.**

Pā'ia *area*

Ho'okipa Beach Park   Good
(but **Superb** for windsurfing)

This convenient park alongside Hāna Highway is a mecca for windsurfers from all over the world. Although it is not a great place to swim, it is the best spot for experienced windsurfers and can be good for surfing as well. Ho'okipa is the home of Maui surfing dating back to the 1930s. This park's high rating comes

from its reputation as a challenging, world-class windsurfing site. Major competitions are held here each year. There are pavilions, showers, restrooms, grills, picnic tables, and a paved parking lot.

Lower Pā'ia Park   Fair

This is an unreliable area, with good swimming when waters are calm but otherwise poor. There are shorebreaks for bodysurfing and offshore breaks for board surfing, but these can be quirky. Windsurfers frequent the area. To the right of the park is a rocky point from which local children jump into the water. There are restrooms, picnic areas, a softball field, and basketball courts.

H. P. Baldwin Park   Superb

Bodysurfers flock to this long, sandy beach, probably the most highly used beach park in this corner of Maui. The surf breaks along the shore and occasionally offshore as well, attracting surfers, especially windsurfers. Swimming is best at the west end of the beach, where large rocks form shallow, sandy-bottom pools. Lifeguards are on duty near the parking area. There are excellent facilities: picnic tables, pavilions, grills, restrooms, showers, plus playing fields suitable for soccer and baseball and plenty of parking. The park is named for Harry P. Baldwin, former delegate to Congress and community leader.

The beach at H. P. Baldwin Park is a mile of white sand.

Ho'okipa Beach Park, the West Maui Mountains in the distance.

Kahului/Wailuku *area*

Kanahā Beach Park Excellent

This great windsurfing beach appeals to all skill levels. Close to the surfing shops in Kahului, it's where many of the surfing schools offer lessons. Windsurfers zipping by at high speeds can be dangerous to swimmers, however. Nevertheless, if you keep to the area designated for swimmers, this is the best swimming beach in the area, and it has a lifeguard. Just west of the Kahului Airport, the beach is on Alahao Street. Kanahā Pond State Wildlife Sanctuary, a bird refuge, is nearby. There are restrooms, showers, and paved parking.

Waiehu Beach Park Fair

On clear days there is no better place to get a good view of Haleakalā than from this beach park. While the swimming here is poor, the park is a wonderful out-of-the-way spot for a picnic and for viewing the ocean. Parts of this beach are heavily used by local fishermen. The park is next to the Waiehu Municipal Golf Course and once contained a wharf, destroyed in the tsunami of 1946. The park includes a pavilion, restrooms, showers, grill, and picnic tables.

Waihe'e Beach Park Good

An impressive reef creates a good swimming area off this beach park; however, swimmers must watch for strong currents where the reef ends. Residents come to this beach to gather *limu*. There are restrooms, picnic areas, and a paved parking lot. Access is via Halewaiu Road.

Kanahā Beach Park attracts windsurfers year round on windy days.

activities

There are so many things to do on Maui,

the problem will be deciding how to fit everything in. While many activities are free—as listed in the Exploring and Beaches sections of this book—others require an entrance fee or tour guide. You will find many friendly, knowledgeable people on Maui whose main concern will be to see that you have a great vacation.

If you are calling any of the companies listed here from the mainland or a neighbor island, the area code is 808 (it's necessary to dial the area code from the neighbor islands).

When taking any kind of tour or engaging in any activity for which you pay a fee, it is customary to tip the guide (see page 212).

Note to Hawai'i residents: whenever booking reservations, be sure to inquire if *kama'āina* rates are available. It never hurts to ask. To out-of-staters: you have to have a Hawai'i driver's license in order to receive *kama'āina* rates—a bonus for living in the most expensive paradise on earth.

Page 164:
'Ukulele, a linocut
by Dietrich Varez.

Page 165:
**Body boarding
at Honolua Bay.**

Above: Sea
kayaks on Big
Beach, Mākena.

Right: Snorkeling at
'Āhihi-Kīna'u Natural
Area Reserve, Mākena.

Watersports

THE WARM OCEAN WATERS of the Hawaiian islands allow for water activities throughout the year. Surfing, canoeing, swimming, and fishing are traditional Hawaiian recreational activities, supplemented today with snorkeling, scuba diving, windsurfing, kayaking, and parasailing. Surfers and windsurfers flock to Maui's north shore in the winter, and scuba divers find some of the best sites in the world off her shores. Be on guard in the water, as Maui has few lifeguards at its beaches.

The waters teem with interesting sea creatures, including giant green sea turtles, bright orange clown fish, shy mottled moray eels, graceful manta rays, and gentle, smiling dolphins. From late November through early May, there is a good chance of spotting humpback whales, which each year migrate thousands of miles from the northern Pacific to Maui to frolic, breed, and bear their young.

The National Weather Service recreation forecast for Maui is available by calling 871-5054.

Snorkeling

Another world awaits exploration along Maui's shores. The many good snorkeling areas are described under Beaches (pages 141–63). In addition, there are many offshore snorkeling spots, with access provided by organized tours and cruises. Snorkeling at Molokini Islet, a crescent-shaped top of an eroded volcano, is everyone's favorite. Molokini lies in the waters off Wailea and Mākena, on Maui's southern coast. Its clear, protected waters attract colorful and curious fish. Many of the boating tours listed below under Boating Excursions (page 177) offer snorkeling as part of the trip and carry all necessary gear. The only drawback to Molokini is that it's crowded. In addition to zillions of fish, there are zillions of people—which makes the trip there perhaps overrated, though still a fine experience.

For over twenty-five years, **Trilogy** (661-4743), owned by the respected Coon family, has been offering first-rate snorkeling tours from Lahaina Harbor to Lāna'i and Molokini aboard sailing catamarans. The all-day Discover Lāna'i snorkel sail is their most popular. Breakfast, featuring Mom Coon's homemade cinnamon rolls, is served on board, and a barbecue chicken lunch is enjoyed at a private picnic pavilion on the island of Lāna'i. The warm, pristine waters of Lāna'i offer incredible fish sightings. For those who want to sleep in (the Lāna'i trip departs at 6:15 A.M.), there is a Lāna'i sunset sail that departs

Trilogy catamarans sailing off Lahaina.

later in the morning (a favorite trip among a lot of people). In addition, a Lānaʻi snorkeling trip can be combined with a Jeep tour of Lānaʻi and/or a Zodiac dolphin-watch trip along Lānaʻi's coast. Another option is a half-day excursion to Molokini, leaving Māʻalaea Harbor at 6:30 A.M. Trilogy also sails out of Kāʻanapali Beach for a snorkeling tour of that coast. Scuba diving is available on most Trilogy trips, and there is whale watching from December through April.

Also operating from Lahaina Harbor is the *Lahaina Princess* (667-6165), a fast-cruising yacht whose primary stop is Molokini. A fun feature for the kids is a water trampoline. The same company offers 2-hour snorkeling trips aboard the *Island Princess*, which are quite a bit less expensive than the Molokini tours.

One of the best Molokini tours is offered by **Maui Classic Charters** (879-8188) from Māʻalaea Harbor aboard their brand-new *Maui Magic*. The trip, which begins with a traditional chant asking the gods to welcome the group to the water, focuses on Hawaiʻi's cultural history and legends. The boat cruises down the coast past La Pérouse Bay to Kanaio Beach, with narration describing ancient sites along the way. The *Maui Magic* is the only boat on Maui

Fun on the *Trilogy IV* during a Kāʻanapali snorkel trip.

Opposite: The back side of Molokini is a favorite diving site.

licensed to cruise this coast. There's a stop for snorkeling in the bay, and then the boat heads for Molokini, where burgers (beef and veggie) are cooked up on the grill—and there's plenty of time for snorkeling. The same outfit also sails to Molokini aboard the *Four Winds II*, a glass-bottomed catamaran with an onboard waterslide. During whale season, a naturalist accompanies the afternoon trip. Snuba—a cross between snorkeling and scuba—is available.

The **Ocean Activities Center** in Kīhei (879-4485) has operated snorkeling tours to Molokini from Māʻalaea Harbor for over twenty-five years. They provide transportation from major hotels and also offer whale watching in season.

The fastest trip to Molokini is aboard the *Kai Kanani* (879-7218 or 874-1111), which sails from the Maui Prince Hotel in Mākena, about as close as you can get to Molokini and still be on land—thus allowing more time for snorkeling. The return trip on this pleasant, low-key tour is a leisurely cruise along Maui's rugged south shore, where you can spot ancient *heiau* from the boat. The *Kai Kanani* also offers whale-watching trips in season, accompanied by a naturalist from Earthtrust, a wildlife conservation group.

Scuba Diving

Excellent scuba diving is possible year round at many spots off Maui for beginning and advanced divers. Among favorite diving areas are: along the Hāna coast, Waiʻānapanapa State Park, Hāna Bay, and Nuʻu Landing; along the southwest coast, Mākena Beach, Hāloa Point, Wailea and Ulua beaches, and McGregor Point; in the Lahaina area, Olowalu and Black Rock; and, at Kapalua, Kapalua Bay, D. T. Fleming Beach Park, Honolua Bay, and Hononana Bay.

Certified divers may rent equipment and go out on their own or may arrange a chartered excursion. Those unfamiliar with local conditions are encouraged to take an escort, as this sport is potentially dangerous, even for trained divers. Introductory classes are available for those seeking certification.

Dives take place wherever conditions are best at the time; this generally means the north shore in summer and the south in winter, as this is the prevailing pattern of calm waters. Depths range from 20 to 150 feet, with most areas falling in the middle of that spectrum. An excellent island-by-island guidebook is available, which the local diving community considers the ultimate resource for diving Hawaiʻi's waters: *Hawaiʻi Below: Favorites, Tips, and Secrets of the Diving Pros,* by Rod Canham (Watersport Publishing). A handy overview of Hawaiʻi's diving is offered in *Below Hawaiʻi: A Diver's Guide,* by Astrid Witte and Casey Mahaney (Island Heritage Publishing).

Molokini, a quick boat ride away from Maui, is one of the most popular dive spots in Hawaiʻi. Exploring the waters around the crescent-shaped islet is an experience that many divers repeat as often as possible. Taking any ocean creatures from this marine conservation district is prohibited. As a result, the area is brimming with ocean life, from eels to turtles, from white-tip reef sharks (harmless) to manta rays.

Diving the back side of Molokini instead of the bay affords a truly spectacular underwater view of the volcano's sharp decline and hints at the depth of surrounding waters. The back side of the islet has strong currents, so extreme caution is advised.

There are a number of shops on Maui that rent scuba and snorkeling equipment and have diving maps. Some of the diving charter companies and retailers also organize whale-watching cruises and photographic tours. Most of them certify new divers after the required courses, which generally last five days.

Mike Severns and his wife, Pauline Fiene-Severns, are both biologists who have photographed and written about Hawaiʻi's underwater world for many years. Their book *Molokini Island* (Pacific Islands Publishing, Wailuku) has exquisite full-color photos of the strange and beautiful creatures that frequent that islet's underwater habitat. **Mike Severns Diving** (879-6596), Kīhei's first dive boat operation, takes divers to sites off Mākena and Molokini. Their knowledge of marine life sets them apart from other ventures. They also offer coral-spawning charters, April through July, and are the only outfit in the world to offer a daytime coral-spawning trip (for info, e-mail them at severns@mauigateway.com).

Another premier Kīhei dive shop is **Ed Robinson's Diving Adventures** (879-3584), the only Maui dive company to have been rated one of the "top ten" in the Indo-Pacific area five years running by *Scuba Diving Magazine*. Ed too is an underwater photographer, whose beautiful photos have appeared in many publications and books, including *An Underwater Guide to Hawaiʻi* by Ann Fielding (University of Hawaiʻi Press). Ed and his wife, Suzzy Parker-Robinson, also will help with accommodations on Maui; see their website: www.mauiscuba.com.

Other recommended Kīhei shops include **Dive & Sea Maui** (874-1952), **Mākena Coast Charters** (874-1273), and **Prodiver Maui** (875-4004). **Maui Dive Shop** has locations in Kīhei (879-3388) and Lahaina (661-6166).

In Lahaina, **Extended Horizons** (667-0611), which offers dive tours from Māla Wharf to Lānaʻi, was established in 1983 and has an excellent reputation, both locally and internationally. Other Lahaina choices are **Captain Nemo's** (667-5331), **Dive Maui** (667-2080), **Lahaina Divers** (667-7496), **Pacific Dive** (667-0901), and **Tropical Divers** (669-6284).

A great resource for Lahaina diving is **Trinity Tours** (661-8085), run by Tanna Swanson Branum, divemaster and owner of the

Guest House B&B (see Accommodations). Tanna will help you with accommodations, give you diving lessons in her pool, and set up diving trips.

Winter surfing at Honolua Bay on the northwest coast.

Surfing

While many Polynesians enjoyed riding the surf in their outrigger canoes, Hawaiians alone developed the art of riding boards specifically designed for play atop the rolling waves. The sport of surfing was perfectly suited to these strong, island-based people, who lived constantly within reach of the sea and its changing waves and who valued courage and agility.

In modern times, this ancient sport has been refined and extended beyond anything its

The ancient Hawaiians prayed for good surf with chants such as:

*Kū mai! Kū mai! Ka nalu
    nui mai Kahiki mai,
Alo poʻi pū! Kū mai ka
    pōhuehue.
Hū! Kai koʻo loa.*

Arise, arise, great waves
    from Tahiti,
Powerful curling waves,
    arise from this chant.
Well up, long-raging surf.

inventors could ever have imagined. Its popularity has spread around the globe, and professional surfers demonstrate their skill and daring while vying for six-figure purses. The manufacture of surfing equipment has also developed, along with the emergence of new materials and technologies, and in recent years several new variants to surfing have been introduced, including windsurfing and kiteboarding. The areas best suited to surfing and windsurfing are noted in the Beaches section (pages 141–63).

Board surfing

This is the original sport. No one knows how long ago it developed, but Hawaiian petroglyphs dating back to about the 8th or 9th century show people board surfing, and as early as the 15th century Hawaiians had so refined the sport that contests between champions were held for what even today would be considered high stakes. Ancient Hawaiians gambled with unbridled enthusiasm at every opportunity, wagering their property, their wives, even their lives on the outcome of a single competition.

Surfing, like all things Hawaiian, declined dramatically during the first century or so of European immigration to the islands. The missionaries frowned upon what they perceived to be idle pleasures, while Hawaiians were busy adapting to Western lifestyles. By 1853 Lahaina was the only place in the islands where surfing was still a popular sport. And in 1892 the anthropologist Nathaniel B. Emerson wrote that "today it is hard to find a surfboard outside of our museums and private collections." But surfing, both on boards and in canoes, began to be promoted again in Hawai'i early in the 20th century, when the islands first began to become a tourist destination. Surfing's international fame spread with demonstrations in Atlantic City, Southern California, and Australia by surfing champion and Olympic gold medal swimmer Duke Kahanamoku, who put Hawai'i on the map in the 1912 Olympic games in Stockholm.

By the 1960s a surfer culture had arrived in Hawai'i, with long-haired "surf bums" populating favorite surf towns, especially on O'ahu's and Maui's north shores. Today, professional surfing is a highly regarded sport, and surfers travel the world to participate in big-wave competitions, including those in Hawai'i.

When the surf's up, Hawai'i school kids head for the beaches at first light, and workers bring their surfboards along for a lunchtime break. Waves are measured in feet, from trough to crest. However, Hawai'i custom doesn't measure wave faces objectively, but instead—in a sort of macho understatement, according to one local surf forecaster—measures them by about 50 to 70 percent of face height. So when you hear there is 15-foot surf, the waves may have a 30-foot drop as they come thundering to shore. The National Weather Service is trying to get Hawai'i surf forecasters to measure the wave face accurately from trough to peak, like the rest of the world.

One of the activities you can do on Maui that's great fun is to take a surf lesson. **Goofy Foot Surf School** at 505 Front Street in Lahaina (244-9283) offers group lessons three times a day for beginners, from young *keiki* to gray-haired *tūtū*. They guarantee that you'll stand by the end of your first 2-hour lesson, or the lesson is on them. Classes are small, limited to five people, and beginners start on soft boards in small waves. In classes for intermediate surfers, students have the opportunity to ride bigger waves in a supervised setting. A 2-hour group lesson is $55; private lessons are available, as are all-day surfing parties for large groups and a supervised day camp where surfing is the activity. A great deal is that after

In ancient Hawai'i, longboards (*oro*), reserved for the use of *ali'i*, were up to 18 feet long and could weigh as much as 150 pounds. Made of native *wiliwili*, the longboards were often stained a glossy black. Ordinary boards (*alaia*) were about 6 feet long and made of *koa* or breadfruit. In a bind, the resourceful Hawaiians surfed without boards, using just their bodies, or rode the waves on whatever was at hand. The 19th-century historian John Papa I'i reported seeing boys surfing at Lahaina using banana trunks for boards.

you've taken a class from them you can rent one of their surfboards for $15 and hang out while they're teaching, catching a tip or two along with the waves.

Pro surfer **Buzzy Kerbox** (573-5728), winner of major contests and cover feature for many surfing magazines, offers individual or group lessons and specializes in beginners. This accomplished waterman, who has done stunt work for such films as *Water World,* is one of Maui's top surfing instructors.

For private surfing lessons in Lahaina and other areas of West Maui, check out the **Nancy Emerson School of Surfing** (244-7873) or **Surf Dog Maui** (669-3760); in Kīhei, **Big Kahuna Adventures Maui** (875-6395) or **Tommy Castleton's Maui Waveriders** (875-4761); and in the Kahului area, **Action Sports Maui** (871-5857) or **Alan Cadiz's HST** (871-5423).

Local Motion rents surfboards at their stores in Kīhei (879-7873) and Lahaina (661-7873). Most of the serious surfboard rental outfits are in Kahului and Pā'ia, including **Extreme Sports Maui** (871-7954), **Hāna Highway Surf** (579-8999), **Hawaiian Island Surf & Sport** (871-4981),

Dietrich Varez, *He'e Nalu,* (board surfing), linocut.

Hi-Tech Surf Sports (877-2111 and 579-9297), **Lightning Bolt Maui** (877-3484), and **Second Wind Sail, Surf & Kite** (877-7467). The activities desks at the major hotels are also good resources for renting surfboards.

Bodysurfing

This cross between board surfing and swimming stems from the same principle as board riding except that the body replaces the board as the vehicle. The ancient Hawaiians called this activity *kaha nalu* or *pae* or *paep'o*. There are two basic techniques for accomplishing this feat: keeping the body straight with the arms pinned against the sides while riding the shoulder of the wave just ahead of the breaking water, or keeping one or both arms straight out in front for greater maneuverability. The former technique seems to work best in offshore breaks, while the latter seems best in the large, shallow shorebreaks.

Most expert bodysurfers use both techniques, sometimes while riding the same wave. Though purists decry the practice, virtually all bodysurfers also use fins to increase propulsion and enhance their ability to catch a wave.

Paipo boarding

The term *paipo* is a post–World War II corruption of the Hawaiian word *paep'o;* it refers to what essentially is a belly board. This type of wave-riding board is short and thin—3 or 4 feet long and only a quarter to half an inch thick—either flat or with a slightly concave surface to fit the body. They are usually homemade and are used mostly by Hawaiians. Their use requires skill, and they have been largely superseded in popularity by the now well-known boogie board.

Body boarding

The body board, developed from the paipo board described above, was invented in Hawai'i in the early 1970s by Tom Morey. Made of flexible foam, the boards are a couple of feet wide, about 4 feet long, and about 3 inches thick. The latest development along this line is a high-performance body board (now termed "turbo board"), invented by Russ Brown in 1983. Considered the Porsche of body boards, it is stiffer and faster than the standard model. These inexpensive water toys have become ubiquitous in Hawai'i and are readily available for rent and for sale.

Sand sliding

This too is an ancient pastime that has been given a modern twist. The original idea was to throw oneself onto the sand at the precise moment when a receding wave had left just a thin sheet of water on which the body would then slide. Precise timing was (and is) essential, as too early a leap results in a mere sinking into the sand, and too late a one ends in an abrupt, abrasive halt.

Bare-body sand sliding is seldom seen anymore, but paipo boards and the more recent body boards are also used in this fashion. Nowadays, the hot trend is the skimboard, a short foam board

about three quarters of an inch thick that is thrown onto the receding wave, then jumped upon.

Skilled standing riders have developed some fancy skateboard-like maneuvers on this type of board, and contests for them have been held on O'ahu.

Windsurfing *and* Kiteboarding

Windsurfing is a marriage of surfing and sailing that is even more complicated than it appears because it requires techniques and styles that are being improved on all the time. This modern variation of the ancient sport of surfing was conceived in 1970 by Californian Hoyle Schweitzer and developed by his friend Jim Drake (actually, the very first windsurfer was Hawai'i surfing pioneer Tom Blake, who in 1935 rigged his surfboard with a crude sail). The popularity of this new sport has spread like wildfire, and today a circuit of amateur and professional contests is well established. The sport is even included in the Olympic games.

On Maui, windsurfing has grown in quantum leaps, and Ho'okipa Beach, on the island's north coast, has become an internationally recognized site of world windsurfing championships. Windsurfing contributes millions of dollars annually to Maui's economy.

Most of the windsurfing schools are in Kahului and Pā'ia, near the best windsurfing beaches. They include **Alan Cadiz's HST** (871-5423), **Extreme Sports Maui** (871-7954), **Hawaiian Island Surf & Sport** (871-4981), **Maui Windsurf Co.** (877-4816), and **Maui Windsurfari** (871-7766). Most of these schools also rent sailboards, as do **Sailboards Maui** in Pā'ia (579-8432) and **Hi-Tech Surf Sports** in Pā'ia (579-9297) and Kahului (877-2111).

Second Wind Sail, Surf & Kite at 111 Hāna Highway (877-7467) is the closest shop to Kanahā Beach Park, where windsurfers of all levels can enjoy the sport. Second Wind also has a complete line of equipment for kiteboarding—which is like surfing while being towed by a controllable kite—and can set up lessons for this hot new sport.

Windsurfing vans, equipped with four board racks inside the van, can be rented from **Al West's Maui Windsurfing Vans** (877-0090), which will arrange to pick you up at the airport. **Al West's Windsurfing Center** (871-8733) is another Kahului-based school for the sport.

In the Lahaina/West Maui area, **Nancy Emerson School of Surfing** (244-7873) offers windsurfing lessons.

Parasailing off Lahaina.

Parasailing *and* Powered Hang Gliding

Some people prefer to rise above it all—up to 800 feet—in a parasail. Powerboats tow the parasails, and the wind does the rest. You don't have to do anything but sit and enjoy the stunning and ever-changing views of Maui. Since you launch and land directly from a boat, you don't even have to get wet. Rides last 8 to 10 minutes, and tandem as well as single rides are available. This is an activity the physically challenged can enjoy; those in a wheelchair must have another person with them. **Lahaina Para-Sail** (661-4887) and **West Maui Para Sail** (661-4060) are two of the older companies around, both operating out of Lahaina Harbor. **UFO Parasailing** (661-7836) and **Parasail Kā'anapali** (669-6555) are located on Kā'anapali Beach. Maui's parasailing season is mid-May to mid-December; parasailing isn't allowed while whales are in Maui's waters.

Powered hang gliding is another matter. You and your instructor take off from Hāna Airport in a powered two-person trike and explore the Hāna coast and up the slopes of Haleakalā. The instructor sits in front, the student behind; dual controls allow you to learn to fly the trike. Anyone from six years old to whatever can enjoy this adventure. The company that offers this activity is **Hang Gliding Maui** (572-6557), owned by pilot Armin Engert. For everything you need to know about powered hang gliding, check out his website at www.hangglidingmaui.com.

Boating Excursions

One of the best ways to appreciate the beauty of Maui is to venture out to the deep blue frontier, where views of the islands and of underwater life are stunning.

Operating out of Lahaina, **Windjammer Cruises Maui** (661-8600) offers a daily sunset dinner cruise, featuring an all-you-can-eat prime rib and baked salmon dinner, freshly prepared on board, an open bar, as well as authentic Hawaiian entertainment. The boat departs from slip 1 at 5:30 P.M. and returns 2 hours later. Windjammer also offers daily whale-watching sails on the *Spirit of Windjammer,* December–April. Children under twelve are free, and whale sightings are guaranteed. At slip 2 in Lahaina is the *Scotch Mist II* (661-0386), offering a morning snorkel and sail, an afternoon sail, and a "champagne and chocolates" sunset sail. The boat is also available for private charters.

America II (667-2195), a contender for the America's Cup, is anchored at slip 5 in Lahaina Harbor and offers daily whale-watch, trade-wind, and sunset sails. While the other cruises rely mostly on their motors, you will feel the magic of the wind filling the sails as you race across the water in this 65-foot yacht. You can rent a sailboat from **Whale Mist Charters** (667-2833), located at slip 6 in Lahaina. The boat comes complete with captain and crew, and they'll provide box lunches if you want (BYOB).

Expeditions (661-3756), which operates the Lahaina–Lāna'i ferry, offers a variety of package tours for day and overnight Lāna'i stays that include a roundtrip excursion aboard the passenger ferry—a great way to get to Lāna'i.

From Kā'anapali, the Hyatt Regency's luxury sailing yacht, a 55-foot catamaran, the *Kiele V* (667-4727), travels along the Kā'anapali coastline every day but Wednesday. The snorkel sail, from 10 A.M. to 2 P.M., includes a continental breakfast, deli lunch, and open bar. A 90-minute afternoon trade-wind sail leaves at 3:30 P.M. and includes *pūpū* and an open bar.

For those who prefer to stay dry while they view the exotic fish that populate Maui's waters, **Atlantis Submarines** (667-2224) allows you to tour the ocean's reef in a spacious passenger submarine; trips leave Lahaina's harbor every hour on the hour. **Reefdancer** (667-2133), operating out of slip 10 at Lahaina Harbor, takes you on an underwater tour while you sit in an air-conditioned below-decks cabin, looking out large windows.

Kayaking, Rafting, *and* Canoeing

For a relaxing change of pace, paddling your own kayak can be a rewarding experience and a way to get a close-up look at some of Maui's scenic and secluded coastline areas. First-rate kayak tours are offered by **Mākena Kaya**k (879-8426). Owned by Dino Ventura, who was born and raised on Maui, this outfit has experienced local guides who know the underwater terrain well. Depending on weather conditions, the tours explore La Pérouse Bay, the 'Āhihi-Kīna'u Natural Area Reserve, or the area around Mākena Landing. You'll discover secluded coral reefs for snorkeling amid green sea turtles and colorful tropical fish.

On the Hāna side of the island, **Hāna-Maui Snorkel and Kayak Tours** (248-7711) offers awesome 2-hour trips led by naturalist Kevin Coates, who has an intimate knowledge of Hawaiian

culture. He'll take you to the cove where Queen Ka'ahumanu was born in 1768, and you'll snorkel in waters teeming with fish and turtles.

Inflatable rafts, usually accommodating up to sixteen passengers each, are another popular means of plying Maui's waters. **Ultimate Rafting Eco Tours** (667-5678), operating out of Lahaina's harbor, offers 4- and 6-hour snorkel and wildlife-viewing tours to Lāna'i led by marine biologists. Snorkeling equipment is provided, as is plenty of food. They also offer a 2-hour **Ultimate Whale Watch** tour aboard a raft,

December through May (sightings guaranteed).

Also operating out of Lahaina are **Hawaiian Rafting Adventure** (661-733), with expeditions to Lāna'i that include introductory scuba dives, and **Ocean Riders** (661-3586), offering rafting tours of Lāna'i waters, Kaho'olawe, or the north shore of Moloka'i, depending on ocean and weather conditions.

Double-hulled canoes are a Polynesian tradition that have evolved into modern-day powered catamarans. At this time there are no tour operators that we know of who offer trips in authentic canoes.

The French explorer La Pérouse wrote of the craft that went out to greet his ships when he arrived off the shores of Maui in May 1786: "The canoes are equipped with outriggers and each carries from three to five men. On the average, the craft are about 24 feet long, 1 foot in beam, and nearly the same in depth. They do not weigh more than fifty pounds. Frail as these boats are, the islanders nevertheless can travel up to sixty leagues in them, crossing channels twenty leagues wide. The natives are such good swimmers that they stand comparison with seals and sea lions."

Whale Watching

North Pacific humpback whales have been popular attractions in the Hawaiian Islands since 1966, but they have plied those waters for much longer. Some scientists believe the mammals have been here for centuries, but no one knows for certain. Others say there is little evidence they were here more than two hundred years ago.

There is no doubt, however, that Hawaiian waters became dangerous territory for whales in 1819, when two whaling ships, the *Balaena* and the *Equator*, became the first of hundreds to make port in Lahaina. Maui became the whaling capital of the Pacific, the place for restocking provisions as well as seeking rest and recreation. The whaling industry gave rise to at least five shore-based whaling stations by the late 1860s. A decade later they had disappeared, the humpbacks hunted to the very edge of extinction and the industry doomed.

Today, whales still face dangers, but they are showing signs of recovery. Whale watching, meanwhile, has become a growing industry in itself. The motivation to protect the large mammals grew appreciably, and local organizations began to focus on scientific study of the migrating whales. The International Whaling Commission scored an impressive

Opposite: Kayaking at the 'Āhihi-Kina'u reserve, Mākena.

Humpback whales surfacing.

victory when a moratorium on commercial whaling was passed in 1982. In 1987 the commission closed a loophole through which some whaling nations were able to take up to 1,500 whales a year for "scientific" purposes. The Hawaiian islands were designated a Humpback Whale National Marine Sanctuary in 1992.

Still, uncounted numbers of whales, dolphins, seals, and seabirds die each year from entanglement in miles of driftnets set out by foreign fleets fishing the waters of the Pacific. Earthtrust, a Honolulu-based environmental organization, has been instru-

mental in drawing worldwide attention to this irresponsible fishing technology, which not only endangers sea mammals and birds but also threatens massive depletion of many other fish species.

When the whales arrive in Maui's waters, between late November and early May (see page 34), most of Maui's charter boats become instant whale-watching platforms. The boats simply add this recreation to their other specialties and/or run special whale-watching expeditions. Most of the snorkel and boat tours listed above include whale watching in season.

To protect the whales from harassment, boats are restricted as to how close they can get to the whales and are not allowed to come between a whale and her calf. Boat skippers know and respect the necessity of keeping a little distance and cannot be persuaded to go any closer than the regulation distance of 100 yards. Similarly, helicopters and aircraft have strict height limits so as not to disturb these magnificent mammals while they are in Hawaiian breeding grounds.

Photographing whales from a distance with an ordinary camera lens is difficult but much improved with an 80–200 mm zoom lens; shutter speed should be 1/500th of a second or faster. The whales that breach (leap out of the water) tend to do so more than once at a time, affording great photo opportunities. Whale watching, enhanced greatly if using binoculars, can be done from a roadside park or scenic point, from the air, or by boat.

The nonprofit **Pacific Whale Foundation** (101 North Kīhei Road, Kīhei; 879-8860; www.pacificwhale.org) is recognized worldwide as a pioneer and leader in noninvasive marine research, focused especially on whales and dolphins. A fascinating and informative book, with just about everything you may have ever wanted to know about humpback whales, is *Hawai'i's Humpback Whales: A Complete Whale Watcher's Guide*, by Gregory D. Kaufman and Paul H. Forestell of the Pacific Whale Foundation. The book is available in most bookstores in Hawai'i as well as at the foundation's Kīhei headquarters and at their **Ocean Store** at 143 Dickenson Street in Lahaina (667-7447). This store is open daily, 9 A.M.–8 P.M., and offers a wide selection of whale-themed gifts, greeting cards, calendars, posters, tee shirts, videos, and books.

For visitors, the Pacific Whale Foundation sponsors a variety of **Eco Adventures** (879-8811) accompanied by well-informed naturalists. On whale-watching tours, you can listen by means of hydrophones to the mysterious songs of the whales. Dolphin encounter and snorkel tours explore the waters off Lāna'i. Their Molokini snorkeling tour includes a stop at Turtle Arches, a pristine reef habitated by the Hawaiian green sea turtle. Tours depart from both Lahaina and Mā'alaea harbors. All profits benefit the foundation's programs.

The fifth largest of the great whales, humpbacks are known for their haunting songs that travel long distances underwater. A newborn calf weighs 1.5 tons and is 10 to 16 feet in length. It will grow to be 45 tons and 43 to 45 feet long. Breathing through a double blowhole located on the top of their heads, humpbacks move their bodies gracefully through the water, propelled by an up-and-down motion of their tails. A whale's tail (its flukes) is like its fingerprint. No two whales have exactly the same markings or coloration patterns on their flukes, and so scientists are able to identify and track whales over their long lifespans of one hundred or more years.

Fishing

Recreational ocean fishing along Maui's shoreline does not require a license. There is no freshwater fishing here. Opinions on the best fishing areas are like other fish tales—they vary with the telling. Experienced fishermen soon learn to talk with the owners of sporting goods stores to get a fix on the best fishing spots.

With the Pacific as a playground, it is no wonder that Maui spawns numerous charter boats for hire. Some of them are simply for cruising, some for deep sea fishing only. Still others advertise sailing and snorkeling trips or fishing-snorkeling-picnic sails. The boats range from serviceable dive boats to luxurious 58-foot catamarans. Many of the boats for charter also make trips to Molokini Islet, the collapsed volcano that has a sweeping half-moon bay and is a marine conservation area, where no fishing is permitted. Hotel desks have the latest information on the various types of charters and fees, or you can go down to the harbors at Lahaina or Māʻalaea and check out the boats for yourself (most will have returned to the docks by the afternoon).

Although the island of Hawaiʻi is the mecca for fishermen, Maui is justly famous for its game fishing. Record-breaking *aʻu* (marlin or swordfish) have been pulled from local waters, and on a day-to-day basis fishermen take on the *ʻahi* (yellowfin tuna), *aku* (skipjack tuna), *mahimahi* (dolphinfish), *ono* (wahoo), and *ulua* (jackfish). Sailfish can run more than 200 pounds and the blue marlin more than 1,000 pounds. The *mahimahi* and the tuna are strong, fighting fish, a thrill to hook.

On some fishing boats in Hawaiʻi, it is customary for the boat captain and crew to keep the catch; others allow visitors to retain any fish they catch. Ask ahead of time which practice the boat you choose subscribes to in order to prevent any misunderstanding. It is customary to tip the skipper and crew after a successful voyage (roughly 10 to 15 percent is a good tip). Unless stated otherwise, you bring your own food and beverages on fishing trips (coolers and ice are provided).

Aerial Sportfishing Charters (667-9089), established in 1964, sails *Aerial III* and *No Problem* out of Lahaina (slip 9) on daily big game fishing excursions, with a maximum of six passengers. Also operating out of Lahaina (slip 50) is **Luckey Strike Charters** (661-4606) with two boats, the *Luckey Strike II* (50-foot Delta) and *Kanoa* (31-foot Uniflite). Captain Tad Luckey has over twenty-five years of experience seeking out deepwater fish in Maui's waters and offers bottom fishing as well. **Lahaina Charter Boats** (667-6672) operates three boats out of Lahaina Harbor (slip 8): *Broadbill* (36-foot Harcraft), *Judy Ann II* (43-foot Delta), and *Alohilani* (28-foot Topaz). **Finest Kind Sport Fishing** sails three boats out of Lahaina (slip 7): *Finest Kind* (37-foot Merritt), *Reel*

A proud fisherman shows off a 30-pound *ono*.

Hooker (35-foot Bertram), and *Exact* (31-foot Bertram).

The **Ocean Activities Center** (879-4485) owns and operates two boats out of Māʻalaea Harbor. The *No Ka Oi III*, a 37-foot Tollycraft customdesigned for Maui waters, takes visitors on 6- and 8-hour deep sea fishing trips, and the 65-foot *Maka Kai* goes on daily (May–December) evening bottom fishing excursions that include a barbecue steak dinner, drinks, and spectacular sunsets.

Activities on Land

Hiking Tours

Several local organizations regularly schedule group hiking activities and welcome visitors to join their excursions. The **Nature Conservancy of Hawai'i** has a Maui field office (P.O. Box 1716, Makawao, Maui 96768; 572-7849) and oversees several preserves on the island. Monthly guided hikes are offered at the Kapunakea Preserve, above Kā'anapali in the West Maui Mountains, where rare native plants and birds exist in a rainforest environment, and at the Waikamoi Preserve, home to hundreds of native Hawaiian species in subalpine and rainforest areas of Haleakalā. Groups can arrange guided hikes outside of the regular hike schedule; contact the field office at least two months prior to your trip. The Hawai'i chapter of the **Sierra Club** (P.O. Box 2577, Honolulu, HI 96803; 538-6616) offers numerous day hikes throughout the islands and welcomes visitors to join them.

The Maui hike nonpareil, available to only a select few and just once a year (usually in September), is the **Pu'u Kukui Nature Hike** offered by the Kapalua Nature Society. Participants, selected by a random drawing, are airlifted from Kapalua to a constructed boardwalk that traverses the Pu'u Kukui bogs and cloud forests. Encompassing the highest peak in the West Maui Mountains, the Pu'u Kukui Preserve is the largest private natural reserve in the islands. Cost of the daylong trip for the twelve fortunate people who are selected is $500 each (proceeds benefit the watershed management program). Applications are available from the Kapalua Nature Society, 800 Kapalua Drive, Kapalua, Maui 96761; 800-KAPALUA or 669-0244.

About the only outfit leading guided hiking tours into 'Īao Valley is the **Hawai'i Nature Center** (244-6500), which offers daily 1.5-hour educational walking tours in the woods; reservations are required. Though the Nature Center is a facility geared toward children, with a great interactive nature museum, the hikes are better suited to adults, and no children under eight are permitted.

Hike Maui (879-5270) is the premier outfit for group hikes with knowledgeable guides. The fee for half- and full-day hikes includes pickup, transportation, equipment, lunch, and snacks. The company is run by Ken Schmitt, a student of classical Greek and Latin who has a graduate degree in Oriental philosophy. Ken came to Maui in 1979,

Hiking the Waihe'e Ridge Trail (page 70) provides incredible rainforest views.

lived outside in the jungle for three years, then began to share his experience of the land with others by means of guided hiking tours. He now has a crew of seven personally trained guides who lead most of the hikes, which range from 5 to 10 hours. Each is an incredible experience, including swimming among *hau* blossoms in mountain pools and

sampling wild fruits and berries in tranquil cloud forests.

Maui Eco-Adventures (661-7720), a newcomer to the scene, offers terrific hikes in the West Maui Mountains, several to spots inaccessible on one's own. A half-day hike is an easy 2-mile walk in the Maunalei Arboretum; a full-day excursion goes deep into Kahakuloa Valley, private land where several Hawaiian

families still live on *kalo* farms and sustain themselves in the ancient manner. Another full-day hike goes up Makamakaʻole Stream to a waterfall and pool for swimming, with twelve stream crossings expertly accomplished by the well-trained guides. All-day hikes include a great picnic lunch laid out on a tablecloth in the wilderness.

Of Hawaiʻi's original 140 native birds, 70 are extinct and 30 endangered. The scarlet *ʻiʻiwi* (left), the crimson *ʻapapane*, the bright green *ʻamakihi*, and the *pueo*, or Hawaiian owl, are among the 30 native birds that still abound in some areas of the state, including the Kapunakea and Waikamoi nature preserves on Maui. The Nature Conservancy of Hawaiʻi (572-7849) offers monthly hikes deep into these pristine areas.

Biking

Maui is a great place for biking. Although most bikers come to Maui to ride the Haleakalā road, there are other choices. A circle tour of the island, covering some 160 miles, can be made with a good mountain bike—which can't be said of any other of the islands except Hawaiʻi. Most Maui roads have good shoulders

and are well marked. An excellent resource is *Short Bike Rides Hawaii* by William Walters (Globe Pequot Press), available in most Maui bookstores.

A favorite activity on Maui is the guided downhill bicycle tour from the summit of Haleakalā Volcano through colorful flower farms and small towns of Upcountry, down to the beach at Pāʻia. In 38 miles the elevation drops 10,000 feet. An excursion company will pick you up at your hotel, take you to the summit by van in time to see the sunrise, and provide bicycles for the trip down to the coast. Bikes are equipped with special brakes, and participants are issued protective gear and rain jackets. The trip may include breakfast going up and lunch on the way down. The outing takes about 8 hours, and most tours are about $100 per person.

There are many good tour operators for downhill excursions. We like **Maui Downhill** (871-2155), which has an especially friendly and professional crew and offers a variety of tours. If you don't mind being picked up at your hotel at 2:30 or 3 A.M., and if it's not raining, the sunrise tour can be spectacular. Otherwise, a trip later in the morning is warmer and more gentle. Among other reputable tour operators are **Cruiser Phil's** (893-2332), **Maui**

Biking down Haleakalā in the morning mist, Science City in the background.

Mountain Cruisers (871-6014), and **Mountain Riders** (242-9739).

If you are an experienced biker, you might want to consider renting a bike and making the trip on your own. You can go at your own pace rather than at the speed of the slowest rider, and you can stop for lunch and snacks wherever you want. There are two very good outfits that will take you up to the summit and give you a bike and gear for the downhill trip, which you return to them in Makawao the same day, whenever you wish. These are **Upcountry Cycles** (573-2888) and **Haleakalā Bike Co.** (575-9575).

Island Biker at 415 Dairy Road in Kahului (877-7744), across from K-Mart, rents out mountain bikes. **West Maui Cycles** at 840 Waineʻe Street in Lahaina (661-9005), owned by Dave Boote and his wife, Linda, is the biggest bike rental shop on Maui (it's located below Denny's). They provide sales, service, and rentals at reasonable daily and weekly rates. In addition, they rent out water sports equipment, such as surf and boogie boards, snorkel sets, and beach chairs. In Kīhei, **South Maui Bicycles** at 1993 South Kīhei Road (874-0068) has a large selection of rentals.

Horseback Riding

Some of the most spectacular riding trails in the world cross Maui pastures, woodlands, and lava flows. Excursions range from easy, uncomplicated rides to overnight expeditions into Haleakalā Crater. Riding a horse on Maui along a sandy beach or past an ancient Hawaiian *heiau*, into the crater, or along a high meadow is a great experience. There are stables on Maui that offer lessons to novices in preparation for later rides that may be more challenging. **Kula Ridge Stables** (878-2942) and **Piʻiholo Stables** (572-1789), both in the Upcountry area, provide equestrian instruction.

Most stables require that you wear long pants and closed-toe shoes. They provide helmets, which are not mandatory. Several of the horseback-riding tours are wary of taking children.

Visitors to the Kīhei area have the good fortune of being not far from **Mākena Stables** (879-0244), where owners Patrick and Helaine Borge offer just one superb ride a day, varying the route with each trip; if you go back, you're not likely to take the same ride. Led by Pat, rides traverse ʻUlupalakua ranchlands, going up to the Tedeschi Winery or across rugged lava fields down to the coast. The horses are beauties, well trained and responsive to experienced riders as well as novices. Book well in advance, as they limit each excursion to six riders.

Nāpili's **Ironwood Ranch** (669-4991), in the Kapalua area, offers a wide variety of riding tours, from a mountain ride with picnic lunch to a trip through a pineapple plantation and into the West Maui Mountains. The Ironwood Odyssey excursion takes more experienced riders through lush tropical valleys of the West Maui Mountains. Shuttle trans-

Horseback riding on Sliding Sands Trail in Haleakalā crater.

portation is available from Kā'ana-pali and Kapalua, and Japanese-speaking guides are available.

On the other side of West Maui, about 5 miles north of Wailuku, is **Mendes Ranch** (871-5222), a working cattle ranch that offers a *paniolo* horseback adventure and barbecue as well as a combination helicopter/horseback excursion, which includes a 30-minute helicopter tour of the West Maui Mountains. They're equipped to accommodate the physically challenged on their rides.

Pony Express Tours (667-2200), based in Kula, offers both half- and full-day crater trips, providing equipment and food as well as a guide. Two-hour *paniolo* rides across Haleakalā Ranch are also available. Also in Kula, **Thompson Ranch** (878-1910), which has been in business since 1902, offers morning, picnic, and sunset rides for the whole family in the picturesque Upcountry area.

In the Ha'ikū area, near Pā'ia, **Adventures on Horseback** (242-7445 or 572-6211), run by Franklin Levinson, offers an exceptional waterfall adventure ride, limited to groups of six. The horses are extremely well trained and cared for, making the escorted riding experience enjoyable even for less experienced riders. The tour crosses 200-foot oceanside cliffs and rolling green pastureland, winding through a lush rainforest where participants are served a picnic lunch and can swim in a refreshing natural pool. Adventures on Horseback is home to the **Maui Horse Whisperer Experience**, a half- or full-day program of communication with one of nature's most exquisite species. This life-enhancing program is a magical, memorable experience. Check out the website at www.mauihorses.com.

On the Hāna coast, **Hāna Ranch** (248-7238) conducts

guided rides on its sprawling ranchlands. Either *mauka* or ocean rides are available. The trail along seaside cliffs is particularly spectacular. Although Hotel Hāna-Maui guests are given priority booking, non-guests may ride if space is available. A 25-minute drive past Hāna to the Kīpahulu district takes you to **'Ohe'o Stables** (667-2222), which offers a 4- or 5-hour scenic ride through the mountains above 'Ohe'o Gulch. For the truly adventuresome, **Charley's Trail Rides and Pack Trips** (248-8209), based in Kaupō, will take you on an overnight ride up the slopes of Haleakalā to Palikū campground inside the crater, where tents are pitched for the night.

Specialized Tours

Tours of 'Ulupalakua Ranch are offered by **Maui Jeep Adventures** (876-1177). Riding in open-air Jeep Wranglers over rugged ranchlands, visitors see otherwise inaccessible areas of Upcountry and coastal Maui. The focus is on the cultural, historical, geological, and environmental aspects of this diverse land. Originally a 19th-century sugar plantation named Rose Ranch, the ranch shifted over to cattle raising at the turn of the century and for over one hundred years has kept alive the *paniolo* tradition. The 25,000-acre ranch owns land from 'Ulupalakua town all the way down to La Pérouse Bay. The 4-hour tour explores either the *mauka* area of the ranch, at cool heights of 3,000 to 6,000 feet, or the *makai* area, the more rugged of the two trips, with access to a precontact Hawaiian village. Either tour provides an unforgettable experience of Maui's unspoiled wilderness areas.

Another tour unique to Maui is of **Maui Pineapple Company**'s 23,000-acre working pineapple plantation, led by Kapalua Nature Society (669-8088). They'll show you why Hawaiian pineapple is *no ka oi* (the best) on a tour that includes spectacular scenery of the West Maui Mountains—and you can pick your own pineapple to take home. The tour is offered weekdays at 9:30 A.M. and 1 P.M. and takes about 2 hours.

In the Hāna area, **Maui Cave Adventures** (248-7308) offers underground treks exploring the Ka'elekū Caverns. This unique adventure takes you through a 30,000-year-old volcanic lava-tube system where few have ever ventured. The guides, Chuck and Deborah Thorne, are trained vulcanospeleologists (lava-tube experts), and all gear is provided (hardhats, gloves, flashlights, drinking water, and, for longer

Exploring the Ka'elekū Caverns.

hikes, snacks). The 2-hour tour is a fairly easy 1.5-mile walk (participants must be at least nine years old), while 4- and 6-hour trips require that hikers be physically fit.

For gay and lesbian travelers, **Gay Hawaiian Excursions** (891-8603) will set up a wide variety of tours and activities, including whale watching, horseback riding, kayaking, windsurfing, snorkeling, scuba diving, surfing, dinner cruises, and much more. For help in planning your trip in advance, they can be reached at 800-891-8603 (www.gay excursions.com).

Health Clubs

Most local health clubs welcome visitors, and most are open seven days a week. **Maui 24 Hour**

Fitness at 150 Hāna Highway in Kahului (877-7474) is a premiere exercise facility open 24 hours a day, as its name suggests. Amenities include free weights and machines, personal training, group exercise programs, a kids club, cardio machines, and locker and shower facilities. In Kahana, **Maui Muscle Sports Club** at 4327 Lower Honoapi'ilani Highway (669-3539) offers spinning, boxing, and rock climbing in addition to the usual health club fare.

Art Schools

The **Hui No'eau Visual Arts Center** (572-6560) in Makawao offers classes in painting, drawing, printmaking, ceramics, photography, and other visual arts mediums (see page 88). Visitors are welcome. If you're staying in the Upcountry area and you're interested in such an activity, give them a call to see what is going on during your stay. Also welcoming visitors is the **Art School at Kapalua** (665-0007), which offers classes and workshops for people of all ages and experience levels. Figure drawing, still-life painting in oil or pastel, watercolors, plein air painting, and ceramics are just a few of the classes offered. In addition, dance and yoga are taught at the Kapalua art school.

Golf

Hawai'i is a golfer's paradise, and the island of Maui and neighboring Lāna'i offer perhaps the best golf in all the Hawaiian islands—some might even say the world. All courses offer fantastic views.

Green fees are competitive with courses elsewhere, but rates can vary considerably from summer to winter, with low season considered from May through November and high season December through April. Rates vary from $200 at a resort course to $34 at a municipal course. The median green fee during low season is $125.

Carts are included in green fees. Every course on Maui rents clubs, usually for about $35.

The **Maui Golf Company** will help you find a course suited to your needs, offers special discounts, and will book tee times. Call their hotline at 874-8300. (They do ask that you book your other activities with them, such as *lū'au* and bike trips, which helps them pay the bills.) Another outfit that will help set up golf outings is **Prestige Golf Services** (874-1081). Their service not only provides preferred tee times but also can include all transfers, meal arrangements, golf bag transfers—even caddies.

At the time of this writing, the Waikapū Country Club in central Maui is closed and up for sale. It's famous for its clubhouse, designed by Frank Lloyd Wright, originally to be a country home in Connecticut for playwright Arthur Miller and his then wife, Marilyn Monroe. They never built the house because they divorced, but the plans were later used for the Maui clubhouse. Also closed is the Kaluako'i Golf Course at Kaluako'i Resorts on Moloka'i.

All Maui courses open to the public are listed here, with comments about those we've played. The Maui area code is 808.

Dunes at Maui Lani

31 Ku'ualoha, Kahului; 873-0422 (www.mauilani.com)

Maui's newest golf course was designed by Nelson and Haworth, who looked to the traditional courses of Scotland for inspiration. The practice facility includes putting greens and fairway bunkers. 18 holes, 6,840 yards, par 72.

Elleair Maui Golf Club

(public), 1345 Pi'ilani Highway, Kīhei; 874-0777 (www.mauigolf.org/elleair)

Originally known as Silversword, this beautifully landscaped course opened in 1987. It was designed by the Canadian Bill Newis. 18 holes, 6,801 yards, par 71.

Beautiful scenery abounds at Kapalua's Village Course.

Opposite:
Signature hole 8 at the Experience at Kō'ele on Lāna'i.

Kāʻanapali Resort, Kāʻanapali Beach: North and South courses; 661-3691 (www.kaanapali golf.com)

The Kāʻanapali **North Course**, designed by Robert Trent Jones Sr., opened in 1962 and marked the beginning of resort golf in Hawaiʻi as we know it today. The course meanders around a village, hotels, and golf course homes on either side of the main highway, going down to the beach at the 14th, where the ocean is a water hazard and Kāʻanapali Beach is a sand trap. There are rolling hills, but the course is relatively flat. Fairways are wide, but this is still a tight course. There are long par 4s, considered among the most difficult in Hawaiʻi. The GPS (Global Positioning System) is helpful. The clubhouse is a busy, commercial operation. 18 holes, 6,994 yards, par 71.

The Arthur Jack Snyder–designed **South Course** at Kāʻanapali opened in 1967 as an executive course. It was redesigned by Snyder in 1976 to be regulation size. 18 holes, 6,555 yards, par 71.

Kapalua Resort, 300 Kapalua Drive, Kapalua. The three Kapalua golf courses—Bay, Plantation, and Village—are among the most splendid in the world.

They are certified as Audubon Cooperative Sanctuaries in recognition of the Kapalua Resort's efforts in preserving wildlife. The courses are nestled between the West Maui Mountains and the pristine Pacific, on grounds where one of the world's largest pineapple plantations once stood. A small working plantation skirted by the golf courses still grows the sweet West Maui pineapple. 669-8044 (www.kapaluamaui.com)

Kapalua Bay. 669-8820. The Bay Course was the first Kapalua golf course. Designed by Arnold Palmer and Francis Duane, it opened in 1975. Winding through tropical palms and hibiscus, this course fronts the ocean. 18 holes, 6,600 yards, par 72.

Kapalua Plantation. 669-8877. The Plantation Course has varied terrain with fabulous views from every hole. This is a challenging course, but it's easy to find your way from tee to tee. The 7th hole is interesting for its blind start; taking off, you can't see where you'll be going. Hole 17 has a great vista to the west that invites trouble at teeing in that the lovely, wide fairway narrows into a little ribbon where it skirts a ravine; you have to choose between going over the

ravine (difficult) or maneuvering into the little slot (the easier choice). The 18th is long—in fact, the longest hole on the professional tour. The course itself is quite long, with nothing under 120 yards even for the woman player. Wind patterns will make a difference, and they can help or hinder. Unfriendly (heavy) sand such as at the Plantation Course is not uncommon on Maui. The clubhouse is very quiet, with an exclusive feeling; you know you're at an elegant resort. Designed in 1991 by Ben Crenshaw and Bill Coore, the Plantation Course is host each January to the official PGA Tour event, the Mercedes Championships, where the likes of Tiger Woods and Vijay Singh compete for a multimillion-dollar purse. The Plantation Course was judged Hawaiʻi's second best golf course by a group of Aloha Section PGA professionals (Hualālai on the Big Island was number one). 18 holes, 7,263 yards, par 73.

Kapalua Village. 669-8830. Village is a very playable course that climbs to 750 feet above the sea, amid towering Cook pines and fragrant eucalyptus trees. Local guava, passion fruit, and grasses surround the wide fairways. There's a treat at the fifth tee: a large lake surrounded by high pines. Panoramic views are amazing here, as they are at the next four holes (6, 7, 8, and 9). Not as challenging as the Plantation Course, the Village Course nevertheless offers a game that's a lot of fun in an idyllic setting. There is no drink cart, but there's a snack bar at about 14. A new clubhouse recently opened. As throughout the Kapalua Resort, the staff is super friendly. The Village Course, designed by Arnold Palmer and Ed Seay, opened in 1980. 18 holes, 6,632 yards, par 71.

Lāna'i Company. Part of Maui County, Lāna'i offers championship golf on two world-class courses, the oceanside Challenge at Mānele (565-2222) and the upcountry Experience at Kō'ele (565-4653). Each course offers a completely unique experience.

At the **Challenge at Mānele**, hole 17 is the challenge—getting your ball across a ravine. This Jack Nicklaus–designed course, which opened in 1993, is without question one of the prettiest we've ever played, kind of like Pebble Beach without the winds. It's a tough course but fun. You have to have a good short game or

you're in trouble, except at no. 17, where you need a good long game to get the ball over the ravine. Hole 12 is a spectacular shot from one ocean cliff to another with nothing but water between, but the 17th is by far the greater challenge. There are lots of hazards and one good sandtrap; as on most Maui courses, the sand is not soft. Even with a lot of players present, this course, with wide fairways closing into narrow greens, wouldn't seem particularly busy. It's a lovely, quiet place for a spectacular game of golf. 18 holes, 7,039 yards, par 72.

The **Experience at Kō'ele** is right up there with the top golf courses in the world and certainly is one of Hawai'i's finest. There are two distinctly different nine holes. The upper mountain front nine is a great course, high up in a pine forest with glimpses of the ocean in the background. The holes are really interesting, especially no. 8, where you hit down into a canyon from a cliff that's 200 feet above the green. Mist-shrouded trees, lush greenery, seven lakes, rushing streams, and picturesque waterfalls accent the course's beauty. There are lots of wild turkeys on the course (drop-

pings, too). Carts have to stay in the cart path, so prepare for more walking than usual. The back nine is lower down—you feel like you're playing in the garden at the adjacent Lodge at Kō'ele. This challenging course, designed by Ted Robinson and Greg Norman, is not as enigmatic as the Mānele course; it's easier to figure out. The course has been recognized by Audubon International for its environmentally friendly policies. 18 holes, 7,014 yards, par 72.

Mākena Golf Club, 5415 Mākena Alanui, Mākena; 879-3344. The Mākena golf course was designed by Robert Trent Jones Jr. and opened in 1981; in 1993 Jones expanded it into the North and South courses, both of which are adjacent to the Maui Prince Hotel.

Mākena North and the Challenge at Mānele (on Lāna'i) are our favorite Maui courses. This classic Robert Trent Jones Jr. course is what a course in Hawai'i should be like. Although you're not up real high and the views aren't as spectacular as from some of the other courses, the terrain more than makes up for this. Nature is at her most elemental here; you can see three or four different weather happenings at once as the sun, rain, clouds, and winds play off one another. The course is beautifully incorporated into the slopes of Haleakalā, making full use of the natural habitat. Not overly landscaped, the course incorporates ancient rock walls and steep ravines. The course is in excellent shape, with good sand traps. You'll end up using a lot of balls on this course. There's a small pro shop, not fancy. Staff is accommodating and service is personable. It's worth the trip to the tip of south Maui to play this superb course. 18 holes, 6,914 yards, par 72.

The **Mākena South** course goes up the slopes of Haleakalā, passing four lakes, and heads down to the oceanfront at holes 15 and 16, which many describe as the most spectacular oceanfront holes in Hawai'i. 18 holes, 7,017 yards, par 72.

Maui Country Club, 48 Nonohe Place, Pā'ia; 877-7893 (open to the public only on Mondays)

Opened in the 1920s, this course was designed by Hawai'i's first golf pro, the Scotsman Alex Bell. The course is relatively flat, but gusty winds, particularly in winter, present challenges.

Pukalani Country Club (public), 360 Pukalani Street, Pukalani; 572-1314 (www.pukalanigolf.com)

The only Upcountry course on Maui, Pukalani skirts around a residential community at the cool, often windy 1,200-foot elevation of Haleakalā. A restaurant features local-style food and serves breakfast, lunch, and dinner. 18 holes, 6,962 yards, par 72.

Sandalwood Golf Course
(public), 2500 Honoapi'ilani Highway, Waikapū; 242-4653 (www.mauigolf.org/sandalwood)

Opened in 1991, Sandalwood was designed by Robin Nelson and Rodney Wright. It features all-grass practice facilities. Included are a clubhouse, pro shop, and restaurant. The central Maui location, on the slopes of the West Maui Mountains between Kīhei and Wailuku, provides spectacular views of Haleakalā and both the north and south coasts. There is an attractive clubhouse/restaurant. 18 holes, 6,469 yards, par 72.

Waiehu Municipal Golf Course
Waiehu (public); 270-7400 (www.mauigolf.org/waiehu)

West of Kahului, not too far from Wailuku, this fairly difficult course is off the tourist track. It features oceanfront holes and stunning views. The front nine runs along the shoreline, with the back nine on old sand dune land above. The course was designed by Maui civil engineers,

with the front nine opening in the 1920s and the back nine forty years later. 18 holes, 6,330 yards, par 72.

Wailea Golf Club. The three Wailea courses—Blue, Gold, and Emerald—are on Maui's sunny south coast. Beautifully landscaped, they consistently receive top honors. 875-5111 (www.waileagolf.com)

Wailea Blue (120 Kaukahi Street, Wailea), designed by Arthur Jack Snyder, opened for play in 1972 (the same year Snyder designed Wailea's Orange Course, which was converted in the 1990s by Robert Trent Jones Jr. into the 36-hole Emerald and Gold courses). Here golfers encounter four lakes, 74 bunkers, wide fairways, and a fair number of hills. 18 holes, 6,700 yards, par 72.

Wailea Emerald (100 Wailea Golf Club Drive, Wailea), designed by Robert Trent Jones Jr., opened in 1994. It is consistently ranked among the top ten courses in the U.S. 18 holes, 6,825 yards, par 72.

Wailea Gold (100 Wailea Golf Club Drive, Wailea) was also designed by Robert Trent Jones Jr. This is a classic resort course, very green, beautifully landscaped, with wide fairways, but without the variety found at, for example, the Kapalua courses; all the holes tend to look alike. Wailea Gold is all golf course, with no homes along the route—just ancient lava rock walls indicating that Hawaiians once lived here in numbers. The course is very playable; it's challenging, but you won't use every club in the bag. If you hit with accuracy and avoid the bunkers, there is little to get in your way. You do need to be accurate around the greens, though, because of the sand traps. If you want to analyze your game, you can purchase a personal video of yourself playing. There is a large, well-stocked pro shop. Wailea Gold, ranked among America's top ten courses, is host to the Senior PGA Tour's Skins Game in January. 18 holes, 7,070 yards, par 72.

The Bay Course at Kapalua (top) and the Wailea clubhouse and Sea Watch Restaurant.

Golf Schools

Kā'anapali Golf College
2290 Kā'anapali Parkway, Kā'anapali; 661-0488

Half and full-day sessions are offered. Executive Director Roger Fredericks has helped many of the Senior PGA Tour's top players with their game, among them Gary Player and Raymond Floyd. As a certified flexibility technician, he's able to provide individual assistance based on what a person is able to do.

Kapalua Golf Academy
300 Kapalua Drive, Kapalua; 669-6500 (www.kapaluamaui.com)

This newly completed facility is state-of-the-art in every way. Head pro Jerry King has the state's largest group of PGA professionals on his staff. A half-day golf school begins at 7 A.M. and goes through putting and chipping, pitching and bunker play, and an hour and a half of full swing with video analysis, after which you lunch with golf professionals. Maximum number of students per instructor is four. Two- and three-day sessions are also offered at the school, as is private instruction.

Tennis

NEARLY EVERY RESORT HOTEL has a tennis complex, with many courts lighted for evening play. Those listed here are open to the public for a fee. A listing of free public courts appears at the end of this section.

Hyatt Regency Maui Tennis Center, 200 Nohea Kai Drive, Kāʻanapali; 661-1234. This six-court facility is at the north end of the Kāʻanapali Resort, adjacent to the Kāʻanapali Golf Course. Clinics are held Mondays through Saturdays at 9 A.M.

Kapalua Resort, 100 Kapalua Drive, Kapalua; 669-5677. There are two tennis complexes at Kapalua Resort—the Village Tennis Center and the Tennis Garden—with a total of twenty plexipave courts, eight with lights. Kapalua is consistently ranked among the top tennis destinations in the world by *Tennis* magazine. Court fees are low compared with similar facilities. Each of the facilities has a slew of clinics for juniors, men, women, and drop-in matchmaking.

Maui Marriott Beach and Tennis Club, 100 Nohea Kai Drive, Kāʻanapali; 661-6200. Combined with the Marriott's fitness center, the tennis facility has five plexipave courts, three lighted for night play. Clinics and round robins are offered daily.

A tennis clinic at the Mānele Bay Hotel, Lānaʻi.

Mākena Tennis Club, 5415 Mākena Alanui, Mākena; 879-8777. This club has six courts, two of them lighted.

Royal Lahaina Tennis Ranch, 2780 Kekaʻa Drive, Kāʻanapali; 661-3611. The center court seats 3,500, and there are ten surrounding courts. A range of clinics are held weekdays. Facilities include a pro shop and snack bar.

Sheraton Maui Tennis Club, 2605 Kāʻanapali Parkway, Kāʻanapali; 662-8208. Three night-lit courts are open until 8 P.M., with daily clinics. The staff prides itself on its match-setting service.

Wailea Tennis Club, 131 Wailea ʻIki Place, Wailea; 879-1958. Nicknamed "Wimbledon West," this club has eleven plexipave courts, including three lit for night play, and a stadium court that can accommodate up to 1,000 spectators. There are regularly scheduled clinics and round robins. Joe's Bar and Grill, one of Maui's best restaurants, is above the pro shop.

Free public tennis courts are maintained by the Maui County Department of Parks and Recreation and are available on a first-come, first-served basis. These are:

Lahaina/Kāʻanapali:
Lahaina Civic Center (1840 Honoapiʻilani Highway), five lighted courts; **Maluʻuluolele Park** (Front and Shaw Streets), four lighted courts

Kīhei: **Kalama Beach Park** (Kīhei Road), four lighted courts; next to the **Maui Sunset** (Waipuʻilani Road), six unlighted courts

Hāna: **Hāna Ball Park**, next to the Hotel Hāna-Maui, two lighted courts

Upcountry: **Eddie Tam Center** in Makawao and **Pukalani Community Center** each have two lighted courts

Wailuku/Kahului: **Kahului Community Center** (Oneheʻe and Uhu Streets), two lighted courts; **Wailuku Community Center** (Wells and Market Streets), seven lighted courts; **Maui Community College**, Kahului (Kaʻahumanu and Wākea avenues), two unlighted courts; **Wailuku War Memorial** (1580 Kaʻahumanu Avenue), four lighted courts

Tours *and* Activity Reservation Services

MAUI OFFERS such a large assortment of tours and tour operators that we have included only a small sampling of companies herein. Activity/tour desks are located in or near most hotels, condominiums, and shopping areas. It should be noted that some of the best activities are not promoted by many reservation services because of their low or nonexistent commissions to such services. If you see something you'd like to do listed in this book, it might be best to book on your own.

That said, it should be remembered that the guidance of an area resident can be invaluable. Among the more knowledgeable companies we have found on Maui are **Activity Warehouse**, with outlets in Lahaina (667-4000 and 662-0111) and Kīhei (875-4000). **Captain Nemo's Ocean Emporium** at 150 Dickenson Street, Lahaina (661-5555), one-half block off Front Street, is a fine dive shop as well as tour agent, with years of experience on Maui. **Tom Barefoot's Cashback Tours** at 834 Front Street, Lahaina (661-8889), has been in business for over twenty-five years. In Kīhei, the **Ocean Activities Center** at 1847 South Kīhei Road (879-4485) books Molokini snorkel tours as well as whale-watching expeditions.

Land Tours

There are a number of sightseeing tour companies operating on Maui, some of them highly specialized, others prepared to show visitors the best of Maui.

Dave and Kathy Campbell of **Temptation Tours** (877-8888) offer an assortment of luxurious upscale tours of Hāna and Upcountry, from full-day excursions to Hāna to a Haleakalā sunrise tour with a visit to an exotic protea farm. They'll pick you up at your hotel in their comfortable "limo-van" and provide an elegant picnic lunch.

Maui Tours and Transportation (874-5561) has a fleet of late-model minibuses and vans for tours to Upcountry, including Tedeschi Winery, and ʻĪao Valley. They will pick you up at your hotel. **Roberts Hawaiʻi** (539-9400) is one of the state's leaders in tours and transportation. The family-owned company has been in business for over sixty years. On Maui, they offer minibus tours of Haleakalā, ʻĪao Valley, Lahaina, and Hāna, as well as a one-day trip to Oʻahu with tours of Pearl Harbor, Punchbowl, and ʻIolani Palace. **Trans Hawaiian Maui** (877-7308) offers Hāna and Haleakalā tours in either vans or limos and has guides that speak a number of foreign languages.

Our favorite tour: **Rent-a-Local** (877-4042). These are the folks Yoko Ono and Oprah call when they want to go exploring. A local guide will meet you at your hotel and give you a private tour in your own rental car, geared to whatever interests you, with no predetermined schedule or itinerary. A tour might include a swim at a waterfall, a hike off the beaten track, shopping, restaurants—whatever your heart desires. This is truly a way to experience the aloha spirit. Tours are 8 to 12 hours and can be for one to six people.

For visitors making the Hāna drive on their own, **Hāna Cassette**

Guide (572-0550) comes complete with a 90-minute tape or CD to listen to while you drive plus a Hāna coast map and flower guide and a free video—all for $20 (free use of a tape player if one's not in your car). Several of the gardens mentioned in the tour are closed, and not all information provided is completely accurate. But the detailed map itself is extremely useful, and the flower guide will help you identify the colorful trees and flowers along the route. The only place to get this cassette guide is at their outlet at the Shell Service Station at 370 Dairy Road (Highway 380) in Kahului, just before the Hāna Highway (36). They also offer a Haleakalā cassette tour for $10 that includes ʻĪao Valley.

Air Tours

Flights aboard small airplanes and helicopters afford visitors a view of Maui from a wonderfully different perspective. Prices vary depending on the length of flights. Some flights include airborne tours not only of Maui but also cross over to the nearby islands of Lānaʻi and/or Molokaʻi or even go on for a day to Oʻahu or the Big Island.

Pacific Wings (873-0877) offers tours to Kīlauea Volcano on the Big Island, to Hāna, and to Kalaupapa on Molokaʻi. For the truly adventuresome, they'll give you a flying lesson that includes landings on Molokaʻi and Lānaʻi. **Maui Air** (871-8152 or 877-5500) offers scenic 2-hour air tours to the Big Island in twin-engine, ten-seat aircraft, departing from Kahului Airport and Kapalua–West Maui Airport. Although seeing the active Kīlauea volcano is the highlight of the tour, you'll also see the summit of Mauna Kea, the beautiful Hāmākua coast on the Big Island, and glimpses of Hāna.

Most helicopter services operate out of the heliport at Kahului Airport (there's a sign for the heliport on the main access road to the airport). An advantage helicopters have is that they can slide deep into narrow valleys, allowing sightseeing in remote areas that are difficult to enter by land. Many of the companies offer passengers custom videos of their flight.

Family-owned and operated **Blue Hawaiian Helicopters** (871-8844) has more than fifteen years experience in the business, with excellent military-trained pilots. Many major motion picture companies have employed the services of Blue Hawaiian for their aerial shooting needs, including the filming of *Jurassic Park*, made on Kauaʻi in 1992. Top-of-the-line stereo headsets cancel all outside noise so that passengers may clearly hear the pilot. These Vietnam vets do a pretty good job with their narration, having been certified as tour guides and thus being knowledgeable about Hawaiʻi's history and culture. Maui tours include a spectacular trip across the West Maui Mountains and the Pailolo Channel to the 3,000-foot cliffs of Molokaʻi, the world's highest sea cliffs. They also offer a trip to Hāna with viewings of Haleakalā crater, and a tour that covers all of Maui. The owners of Blue Hawaiian, David and Patti Chevalier, have received numerous awards for their innovative programs and concern for safety. They emphasize that the point is not the thrill but the educational experience.

Other helicopter companies offer similar ranges of tours, mostly focusing on West Maui and Hāna/Haleakalā but also with trips to other islands. Reputable companies with excellent safety records are **Alexair Helicopters** (877-4354), **Hawaiʻi Helicopters** (877-5922), and **Sunshine Helicopters** (871-0722).

Just *for* Children

MAUI IS AN EXCELLENT PLACE to bring children on vacation. The near-perfect climate allows them to spend time outdoors at the beach or in a park. In addition, most hotels offer supervised daily programs for children.

A favorite attraction for children is the **Sugar Cane Train** (667-6851), run by the old Lahaina–Kāʻanapali & Pacific Railroad, which once hauled cane to the mill in Lahaina and transported workers between their homes and the canefields. Six miles of track have been restored, and the Sugar Cane Train, pulled by the steam locomotives *Anaka* or *Myrtle*, chugs from Kāʻanapali to Lahaina and back, with singing conductors providing entertainment. A highlight of the 30-minute trip is crossing Hāhākea trestle, rising 35 feet above a streambed. The Lahaina station is in the Victorian style, befitting its Hawaiian monarchy-era origins. Passenger cars are fitted with wooden seats; the locomotive's cab is trimmed in mahogany. There are six daily departures, between 8:55 A.M. and 4 P.M., from three stations, evident from Highway 30 between Lahaina and Kāʻanapali. To spend a day sightseeing in Lahaina without the hassle of parking, visitors may leave their cars at the Puʻukoliʻi station for the day and take a later train back from Lahaina. No reservations are needed; tickets may be purchased at the train stations. Roundtrip fares are $15 for adults, $8.50 for children 3–12 (2 and younger free). Schedules and fares vary from time to time, so it is best to call for current information.

Hawaiʻi Nature Center (244-6500), at the gateway to ʻĪao Valley, just above the Kepaniwai Heritage Gardens, is a nonprofit environmental education organization with programs geared to children. There's a hands-on interactive science center with fun for the entire family—but especially for kids, who may have to be dragged away. Local *tūtū* (grandparents) always bring the grandkids here. The center is open daily, 10 A.M.–4 P.M. ($4 children, $6 adults).

Keiki Zoo Maui at 370 Kekaulike Avenue in Kula (878-2189 or 878-1940) is a nonprofit facility whose aim is to nurture interactive contact between humans and animals. Among the animals are *nēnē*, Hawaiʻi's state bird, along with sheep, cows, and horses. Appointments are needed for tours, Tuesday–Friday, 10 A.M.–2 P.M., and Saturday, noon–3 P.M. Admission is $5 for kids, $4 for adults.

The **Art School at Kapalua** (665-0007) runs a summer enrichment session for ages 5–9, an all-day program with a variety of creative, intellectual, and athletic activities. Five spaces are kept open for visiting children ($40/day).

The Sugar Cane Train.

Entertainment

Polynesian Shows

On nearly every island in the Pacific, Polynesian or not, the "Polynesian Show" has become virtually de rigueur for tourist entertainment. These shows stage performances based on the traditional music, dance, and costumes of Hawai'i, Tahiti, Samoa, New Zealand, and, occasionally, Tonga and the Cook Islands; sometimes Melanesian Fiji is included.

Available on Maui at all *lū'au* and dinner shows, these spectacles are glitzy, show-biz interpretations. The Tahitian *tamure* almost invariably highlights the evening with its fast-paced hip-swiveling, its grass skirts, tall headdresses, and wildly beating drums. Another showstopper is the Samoan fire dance or its close kin, the knife dance (often combined as the fire-knife dance). Hawaiian hula is usually the *'auana*, or modern variety, though some shows include a traditional *'ōlapa* or *kahiko* hula as well. The Maori (New Zealand) contributions are always a *poi* dance (*poi* in Maori are the white balls on string that the women manipulate so expertly in their dances) and the fierce *haka*, in which men challenge each other (and their audience) with spears and protruding tongues.

Lū'au

Undoubtedly, the *lū'au* is the most famous feast on visitors' entertainment menus. This highly civilized Polynesian custom resembles the American Thanksgiving feast, except that the *lū'au* can be given at any time, for any reason. One good traditional reason for a *lū'au* is to honor and entertain visitors, so your attendance at one is entirely appropriate. The feast is named after the *kalo* tops *(lū'au)* that are always served. Cooked with coconut cream, they are delicious.

Other traditional fare on such occasions includes a whole pig (or even chicken or fish), which is baked *(kālua)* in a pit in the ground *(imu),* and such dishes as *laulau,* small packages of fish, pork, chicken, or beef, with *kalo* tops, wrapped in *ti* or banana leaves and baked; *poi,* a thick, purplish gray paste made from the cooked and pounded base of the *kalo* plant (the nutritious staple food of the Hawaiians); sweet potatoes; *lomilomi* (smashed) salmon with chopped tomatoes and onions; and *haupia,* a thick, creamy coconut pudding. The introduction of European and Asian foods to Hawai'i has added great variety to the culinary concoctions that are now traditional

A hula dancer in Victorian-inspired dress performs beneath the palms.

at a *lū'au*. There is usually so much to choose from that the *lū'au* can please the palate of almost everyone.

Though the focus of the feast is food, a *lū'au* includes a host of entertainment. Music, dance, and usually a bit of comedy enhance the festive atmosphere and add to the fun. Prices at the different venues range from about $65 to $90 per person; there is always an open bar, and prices for children are reduced.

The best *lū'au* in our view is the **Old Lahaina Lū'au** (667-1998), held nightly at *lū'au* grounds near Māla Wharf. What we like about this *lū'au* is that the show strives to be authentic to Hawai'i, with only one Polynesian number as part of the entertainment. Hawai'i's history—from the time of the Polynesian migration, through the monarchy and missionary periods, up until 1950s kitsch—is recreated in dance, with hula related to each period. (As indication of the dancers' talents, the Old Lahaina Lū'au was selected to represent Hawai'i at Macy's Thanksgiving Day parade in New York.) There's no participatory hula (which we admit a lot of people do enjoy), but near the end, in a lovely, romantic touch, couples who wish to may get up and dance under the moonlight to the strains of the "Hawaiian Wedding Song." The food is

excellent—we've never had better *poi*—and the overall ambiance is perfect for a delightful Hawaiian experience. Be sure to get there in plenty of time to explore the beautiful oceanfront grounds, where island craftspeople demonstrate their skills and display their work. Altogether, from the personal lei greeting to the final bows of the performers, this is a memorable evening. Reserve well in advance; this is a popular event.

Other westside *lū'au* are at the **Hyatt Regency** (667-4420), the **Maui Marriott** (661-5828), and the **Royal Lahaina Resort** (661-3611). All are on Kā'anapali Beach and feature Polynesian revues.

The **Wailea Sunset Lū'au** (879-4900), at the Renaissance Wailea Beach Resort, is a wonderful low-key event offered three nights a week at the resort's oceanfront *lū'au* gardens. The Polynesian show features traditional Hawaiian hula, Tahitian drums and dancing, dancers from Fiji, and a Samoan fire-knife dance finale. A similar show, also low-key and fun, is offered four nights a week at **Wailea's Finest Lū'au** (879-1922) at the Outrigger Wailea Resort, with world champion Ifi So'o performing the fire-knife dance.

Not a true *lū'au*, the **Feast at Lele**, beachfront at 505 Front Street in Lahaina (667-5353),

is a sophisticated blend of fine food, dance, music of the Pacific islands, and warm hospitality. The five-course gourmet dinner is overseen by James McDonald, chef at the nearby Pacific'o and I'o restaurants, two of Lahaina's top dining spots. The Feast at Lele (Lele was the Hawaiian name for Lahaina) reflects the entertainment and food of four Pacific island nations: Hawai'i, Tonga, Tahiti, and Samoa. A seaside setting with flickering torches makes this dinner and show an unforgettably romantic evening. Currently, the show is offered Tuesday through Saturday.

Hula

If a *lū'au* epitomizes the culinary traditions of our island culture, hula captures its heartbeat. Dance was an integral part of the ritual life of the ancients, and the old hula has never died. New dances derived from it became popular entertainment for visiting sailors, who paid well to witness these altered performances, but Hawaiians didn't fundamentally connect this new and lucrative enterprise with their sacred dance. Reviled by missionaries as obscene, the old dance was taken underground and taught in secret, while the new dance thrived in places where religious reformers held no sway. Thus there developed two distinct classes of hula, the ancient and the modern.

Hula *'ōlapa,* more recently known as hula *kahiko,* the old style, is performed to the accompaniment of chanting and percussion only. Traditionally, the dance was done to accompany the chant, which was of primary importance, and it was performed on most occasions by men. Though many hula groups today have a preponderance of women, the men's hula is every bit as beautiful and is energetic with a virile grace that seems absent from the aggressive men's dances of other Polynesian cultures. Chanting, too, is an art that has experienced a revival, along with an upsurge of interest in the Hawaiian language, which is always used in the chants.

The women's hula is usually softer than the men's but still has strength and precision. Precision is a vital element of this hula style, and while there is ample scope for the enactment of modern tales in the ancient mode, the rules of the dance are strict and are strictly followed.

It is interesting to note that the most famous symbol of the hula, indeed, perhaps of Hawai'i—the grass skirt—is not Hawaiian at all. The grass skirt was introduced from Micronesia by laborers from the Gilbert Islands in the early 19th century. Hawaiians subsequently used

Hula dancer with traditional bamboo *pūʻili*.

native materials, such as *ti* leaves, in a similar fashion, but they were always fresh and green out of respect for the gods, a strictly Hawaiian innovation.

Prior to European visitations, the garments worn by Hawaiians were made of barkcloth *(kapa).* During the reign of King Kalākaua, when by royal decree the hula was again performed in public (helping to earn him the nickname "the Merrie Monarch"), European clothing of the time was worn in the dance, and hula dating from that era are still performed in costumes of the period.

Hula *ku'i,* a transitional form that combines traditional hula movements with those of 19th-century European ballroom dance, arose at this time. Prior to this innovation, men and women seldom danced together; in most ancient hula performed today, they still do not.

Hula *'auana,* the modern style, is much more flexible than its ancient forebear, just as modern ballet more freely extends the forms of classical ballet. Its costuming is keyed to the story

being told and is limited only by the imagination. Modern hula is usually accompanied by both melody and lyrics as well as ukuleles, guitars, and other instruments, and the songs may be in any language, though English and Hawaiian are most common.

There are several *hālau* on Maui that perform both modern and traditional hula. Cliff Ahue and his *hālau* perform hula *kahiko* at the Kapalua Shops Thursday mornings (the time and day are subject to change; call 669-0244 for current information). Traditional and modern hula are performed nightly at 6:30 P.M. in the courtyard of the Kā'anapali Beach Hotel (call 661-0011 to confirm time). Both of these shows are free, as are hula shows Friday evenings at Whalers Village in Kā'anapali and Sunday afternoons at Lahaina Cannery Mall. In Hawai'i, every Friday is Aloha Friday, and on Aloha Fridays employees often perform hula in hotel lobbies and local artisans display their wares.

Check tourist publications and the *Maui News,* Maui's daily newspaper, for listings of when and where *ho'olaule'a* or other community events are scheduled that feature hula, because what you see can be significantly different from what you may see in a Polynesian revue, especially if you catch a good *kahiko.*

Hawaiian Music

There is no sound more clearly associated with the tropical beauty of these islands than the lovely Hawaiian melody accompanied by the ukulele. Though neither melody nor harmony had existed in Polynesian tradition prior to European contact, the people of the islands demonstrated remarkable natural affinity and talent for both. They also enthusiastically adopted the stringed instruments the visitors introduced, and each Polynesian group has developed a distinctive musical style during the past century or two.

The guitar is probably the instrument most commonly used by contemporary Hawaiian musicians, but its baby brother, the ukulele, is most strongly identified with Hawai'i. 'Ukulele is, in fact, a Hawaiian word. It means "leaping flea" and was first applied as a nickname to Edward Purvis, a popular 19th-century player of the instrument who jumped around while he strummed. Brought to Hawai'i by Portuguese laborers in 1879, the diminutive instrument was known to them as braquinho.

The other stringed instrument immutably linked with Hawai'i is the steel guitar, played horizontally with a metal slide. The distinctively Hawaiian slack-key guitar derives from a tuning effect achieved by loosening the strings of a steel guitar.

Today's island music has continued to evolve and is now less stereotypical—more grounded in true expression of the feelings of island life—than music written in the '30s and '40s to appeal to tourists. Most of the large resort hotels have live Hawaiian music in their cocktail lounges and sometimes in restaurants during dinner hours.

Theater

The show 'Ulalena, a presentation of Maui Myth and Magic Theatre at 878 Front Street in Lahaina (661-9913), is not to be missed. The show is a magical retelling, in dance and music, of the story of Hawai'i's mythical and historical events. When Pele unleashes her fury, cascades of shimmering red cloth sweep from the stage and billow across the audience to the very back of the theater. Actors dance on stilts in a riveting representation of bamboo trees in a rainforest. This splendid production equals in style and inventiveness anything that Broadway has to offer. Although the production company is based in Montreal, Hawai'i artists, dancers, musicians, and scholars were consulted for cultural accuracy and most of the performers are from the islands. Tickets are $40 ($30 for children), which may seem steep, but the show is sensational. Dinner/show packages are available, a bargain at $60, with several restaurant partners, including Longhi's, Hard Rock Café, Ruth's Chris Steak House, Lahaina Fish Co., and Kimo's. There are currently two shows per night, Tuesday–Saturday.

Another popular attraction in Lahaina is the **Hawai'i Experience Domed Theater** at 824 Front Street (661-8314), with a domed screen over three stories high, showing an exciting and informative film featuring breathtaking photography of Hawai'i's scenic wonders. The 40-minute film, Hawai'i: Islands of the Gods, is presented daily on the hour, 10 A.M.–10 P.M. Seating is planetarium-style, designed with clear views of the 180-degree screen from every seat. This short program is well worth the ticket price: $6.95 adults, $3.95 children (4–12).

The **Maui Arts and Cultural Center**, facing the harbor in Kahului (242-2787), hosts a full menu of cultural events at its Castle Theater, with dance performances, concerts, and film screenings. Mainland and international artists often visit here, as do exceptional local performers.

As part of the Maui Film Festival, outstanding contemporary films are screened Wednesdays. A schedule of current events is published in the *Maui News*.

'Iao Theater at 68 North Market Street in Wailuku is host to **Maui OnStage** (244-8680), a mostly local community theater group that offers drama that is occasionally on the cutting edge. The **Maui Academy of Performing Arts** (244-8760) is a growing organization that stages several plays and other events each year, many of which are for children's entertainment. Since 1974, its educational programs on creative dramatics and theater arts skills have been strongly supported by the community. The **Baldwin Theater Guild** (984-5673) is another fixture on Maui, in existence since 1964, presenting a number of theatrical productions and workshops during the year. Again, the *Maui News* is the best source for information about current productions.

Nightclubs

Some vacationers welcome evenings as a time to relax. For others, nightfall means jumping into high gear and dancing and schmoozing until the wee hours. Though Maui nightlife is generally subdued, there are a few places to party all night (well, at least until midnight). As for nightclubs, the most reliable source of what's happening at the moment is the *Maui News*. For the places we've listed below, it would be wise to call ahead, since times and programs are subject to change.

In Lahaina, you can just stroll down Front Street in the evening and take your pick of the music floating out of the various establishments. **Maui Brews**, 900 Front Street (667-7794), has dancing and live music nightly, and **Moose McGillycuddy's**, 844 Front Street (667-7758), has live bands on weekends. **Hula Grill's Barefoot Bar**, in Whalers Village (667-6636), situated right at the edge of the sand on Kā'anapali Beach, is a happening place with live Hawaiian music and hula nightly; you can learn to dance Hawaiian style here.

At **Pizazz Café**, 1279 South Kīhei Road (891-2123), a good jazz group plays every night but Monday, and there's a small dance floor. **Hapa's Brew Haus**, in the Līpoa Shopping Center in Kīhei (East Līpoa Street off South Kīhei Road; 879-9001), has live music and deejays. Maui's Willy K owns Monday nights and rocks. Hapa's also presents a popular Broadway revue dinner theater every other week; call for current info. Next to Hapa's, **Henry's Bar and Grill** (879-2849) has live music and pool tables—and sometimes dancing. **Life's a Beach,** 1913 South Kīhei Road (891-8010), has live music, pool tables, and a bar; no dancing.

Tsunami, the Grand Wailea's elegant nightclub (875-1234), has an attractive high-tech interior and features a deejay playing club music for dancing. The club boasts a state-of-the-art sound, lighting, and video system as well as a 10,000-square-foot dance floor where the action continues until 4 A.M. on weekends.

The dance nights at **Casanova**, 1188 Makawao Avenue in Makawao (572-0220), are legendary; Wednesday is ladies' night, and Friday brings live Latin music. Sunday nights are reserved for New York deejay Dante. Other nights Casanova offers the best in live contemporary Hawaiian music, featuring such big names on the local music scene as Willie K and Amy Gilliom, Kapena, O'shen, 3plus, Hapa, Cecilio and Kapono, and Pound4Pound. **Charley's** (579-9453) is a favorite restaurant and bar in Pā'ia where impromptu performances in past years have been presented by such famous Maui visitors as Willie Nelson and Ringo Starr; no dancing but plenty of good live music.

Calendar
of Events

THE EVENTS LISTED HERE
occur annually, sometimes varying from one month to another.
Current information may
be obtained from the Maui
Visitors Bureau (1727 Wili Pa
Loop, Wailuku, Maui 96793;
800-525-MAUI, 808-244-3530;
www.visitmaui.com).

January
Makahiki festival on Moloka'i
(celebration of hula, Hawaiian
arts and crafts, games,
and food)
Festival of Hula, Lahaina
Cannery Mall (Maui *hula
hālau* competition)
Chinese New Year, Front Street,
Lahaina, and Market Street,
Wailuku (lion dance, fire
crackers, and other colorful
events)
Hula Bowl, War Memorial
Stadium, Wailuku (college
all-star football)
Mercedes Championships, Plan-
tation Golf Course, Kapalua
Resort (PGA Tour winners
compete in the season opener)
Senior Skins Game, Gold
Course, Wailea Resort (senior
PGA Tour professionals
compete for a six-figure purse)

February
Whale Week on Maui (events in
honor of the humpback whale)
Annual Whale Day Celebration,
Kalama Beach Park (live
Hawaiian music and hula,
great food by Maui's top
restaurants, and children's
entertainment)
Whalefest, Lahaina (weeklong
celebration in honor of the
humpback whale)
Kea Lani Food and Wine Masters,
Kea Lani Resort (top chefs
provide demonstrations and
signature dinners)
**Maui Scholastic Surf Champion-
ship**, Ho'okipa Beach Park
(Maui County surf cham-
pionship)

March
Art Maui, Maui Arts and Cultural Center, Kahului (juried
show of multimedia works by
the best Maui artists)
East Maui Taro Festival
(a celebration of the staple of
the Hawaiian diet, with
exhibits, food, and music and
hula performances)
Maui Marathon, Kahului to
Kā'anapali

April
Celebration of the Arts, Ritz-
Carlton, Kapalua (Easter
weekend celebration of the
people, arts, and culture of
Hawai'i, with workshops,

demonstrations, and enter-
tainment)
David Malo Day, Lahainaluna
High School (*lū'au* and hula
to celebrate Hawai'i's famous
scholar, April 21)
Ulupalakua Thing! Maui
County Agricultural Trade
Show (exhibition and
sampling of local products)
Just Desserts, Maui Prince Hotel
(annual fundraiser for the
Maui Humane Society)
Earth Maui 5K Fun Run,
Kapalua Resort (run or walk
for Hawai'i's environment)
**Da Kine Hawaiian Pro Am
Wave Sailing Championship**,
Ho'okipa Beach Park
(top windsurfers compete
in the Maui event of the
Professional Windsurfing
Association's World Tour)

May
Humpback whales leave Maui
to summer in the north
Moloka'i Ka Hula Piko,
Pāpōhaku Beach Park,
Moloka'i (celebration of the
legendary birth of hula)
Lei Festival, Outrigger Wailea
Resort (flower lei competition
in celebration of May Day;
entertainment includes the
Aloha Festival royal court)
In Celebration of Canoes, Front
Street, Lahaina (weeklong
festival featuring master canoe
carvers, a parade of Polynesian

canoes, cultural demonstrations, and a concert)

Maui Music Festival, Kāʻanapali Resort (two days of contemporary jazz)

Barrio Festival, War Memorial Gym, Wailuku (celebration of Filipino food, dance, and music)

Seabury Hall Crafts Fair, Makawao

Da Kine Classic Windsurfing Event, Kanahā Beach Park

Verizon Hawaiʻi Hall of Fame, Plantation Golf Course, Kapalua Resort (36-hole stroke play Pro-Am tournament)

Kapalua Jr. Vet/Sr. Tennis Championships, Kapalua Tennis Club (for men and women 35 years and over)

June

Royal Court Investiture, Mitchell Pauʻole Center, Molokaʻi (presentation of the king and queen of Molokaʻi's royal court)

King Kamehameha Day (statewide holiday on June 12, honoring Kamehameha the Great)

Maui Film Festival, Wailea Resort (under-the-stars premieres and special screenings)

Maui Chamber Music Festival, Kapalua, Wailea, and Kahului

Bankoh Ki Hoʻalu Guitar Festival, Maui Arts and Cultural Center (Hawaiʻi's top slack-key guitarists)

Upcountry Fair, Makawao (country fair with livestock auction, farmers' market, and entertainment)

Ox Bow Hoyle Schweitzer Course Race, Kanahā Beach Park (Pacific regional windsurfing championship)

Neil Pryde Slalom, Kanahā Beach Park (windsurfing slalom race)

Shapers Pohai Nā Keiki Nalu, Launiupoko State Wayside Park (surf meet for kids 12 and under)

Kapalua Fun Swim Challenge, Kapalua Resort (1-mile ocean swim to benefit marine conservation efforts)

July

Makawao Parade and Rodeo (to celebrate the 4th, Maui style)

4th of July Celebration, Kāʻanapali Resort (music, children's activities, and fireworks)

Oʻ Bon Festival, Jodo Mission, Lahaina (Bon dance and lantern boat ceremony on the first Saturday in July)

Pineapple Festival, Lānaʻi City (arts and crafts, entertainment, and food)

Kapalua Wine and Food Festival, Kapalua Resort (world-famous winemakers, chefs, and visitors assemble for gourmet meals)

Kīhei Sea Festival, Kalama Beach Park (ocean sports, music, and food)

Wailea Open Tennis Championships, Wailea Tennis Club (a popular event attracting both local and out-of-state players)

Polo, Olinda Polo Field (Sundays at 1:00 P.M.)

Quicksilver Cup, Kanahā Beach Park (windsurfing contest featuring professional and amateur men and women)

August

Maui Onion Festival, Whalers Village (events related to the Maui onion; first weekend in August)

Maui Pineapple Festival, Queen Kaʻahumanu Center, Kahului (Hawaiʻi's king of fruits reigns supreme)

Tahiti Fête, War Memorial Gym, Wailuku (Tahitian solo and group dance competition)

Hawaiʻi State Windsurfing Championships, Kanahā Beach Park (professional and amateur men and women)

September

Maui Writers' Conference, Outrigger Wailea Resort (six inspiring days learning the art and craft of writing, with top authors and agents)

A Taste of Lahaina (cooking demonstrations, wine tasting, entertainment, and a kids' zone)

Lānaʻi Aloha Festival, Dole Park (dance, parade, and *hoʻolauleʻa*)

Puʻu Kukui Nature Walk, Kapalua Resort (Hawaiʻi's most exclusive hike, for which participants are selected by lottery)

Hāna Relay, Kahului to Hāna (54-mile relay run by six-person teams)

Haleakalā Run to the Sun, Kahului to Haleakalā National Park (36.2 miles uphill, from sea level to 10,000 feet)

Maui Channel Relay Swim, Lānaʻi to Maui (Labor Day weekend)

Bankoh Nā Wāhine o Ke Kai, Hale o Lono Harbor on Molokaʻi to Oʻahu (women's 40.8-mile six-person outrigger canoe race)

Wilson Kapalua Tennis Open, Kapalua Resort (Hawaiʻi's hottest tennis stars heat up during this Labor Day event)

October

Maui Aloha Festival (Hawaiian pageantry, canoe races, *hoʻolauleʻa*, parades, and a variety of entertainment and stage shows)

Molokaʻi Aloha Festival (parade, *hoʻolauleʻa*, *poke* contest, and royal ball)

Maui County Fair, Wailuku War Memorial (the state's oldest fair, featuring a grand orchid exhibition, arts and crafts, ethnic foods, and a parade to kick off the four-day event)

Halloween in Lahaina, Front Street (a people-watching event with scores of outrageous costumes, beginning with a parade for kids at 4 P.M.; *the* place to be on October 31)

Kuʻu Home O Wailuku Hoʻolauleʻa, Market Street, Wailuku (Hawaiian cultural event)

Bankoh Molokaʻi Hoe, Molokaʻi to Oʻahu (40.8-mile six-person championship outrigger race)

Terry Fox Run/Walk, Four Seasons Resort, Wailea (10K run/walk to benefit cancer research and care)

XTERRA World Championship, Wailea Resort (internationally acclaimed off-road triathlon with 1.5K ocean swim, 30K mountain bike course, and 11K footrace)

Ducks Unlimited, Lānaʻi Sporting Clays (four days of sporting clays events)

November

Humpback whales return to Maui's waters

Hawaiʻi International Film Festival (award-winning films are screened at the Maui Arts and Cultural Center)

Hula O Nā Keiki, Kāʻanapali Beach Hotel (youngsters' solo competition in ancient and modern hula)

Christmas House, Hui Noʻeau Visual Arts Center (holiday arts and crafts featuring the work of Maui's best artists)

Ice-Carving Exhibition and Competition, Lahaina (ice carvers from Hawaiʻi and Japan showcase their talents in this Thanksgiving weekend event)

Aloha Classic World Wave Sailing Championship, Hoʻokipa Beach Park (amateur windsurfers compete for the World Cup in this four-day event)

Lopez/Hi-Tech Surf Bash, Hoʻokipa Beach Park (Maui's largest surf contest)

Maui Invitational Basketball Tournament, Lahaina Civic Center (top college teams vie in this annual classic)

December

Molokaʻi Main Street Christmas Festival

Gala tree-lighting ceremony, Ritz-Carlton, Kapalua (from December 1, the resort sparkles with lights)

Santa Comes to Wailea, Outrigger Wailea Resort (Santa arrives attired in a red-and-white *lavalava* by means of outrigger canoe)

Nā Mele O Maui, Kāʻanapali Resort (festival to perpetuate Hawaiian culture)

Festival of Art and Flowers, Front Street, Lahaina (flower displays and demonstrations)

Maui Women's Basketball Tournament, Lahaina Civic Center (pre-season college basketball tournament)

the nitty gritty

Getting *to* Maui

Airlines

Hawai'i is such a popular destination that airfares are kept relatively low through volume and competition. There are many airlines serving the islands, most arriving at Honolulu International Airport, where passengers may switch to interisland aircraft to continue their journey. The additional trip usually takes about 20 minutes, but getting from the main terminal building to the interisland terminal increases the stopover time to about 2 hours. If possible, check your luggage all the way through to Maui. If you miss your scheduled interisland flight, don't worry; tickets can be applied to any flight, and flights take off every hour or so. If you arrive in Honolulu early, you might be put on an earlier interisland flight to Maui.

Several airlines fly directly into Maui's Kahului Airport nonstop from the U.S. mainland. At this time they are Air Canada, Aloha (from Oakland, Calif.), American, Continental, Delta, Hawaiian (from Los Angeles), and United. Consult your travel agent for the latest details and flight schedules.

Page 207: The dining room on the SS *Independence* (page 209) has a mural by Eugene Savage, whose work decorated Matson Line steamships in the 1940s.

Flight times are roughly 5 hours from California, 9 hours from Chicago, 11 hours from New York, 8 hours from Tokyo, and 9.5 hours from Sydney. Return flights to the U.S. mainland, taking advantage of the jet stream, are often somewhat shorter. Domestic carriers providing service to and from the U.S. mainland are Aloha, America West, American, Continental, Delta, Hawaiian, Northwest, TWA, and United. Foreign carriers currently serving Honolulu are Air Canada, Air New Zealand, All Nippon Airways, Canadian Airlines, China Airlines, Japan Airlines, Korean Air, Philippine Airlines, and Qantas, among others.

Maui Airports

Maui's principal airport is Kahului, located in the central valley. In addition to helicopter traffic and the occasional private jet, more than one hundred flights a day land here. The airport is a modern, full-service complex with restaurant, lockers, information booth, car rental agencies, and taxi service. Shuttle buses to car rental offices are located just outside the airport, to the right as you exit.

The Kapalua–West Maui Airport opened for service to commuter airlines in 1987. It has a snack shop, gift shop, porter service, and car rental agencies. Hāna's airport is little more than a landing strip, with pickup service available for guests staying at the Hotel Hāna-Maui (248-8211).

Interisland Flights

Carriers providing service between the Hawaiian islands are **Aloha Airlines** (800-367-5250; www.alohaairlines.com), **Hawaiian Airlines** (800-367-5320; www.hawaiianair.com), **Island Air** (800-323-3345), and **Pacific Wings** (888-575-4546; www.pacificwings.com).

If you're staying in West Maui, you might consider flying into the convenient Kapalua–West Maui Airport, serviced by Island Air. Pacific Wings operates scheduled flights to Hāna from both Honolulu and Kahului. For flights to Moloka'i and Lāna'i, see pages 250 and 272.

Seats on interisland flights are not assigned. On Hawaiian Airlines, first-class passengers sit in the first few rows (you'll recognize the larger seats).

Tip: When you're flying from Honolulu to Maui, the best place to sit for views of Waikīkī and Moloka'i is on the left side (facing forward). On the return trip, sitting by the left window again gives great views of the West Maui Mountains.

Cruise Ships

Arriving in Hawai'i by cruise ship is far more complicated now than it was decades ago when most visitors sailed into island ports. Today, the cruise lines that make stops at Hawai'i ports are of foreign registry and are forbidden by U.S. law to transport American citizens from one U.S. port to another.

Norwegian Cruise Lines (800-327-7030; www.ncl.com) offers one-week cruises of the Hawaiian islands aboard the 2,200-passenger *Norwegian Star,* whose homeport is Honolulu. Ports of call include Hilo, Hawai'i; Lahaina, Maui; Nāwiliwili, Kaua'i; and the Fanning Islands in the Republic of Kiribati, 1,000 miles south of Hawai'i.

The *Star,* Norwegian Cruise Line's newest and largest vessel, has ten restaurants and 24-hour room service. The sports deck has a golf driving range and volleyball and basketball courts, while the two-deck fitness center boasts state-of-the-art equipment. Hawai'i-based Mandara Spa offers the ultimate in spa treatments.

There is a huge children's center complete with outdoor pool, movie theater, and computer rooms.

This fast-sailing ship provides visitors with excellent service and exquisite vistas by sea. Travelers can choose from a selection of land tours at island stopovers, including golf outings. This is a wonderful, romantic way to see the islands.

What *to* Bring

Visitors should pack warm-weather clothing to wear in Hawai'i's perpetual spring and summer climate. The usual attire on Maui is casual, and apparel known elsewhere as summer clothing is worn year round. Shorts are acceptable almost anywhere; most businesses require customers to wear shoes (though rubber thongs will usually suffice). Comfortable walking shoes are a must. Sleeveless or short-sleeved shirts are usually best for day wear, but long sleeves, or even a jacket or sweater, may be needed for cool winter evenings and air-conditioned buildings. Deluxe restaurants occasionally have a dress code requiring men to wear jackets but not usually ties. Until the last decade, men wore jackets and ties to work in offices, but today an aloha shirt suffices.

Once here, there's no shortage of places to buy sunscreen, bathing suits, sandals, and the like. Prices tend to be slightly higher than on the mainland. Many hotels provide snorkel equipment for guests, and snorkel and dive tours provide equipment.

Synonymous with Hawai'i are the *mu'umu'u* for the ladies and aloha shirts for men. Stylish takes on the *mu'umu'u* are available in many upscale boutiques. Aloha shirts have been virtually unchanged since designs of the '30s and '40s captured the hearts of Americans who were drawn to the romantic aura of things Hawaiian. Today they look much like the shirts described in the *Honolulu Advertiser* in 1939 as "exotic prints, over which tumble in delightful confusion tropical fish and palm trees, Diamond Head and the Aloha Tower, surfboards and leis, ukuleles and Waikiki beach scenes."

Leaving

Though the Hawai'i Visitors Bureau and the state certainly hope you will purchase souvenirs while you're here, there's no point in trying to take home many agricultural products, as they won't pass agricultural inspection, designed to prevent certain insects from traveling to the mainland. Be cautious when buying leis to take home. Certain flowers, such as roses, *maunaloa,* and jade; berries, such as mock orange and *mokihana;* and leaves, such as *hala*, are prohibited, and leis containing them will be confiscated. You may take coconuts with you, as well as pineapples and papaya that have been inspected. Coffee, jams, and salsas will pass. But don't try to slip through the inspection line with fresh limes, avocados, bananas, or the like. You will definitely be stopped (we know from experience).

If you're leaving the United States, you may take whatever you like, but there's no guarantee of its passing quarantine inspection in your country of arrival.

Getting Around

IT'S POSSIBLE to drive completely around Maui, though some sections of the road are unpaved. When planning tours or simply driving and sightseeing, it is important to remember that Maui falls easily into distinct regions. West Maui, with its exceptional climate, magnificent beaches, the old whaling town of Lahaina, and the resort area of Kāʻanapali, is the region most visitors know best. Kapalua, at the far western end of Maui, boasts two elegant resorts and stunning beaches. The southern shore from Māʻalaea to La Pérouse Bay, which encompasses Kīhei

and Wailea, features more wonderful beaches. The 10,023-foot Haleakalā towers over East Maui, which includes the lush, green cowboy region known as Upcountry. Hāna, a beautiful, sleepy seacoast area that includes a cattle ranch, holds court at the extreme eastern end of Maui. Finally, the central valley features the seat of government at Wailuku and a thriving port and commercial center at Kahului.

Maui has no public transportation. There are a number of air and land tour companies operating on the island, most of them very experienced in packaging tours to specific areas (see Activities). For exploring on your own or for sudden, spur-of-the-moment sightseeing or shopping, a rental car is essential. It is worth mentioning that it is illegal to hitchhike on Maui. When driving on Maui, you may occasionally spot someone standing at the side of the road watching the cars go by. It is doubtful such persons are simply studying Maui's traffic flow—they are most likely hitchhiking but know not to stick out a thumb.

Taxis *and* Shuttles

There's a taxi stand outside the Kahului Airport. Among the taxi companies are:

Kahului/Wailuku, including the airport: **Maui Central Cab** (244-7278), **Jake's Taxi** (877-6139), and **La Bella Taxi** (242-8011 or 242-2772)

Lahaina/Kāʻanapali/Kapalua: **AB-Taxi** (667-7575), **Aliʻi Cab Co.** (661-3688), **Classy Taxi** (661-3044), and **Kapalua Executive Cab Service** (667-7770)

Kīhei/Wailea: **Kīhei Taxi** (879-3000), **Wailea Taxi** (874-5000), **Royal Sedan and Taxi Service** (874-6900), and **Yellow Cab of Maui** (877-7000)

Upcountry: **Caroline's Taxi** (572-9915)

Taxi rides tend to be pricey. **Speedi Shuttle** (875-8070), with courtesy phones at the baggage claim area, will take you to your hotel for $10 to $20, depending on where you're staying. **The Airport Shuttle** (661-6667) services the Lahaina/Kāʻanapali area with reasonable rates.

Limousines

Maui has several limousine services, most operating 24 hours a day. **Arthur's Limousine Service** (871-5555) operates stretch Lincolns and Cadillacs all over the island and will drive you to Hāna and

Haleakalā in style. Chauffeurs wear uniforms and caps and roll out a red carpet for every client. Japanese-speaking drivers are available. In the Kapalua area, there's the classy **Kapalua Executive Limousine Service** (669-2300), which also has Japanese-speaking drivers. **Wailea Limousine Service** (875-4114) has a well-deserved reputation for service and style.

Driving

Any visitor who drives in Hawai'i must have a valid driver's license from another state or a Canadian province or a current international driver's license issued in another country.

Wear your seatbelt. Hawai'i police are known to issue tickets to beltless drivers and riders. Posted speed limits should be followed. Traffic slowdowns from heavy construction or sugarcane and pineapple trucks that crawl down the two-lane roads occur often, and motorists must exercise both patience and caution. Most urban centers are relatively easy to drive in, but Lahaina town can be traffic-clogged at times, and parking is at a premium. While driving generally is good, there are times to remember the local phrase, "ain't no beeg t'ing, brah." Because most areas are accessible by only one road, an accident or other emergency event can tie up traffic for hours.

Driving Times

Sample distances in both miles and driving time from Kahului Airport are:

Haleakalā summit • 37 miles; 1.5 hours
Hāna • 52 miles; 2.5 hours
Kā'anapali • 30 miles; 50 minutes
Kahului • 3 miles; 5 minutes
Kapalua • 36 miles; 1 hour
Kīhei • 10 miles; 20 minutes
Lahaina • 27 miles; 45 minutes
Mā'alaea • 10 miles; 15 minutes
Mākena • 20 miles; 30 minutes
Pukalani • 7 miles; 15 minutes
Wailea • 16 miles; 25 minutes
Wailuku • 6 miles; 10 minutes

Car Rentals

More than a dozen car rental companies flourish on Maui, offering everything from luxury automobiles to four-wheel drives and subcompacts. Staff at hotel desks can put you in touch with any of them, or you can take advantage of the agencies represented at Kahului and Kapalua–West Maui airports. During high season, it's good to book a car in advance; occasionally the rental car agencies run out of vehicles.

Nationally known agencies at or near Kahului Airport include: **Alamo** (800-327-9633, 871-6235), **Avis** (800-321-3712, 871-7575), **Budget** (800-527-0700, 877-283-2468), **Dollar** (800-800-4000, 877-2731), **Enterprise** (800-RENT-A-CAR, 871-1511), **Hertz** (800-654-3011, 877-5167), **National** (800-227-7368, 871-8851), and **Thrifty** (800-367-2277, 871-2860).

Among local companies (area code 808), **Word of Mouth Rent-a-Used Car** (800-533-5929, 877-2436) offers late model cars at reasonable rates. **Maui Rent a Jeep** (877-6626) offers a discount to senior citizens. Other local car rental agencies are **Andres Rent-a-Car** (877-5378), **Kīhei Rent a Car** (800-251-5288, 879-7257), **Maui Motors** (800-249-5222, 877-8091), and **Wheels R Us** (871-6858). For Jeeps, try **Hawaiian Riders** (662-4386), **Maui Sport Rental** (268-3165), or **Regency Rent a Car** (877-280-5337, 871-6147). **Island Riders** (661-9966) specializes in exotic cars like Ferraris, Porsches, and BMWs, as does **Aloha Toy Store** (662-0888).

Accessible vans are available from **Accessible Vans of Hawai'i** (800-303-3750, 871-7785; www.accessiblevans.com), which will meet you at the airport.

Motorcycles and Mopeds

Mopeds may be rented in Lahaina at **Aloha Toy Store** (662-0888) and **Hawaiian Riders** (662-4386). Farther up the road, in the Kahana/Honokōwai area, try **A&B Moped Rental** (669-0027). Mopeds are available in Kīhei at **Kukui Activity Center** (875-1151). Also, **Wheels R Us** rents mopeds at three locations: Kahului (871-6858), Lahaina (667-7751), and Kīhei (875-1221).

Motorcycle enthusiasts can tour Maui on a Harley Davidson for half or full days (solo or in an escorted group) by renting a bike from **Island Riders**. There are two Maui stores, in Lahaina (661-9966) and Kīhei (874-0311). Motorcycle tours as well as rentals are also available from **Ride Maui** (242-1015), based in Wailuku. **Mavrik's Hot Rods n' Harleys** rents bikes at three locations: Kahului (871-7118), Lahaina (661-3099), and Kīhei (891-2299). Motorcycles can also be rented in Lahaina at **Aloha Toy Store** (662-0888), **Hawaiian Riders** (662-4386), and **Lahaina Motorcycle Works** (661-6603).

Riders must be at least 21 years old with a valid motorcycle license or permit and a major credit card.

Bicycles

It's possible to see Maui on a bicycle if you are both experienced and careful. Long-distance bicycling is especially strenuous in east Maui, where Haleakalā rises more than 10,000 feet in 40 miles, though bike enthusiasts come to Maui just to do this climb. On the other hand, a paved bicycle path from Kāʻanapali to Lahaina, only 3 miles away, makes bicycling in that area a pleasure. Bicycles may be rented at the following locations:

Kahului: **Extreme Sports Maui** (871-7954), **Island Biker** (877-7744), and **Bike Shop** (877-5848)

Upcountry: **Haleakalā Bike Co.** (575-9575) and **Upcountry Cycle** (573-2888)

Lahaina: **Hawaiian Riders** (662-4386) and **West Maui Cycles** (661-9005)

Kīhei: **Kukui Activity Center** (875-1151), **Maui Sports and Cycle** (875-2882 or 875-8448), and **South Maui Bicycles** (874-0068)

Tipping

MANY PEOPLE who work in the tourist industry in Hawaiʻi hold down more than one job and count tips as essential to their income. At restaurants, bars, and nightclubs, tip 15 percent of the bill before tax; up to 20 percent for exceptional service and in fine-dining establishments. The same tip applies to taxi drivers, hairdressers and beauticians, and massage therapists.

Give tour guides a 10 or 15 percent tip. Give airport and hotel porters $1 or $2 per bag (at least $5), and leave $1 or $2 per day in the room for housekeeping services. The attendant who valet parks your car should be given $2 each time you take the car out. If the hotel concierge is helpful during your stay, leave a $5 or $10 tip.

Accommodations

MAUI HAS A VARIETY of accommodations, from luxury destination resorts to modest cottages and bed-and-breakfast (B&B) guestrooms. Our choices of what to list are based on two main factors: Hawaiian-style comfort and value. We like hotels that have respect for the Hawaiian culture, from which guests will come away with a little more than the average vacation experience. We love Hawai'i, and we want you to love it too.

Both toll-free and local telephone numbers are provided. Very often the toll-free number is for a nationwide reservation system. Sometimes if you call the local number you may get better rates. Or a travel agent may be able to book a hotel at rates below what is quoted by the hotel to you.

Rates given are for one night and are usually for two people. There is usually a fee for an additional person. We've listed the lowest and the highest rates provided to us. Don't be frightened by the highest rates; they're often for what is called the Presidential Suite or some such. A standard room is fine for most of us mortals. Also, be sure to ask about packages or special rates. Many B&Bs and vacation rentals offer reduced rates for longer stays.

If you'll be on your honeymoon or will be celebrating an anniversary, be sure to tell the hotel.

Rates do not include Hawai'i taxes of 11.25% (7.25% room tax and 4% excise tax). If you plan to pay by credit card, ask in advance if that's okay, especially for B&Bs and smaller establishments. Otherwise, bring along your checkbook—or cash.

Accommodations are listed alphabetically in the following five categories: hotels; inns; condominiums and vacation rentals; bed and breakfasts and cottages; and hostels, cabins, and campsites. For accommodations on Moloka'i, see pages 250–53; for Lāna'i, see pages 274–80. A listing of reservation services is at the end of this section (page 232).

Hotels

Aston Maui Islander

660 Waine'e Street, Lahaina, Maui 96761. 800-922-7866, 808-667-9766, fax 808-667-2792. $98–$276

These low-rise hotel and condo units are located on 10 lush acres in the heart of Lahaina; walk to Front Street, restaurants, beaches, and historic sites. Rooms are plainly furnished, spacious, and clean, many with full

Hotels
are listed alphabetically. By area they are:

Lahaina/Kā'anapali/ Kapalua Area
Aston Maui Islander
Embassy Vacation Resort
Hyatt Regency Maui
    Resort & Spa
Kā'anapali Beach Hotel
Kapalua Bay Hotel
Maui Marriott Resort &
    Ocean Club
Nāpili Kai Beach Resort
Ritz-Carlton, Kapalua
Royal Lahaina Resort
Sheraton Maui
Westin Maui

Kīhei/Wailea Area
Aston Maui Lu
Diamond Resort Hawai'i
Four Seasons Resort
    Maui
Grand Wailea Resort
    Hotel and Spa
Kea Lani Resort
Maui Coast Hotel
Maui Oceanfront Inn
Maui Prince
Outrigger Wailea Resort
Renaissance Wailea Beach
    Resort

Hāna Area
Hotel Hāna-Maui

213

kitchens. There are a pool and lighted tennis court. The highest rate is for a three-bedroom, three-bath suite, with kitchen, for up to eight people. We like this hotel for its friendly, aloha spirit. Aston is a local Hawaiian chain that offers excellent values.

Aston Maui Lu

575 South Kīhei Road, Kīhei, Maui 96753. 800-922-7866, 808-879-5881. $100–$190

The first structure of the Maui Lu, now the reception area, was built in 1956 by Gordon Gibson for his home. He had so many fellow Canadians as guests that he eventually turned the place into a hotel and built another home for himself 3 miles away. The first hotel in Kīhei, the Maui Lu became the area's social hub. Today low-rise guest units stud the 28 acres. The aloha spirit flourishes here. The hotel may be a little worn, and the rooms are modestly furnished, but the sense of old Hawai'i, with friendly staff and beautiful grounds, makes for a very pleasant stay. In the oceanfront units, you'll sleep to the soothing sounds of crashing surf. The large pool, shaped like the island of Maui, is shaded by sway-ing palms. Of the 1,008 coconut palms originally planted by Gibson on the hotel grounds, nearly 900 remain. At the beach near the hotel, totem poles stand absurdly among the palm trees lining the water's edge (see page 153).

Diamond Resort Hawai'i

555 Kaukahi Street, Wailea, Maui 96753. 800-800-0720, 808-874-0500, fax 808-874-8778; info@diamondresort.com (www.diamondresort.com). $280–$340

Nestled in the foothills above the Wailea golf courses on 15 beauti-fully landscaped acres, this Japanese-owned luxury resort has only 72 rooms, each with a separate bedroom and small kitchen. Guests are assured a quiet, peaceful stay. The huge open-air Japanese bathhouse has breathtaking views. The hotel's restaurants offer award-winning Japanese and French cuisine.

Embassy Vacation Resort

104 Kā'anapali Shores Place, Lahaina, Maui 96761. 800-669-3155, 808-661-2000, fax 808-667-5821; embassy@maui.net (www.maui.net/~embassy). $290–$1,500

Here every guestroom is a suite, with a living room and one or two private bedrooms. All suites feature big-screen TV's and mini-kitchens, plus many more ameni-ties. Large bathrooms have soak-ing tubs and separate showers. Accessible suites are available, and there are special services for the hearing and sight challenged. Complimentary full-breakfast buffet is served poolside, and every afternoon the manager hosts a complimentary cocktail reception. There is a year-round Beach Buddies children's pro-gram, 8:30 A.M. to 2:30 P.M. The heated pool is a full acre with a water slide. There are also an exercise center, a video game area, a beauty salon, and a spa. Championship golf and tennis are nearby.

Four Seasons Resort Maui

3900 Wailea Alanui, Wailea, Maui 96753. 800-334-6284, 808-874-8000, fax 808-874-2222 (www.fourseasons.com). $305–$6,000

True luxury awaits guests at this exceptional resort, which makes many lists of top resorts in the world. The superb service and special attention here make you feel like royalty. When you drive up to the hotel, you're greeted like a long-lost friend before your car is whisked off for com-plimentary valet parking. Guest-rooms and bathrooms are immense and beautifully appointed. The grounds are lush and impeccable. Spa and health club facilities are the best anywhere, large, luxuri-ous, and with top-of-the-line equipment. Fitness classes include yoga, aerobics, and spinning. You can exercise outdoors on a shaded lanai, looking out over tropical gardens (or looking at your own personal TV), or in air-conditioned comfort. Or better yet, pamper yourself with a massage or body treatment. The Hawaiian *lomi pōhaku* massage, using hot stones (*pōhaku* is the Hawaiian word for "stone"), is pure bliss. Three championship golf courses across the road make this a golfer's paradise. There's a complimentary daily program for children.

Grand Wailea Resort Hotel and Spa
Grand Wailea Resort Hotel and Spa, 3850 Wailea Alanui, Wailea, Maui 96753. 800-888-6100, 808-875-1234, fax 808-874-2411; info@grandwailea.com (www.grandwailea.com). $390–$10,000

The Grand Wailea is indeed grand. Everything about it is big, from the 2,000-foot-long river pool that meanders through tropical gardens, with waterslides and hot tubs at every turn, to the two-level spa, by far the largest such facility in Hawai'i. The spa offers everything from the sublime (how about a honey steam wrap) to the absurd (a personal sunscreen application). While mom and dad are being pampered, kids are pampered too in their own mini resort, Camp Grande. Guestrooms are spacious and elegantly appointed. A stunning art collection dots the public areas and lush grounds with works by both international artists (Botero and Léger, for example) and well-known local artists, such as Satoru Abe, Sean K. L. Browne, Yvonne Cheng, Herb Kawainui Kāne, Wayne Miyata, and Esther Shimazu.

Hotel Hāna-Maui
Hotel Hāna-Maui
P. O. Box 9, Hāna, Maui 96713. 800-321-4262, 808-248-8211, fax 808-248-7202 (www.hotelhana maui.com). $235–$655

If you can stay a few days in Hāna, the perfect place is the Hotel Hāna-Maui, with its elegantly furnished rooms and suites, lush landscaped lawns, and two heated swimming pools, one a romantic "eternity" pool overlooking the Pacific. Low-key and luxurious—and a favorite celebrity hideaway—the hotel has bungalow-style guestrooms dotting the grounds around the main building as well as cottages on a seaside bluff with dramatic ocean and mountain views from private outdoor spa tubs. All of the buildings are architecturally spectacular. In the lobby and library are examples of rare Hawaiian art, and original watercolors hang in the rooms. Guestrooms are tastefully decorated in tropical style; bathrooms are large. You won't find an in-room TV, and room service is limited. The hotel *is* older than many Maui luxury establishments, but it has aged gracefully. There is a modern fitness center affording an inspiring ocean view, and a variety of massage treatments are available. The hotel offers free bikes to guests for exploring the town. Horseback riding is available at the Hāna Ranch Stables. It's quiet in Hāna —a night's entertainment might be a hula performance by local *keiki*—but it is just this peace and tranquillity that helps keep Hāna a tropical paradise. Special rates are available for honeymooners and those staying five nights or more. To get to this remote hotel, guests may either fly into the small Hāna Airport via Pacific Wings or drive from Kahului, a 2.5-hour trip on the narrow, winding Hāna Highway.

Hyatt Regency Maui Resort & Spa
Hyatt Regency Maui Resort & Spa
200 Nohea Kai Drive, Kā'anapali, Maui 96761. 800-554-9288, 808-661-1234, fax 808-667-4498 (www.maui.hyatt.com). $300–$3,000

Elegant is the word to describe the Hyatt Regency Maui with its magnificent atrium lobby. This big, busy hotel is great for the traveler who likes to be in a sumptuous setting with everything taken care of. Rooms are large and elegantly furnished. The Swan Court restaurant lives up to its reputation for romance. Spa Luana, a new spa and fitness center, allows guests to exercise or be pampered in beautiful surroundings. Once a week the spa hosts talks on native Hawaiian healing arts. Throughout the hotel are examples of fine art, mostly Asian and Pacific, which add further grace to the setting. Exotic wildlife, like swans and parrots, populate the grounds. There is a tennis center, and the Kāʻanapali Golf Course borders the hotel. Camp Hyatt takes children as young as three.

Kāʻanapali Beach Hotel

2525 Kāʻanapali Parkway, Kāʻanapali, Maui 96761. 800-262-8450, 808-661-0011, fax 808-667-5978; info@kaanapalibeachhotel.com (www.kaanapalibeachhotel.com). $170–$585

For a true local flavor, this place can't be beat. General manager Mike White actively promotes tourism based on the lure of Hawaiian culture, and his efforts have been recognized by no less than the White House. Nestled amid luxury hotels on tony Kāʻanapali Beach, the Kāʻanapali Beach Hotel may not have as lushly planted grounds or as elegant restaurants as its neighbors, but what it does have is gardens planted with native Hawaiian plants such as *kalo*, a nightly hula show that emphasizes Hawaiian dancing and drumming, and daily activities

such as lei making, *lau* printing, and cultural garden walks. The Tiki Bar in the garden is a great place for a mai tai while you watch the authentic hula show (6:30 P.M.). Local craftspeople set up in the lobby several mornings a week. All rooms have A.C. and are furnished in a tropical style. There's a big whale-shaped swimming pool, and beautiful Kāʻanapali Beach is steps away. The staff is the friendliest you'll find anywhere. The upscale Whalers Village Shopping Center is within walking distance.

Kapalua Bay Hotel, One Bay Drive, Kapalua, Maui 96761. 800-325-3589, 808-669-5656, fax 808-669-4694 (www.luxurycollectionhawaii.com). $295–$800+

A luxury resort on one of the world's finest beaches, this boutique hotel is adjacent to three championship golf courses and two tennis complexes. There are 196 elegantly appointed rooms and suites as well as 14 oceanfront villa suites with kitchens, laundry facilities, and one or two bedrooms. The elegant Bay Club, atop a lava rock promontory fronting Kapalua Bay, is one of Maui's finest restaurants. A beautiful butterfly-shaped swimming pool is perfectly heated to 81 degrees. Beach activities include swimming, snorkeling, and kayaking.

Kea Lani Resort, 4100 Wailea Alanui, Wailea, Maui 96753. 800-659-4100, 808-875-4100, fax 808-875-1200. $305–$615

Opened in 1991, this luxurious oceanfront resort is comprised of 12 Mediterranean-style white buildings, ranging from two to six stories in height. It overlooks Wailea's Polo Beach, a sandy swimming beach. All rooms are suites, one or two bedrooms, making this a good family value. There are also 37 two- and three-bedroom oceanfront villas, each with a private plunge pool. For the sybaritic, the resort's luxurious spa has recently been expanded and enhanced. And for the more practical minded, a new business center has PCs and Macs as well as all other necessary office equipment.

Maui Coast Hotel, 2259 South Kīhei Road, Kīhei, Maui 96753. 800-895-6284, 808-874-6284, fax 808-875-4731. $155–$309

Word is getting out as visitors discover this unpretentious two-story hotel in Kīhei, which opened its doors in 1993 and offers clean, modestly priced accommodations. The 264 guestrooms include 114 one- and two-bedroom suites (the highest room rate is for two bedrooms, making this a real bargain). There are a swimming pool, two outdoor spas, two lighted tennis courts, and laundry facilities. Restaurants, golf, and beaches are nearby, and Kīhei beach parks are conveniently located directly across the street.

Maui Marriott Resort & Ocean Club, 100 Nohea Kai Drive, Kāʻanapali, Maui 96761. 800-763-1333, 808-667-1200, fax 808-667-8181. $299–$1,500

This oceanfront hotel is directly across from the 36-hole Kāʻanapali Golf Course. There are a tennis club and a fitness center, as well as a new pool system with an island bar, a waterslide, and a sandy beach. Massage and beauty services include a tent at the beach for private massage. Hawaiʻi cultural activities such as lei making, hula lessons, and Hawaiian language instruction are offered daily. Kāʻanapali Kids provides year-round activities and field trips. The Marriott Lūʻau is a popular event (every day but Monday). The hotel has just undergone total renovation, making it a choice Kāʻanapali destination. Special packages include "room and golf," "romance," "Maui grab bag" (choose between breakfast and a car), and "everything under the Maui sun."

Maui Oceanfront Inn

2980 South Kīhei Road, Kīhei, Maui 96753. 800-263-3387, 808-879-7744, fax 808-874-0145; info@mauioceanfrontinn.com (www.mauioceanfrontinn.com). $159–$379

A new owner and major renovations have turned this once unappealing hotel into a rare find. Located on lovely Keawakapu Beach at the gateway to Wailea, the hotel is decorated in pleasing Hawaiian-style decor. Rooms are small; one-bedroom suites would be more comfortable than single rooms for longer stays. However, the friendly ambiance, oceanfront café that serves breakfast and lunch, and easy access to Wailea and Kīhei more than make up for the small rooms. Located on the property is a fine restaurant, Sarento's on the Beach.

Maui Prince (Westin)

5400 Mākena Alanui, Mākena, Maui 96753. 800-321-6248, 808-874-1111, fax 808-879-8763 (www.westin.com). $300–$1,500

For championship golf on the Mākena North and South courses (see pages 191–92), this is the place to stay. The Prince Court restaurant has excellent food and service in a pleasant room enhanced by the resplendent oils of Maui painter Ed Lane. There is also an acclaimed Japanese restaurant and sushi bar, Hakone, on the premises. Guestrooms are modest, especially the bathrooms by today's luxury standards. The surroundings, steeped in Hawaiian history, are incredible. An ancient roadway, used by Hawaiʻi's kings, fronts the beach, and the ʻĀhihi-Kīnaʻu Natural Area Reserve is nearby. Molokini Islet, known for its spectacular snorkeling, is a mere 20 minutes away via the *Kai Kanani,* which operates out of the hotel (see snorkeling, page 170).

Nāpili Kai Beach Resort

5900 Honoapiʻilani Road, Nāpili, Maui 96761. 800-367-5030, 808-669-6271, fax 808-669-0086; nkbc@maui.net (www.napilikai.com). $185–$660

Guests return season after season to this 10-acre beachfront West Maui low-rise resort that offers 163 comfortable rooms and studios or suites with kitchenettes. All rooms have private lanais and offer the ambiance of old Hawaiʻi; most are air-conditioned. Amenities include four swimming pools and large whirlpool, seasonal children's program, two 18-hole putting greens, exercise room, barbecue areas, and laundry facilities. The Sea House Restaurant offers oceanside dining for breakfast, lunch, and dinner. Get to know the staff at weekly mai tai parties. Tennis and golf are just a few minutes away at Kapalua Resort. Ask about special packages, such as five nights room and car or family reunion specials.

Wailea Resort

3700 Wailea Alanui, Wailea, Maui 96753. 800-688-7444, 808-874-7976, fax 808-874-8176 (www.outrigger.com). $295–$1,000

This older resort hotel, the first to open in Wailea, had major renovations in 2000, updating all guestrooms and public spaces. In decor and art, the theme is Hawaiiana, low-key and comfortable. The lobby lanai, with great old-style Hawai'i furniture, and the Hula Moons restaurant evoke a nostalgia for days gone by, while data ports in all the rooms and high-speed Internet access bring the hotel into the 21st century. There is a new Voyager Club with VIP guest services. The new Shops at Wailea, immediately adjacent to the hotel, feature luxury shopping and fine dining. For golfers, the Wailea Gold, Emerald, and Blue courses are minutes away.

Renaissance Wailea Beach Resort

3550 Wailea Alanui, Wailea, Maui 96753. 800-992-4532, 808-879-4900, fax 808-879-6128 (www.renaissancehotels.com). $280–$3,000

This is definitely one of the nicest Wailea resort hotels, exceptional for its low-key luxury and friendly, personal service. The grounds have lush tropical land-scaping, with waterfalls and pools. The hotel fronts palm-fringed Mōkapu Beach, a small but beautiful crescent of sand. If you stay in the luxury Mōkapu Beachfront rooms, you will hear only the soft sounds of the waves. Camp Wailea offers year-round activities for children. There is a variety of dining, from the poolside Maui Onion, famous for its onion rings, to the gourmet Palm Court or the Hana Gion, an intimate Japanese restaurant. Three nights a week there's a sunset *lū'au* on an oceanfront lawn, complete with Hawaiian hula, Tahitian drums and dancing, and a Samoan fire dance. Complimentary shuttle service is provided to shopping, golf, and tennis within the Wailea Resort area.

Ritz-Carlton, Kapalua

One Ritz-Carlton Drive, Kapalua, Maui 96761. 800-262-8440, 808-669-6200, fax 808-665-0026 (www.ritzcarlton.com). $325–$2,500

Among Hawai'i's finest hotels, the award-winning Ritz-Carlton, Kapalua, offers an unforgettable vacation experience. If we had to select any one place to stay on Maui, it would be here, both because of the hotel's luxury accommodations and the staff's commitment to service, as well as for its integration of Hawaiian history and tradition into daily resort activities. The hotel has a Hawaiian cultural advisor, Clifford Nae'ole, on staff who offers informal tours of the grounds every Friday. A monthly moonlight *mo'olelo* (storytelling) program brings *kūpuna* (Hawaiian elders) to the hotel for evenings of stories and entertainment. Every Friday the staff presents informal song and hula in the hotel lobby, offering an opportunity to see authentic performances rather than glitzy staged productions. Easter weekends, the hotel celebrates the arts in Hawai'i with demonstrations and participatory events.

The hotel's stunning architecture fits comfortably in the 50 hillside acres, surrounded by towering Cook Island pines and ironwood trees. Guestrooms are large and beautifully appointed, with featherbeds and down pillows. (We only wish the furnishings were less generic Ritz-Carlton and more local-style Hawaiian.) The Ritz-Carlton Club is a private floor with 72 guestrooms offering special amenities, including a club concierge and complimentary food and beverage service throughout the day. Hotel food services are excellent, with five restaurants to choose from. The signature restaurant, the Ānuenue Room, offers gourmet contemporary island cuisine that has earned it Zagat's "Extraordinary" award. Activities include golf at Kapalua's famous championship courses (see pages 190–91), tennis, and all water sports. There are a beautiful white sand beach and a magnificent heated swimming pool. The fitness center has a sauna and steam room. You can treat yourself to a massage or body treatment using special Hawaiian ingredients. Although it's the last resort hotel along Maui's spectacular northwest coast, the Ritz-Carlton, an oasis of serenity, is only 5 minutes from the West Maui airport.

Royal Lahaina Resort

2780 Keka'a Drive, Kā'anapali, Maui 96761. 800-222-5642, 808-661-3611. $200–$1,500

This large hotel on beautiful Kā'anapali Beach has a nice, tropical feel with Hawaiian-style decor. The most desirable rooms are cottages situated in garden settings. Owned by the tour company Pleasant Hawaiian Holiday, the hotel offers a variety of affordable packages.

Sheraton Maui

2605 Kā'anapali Parkway, Kā'anapali, Maui 96761. 800-782-9488, 808-661-0031, fax 808-661-0458 (www.sheraton-hawaii.com). $340–$800

With the best Kā'anapali Beach location, on a sandy beach bordered by famous Black Rock (Pu'u Keka'a), the Sheraton Maui combines a reverence for the old matched with resort amenities for the 21st century. There are three restaurants and three lounges. The large swimming pool has meandering lava rock waterways and heated spas. A program for kids, Keiki Aloha Club, is available during the summer, and kids 12 years or younger eat free when dining with a paying adult. Two famous golf courses are within walking distance, the Kā'anapali North and South courses. Every evening, witness the torch-lighting ceremony as a Hawaiian youth climbs Black Rock and plunges into the sea, replicating the brave feat of Maui's most famous king, Kahekili (see page 60). This is followed by a program of authentic Hawaiian song and dance. Black Rock is one of Maui's favorite snorkeling sites, or sail on a catamaran directly from the Sheraton's beach.

Westin Maui

2365 Kā'anapali Parkway, Kā'anapali, Maui 96761. 800-937-8461, 808-667-2525, fax 808-661-5764 (www.westin.com). $280–$3,500

Located on 12 impeccably landscaped oceanfront acres, the Westin Maui has 728 rooms and 28 suites, including rooms for travelers with disabilities. Every room has a new "Heavenly Bed," with the best mattress and pillows imaginable. Cascading waterfalls and meandering pathways surround five free-form heated swimming pools, one with a 128-foot ride, another reserved only for adults. The full-service spa and beauty salon offers body treatments, massage, and aerobic classes. The gym has state-of-the-art fitness equipment, and there are a steam room, a sauna, and a whirlpool spa. Kā'anapali golf courses are nearby. Day and evening Keiki Kamp keeps the children busy.

Inns

Heavenly Hāna Inn, 4155 Hāna Highway, P. O. Box 790, Hāna, Maui 96713. 808-248-8442; hanainn@maui.net (www.heavenlyhanainn.com). $185–$250

This tranquil Japanese-style inn has three two-bedroom suites, each with its own entrance, lanai, and large Japanese bath. The room rate includes a gourmet breakfast with a selection of menus focusing on American-style, Japanese, and Hawaiian cuisines. A maximum stay of two days is recommended.

Kula Lodge

Highway 377, R.R. 1, Box 475, Kula, Maui 96790. 800-233-1535, 808-878-1535, fax 808-878-2518; info@kulalodge.com (www.kula lodge.com). $110–$165

On the road to Haleakalā, at 3,200 feet, the Kula Lodge offers five rustic chalets that sleep from two to four. Fireplaces and quilts are provided for cool nights. The views are magnificent, day and night. There's a convenient restaurant serving breakfast, lunch, and dinner. Maui artist Curtis Wilson Cost has a gallery at the lodge.

Lahaina Inn

127 Lahainaluna Road, Lahaina, Maui 96761. 800-669-3444, 808-661-0577. $99–$169

A restored 12-room Victorian inn just off Front Street, this establishment is furnished with antiques and period fabrics and wall coverings. Nine double rooms and three parlor suites are individually decorated in keeping with the style of the late 1800s, though updated with private baths, telephones, and air conditioning. A continental breakfast is included with the room. David Paul's Lahaina Grill is on the street level of the inn.

Old Wailuku Inn at Ulupono

2199 Kahoʻokele Street, Wailuku, Maui 96793. 800-305-4899, 808-244-5897, fax 808-242-9600; Maui BandB@aol.com (www.mauiinn.com). $120–$180

This delightful inn has been receiving awards since it opened in 1997. It was recently rated by *Travel & Leisure* as number five of the top ten B&Bs in the U.S. Innkeepers Janice and Tom Fairbanks are Hawaiʻi natives and will share their knowledge of island history and culture. They have lovingly restored the 1924 house to reflect the simple elegance of a plantation home, with handmade Hawaiian quilts on the beds and handwoven *lauhala* mats on the original *ʻōhiʻa* and eucalyptus wood floors. The location, an old county seat town, adds to the sense of days gone by. Although the inn is off the tourist route, it's not far from many sightseeing attractions and great restaurants. The inn is listed on the Hawaiʻi Register of Historic Places. Janice serves a delicious gourmet breakfast, which guests share together on the sunny dining porch. Many Hawaiʻi residents stay here when they visit Maui, and you're likely to run into a local celebrity or two at breakfast.

Pioneer Inn (Best Western)

658 Wharf Street, Lahaina, Maui 96761. 800-457-5457, 808-661-3636, fax 808-667-5708 (www.pioneerinnmaui.com). $100–$165

The historic Pioneer Inn, opened in 1901, fronts Lahaina's busy harbor at one side and bustling Front Street at the other. The first floor of this green and white landmark building is taken up with a restaurant and bar and numerous (too many!) postcard and tee-shirt shops. There are 45 air-conditioned rooms, each with a private lanai overlooking the courtyard and pool or Lahaina's famous banyan tree next door. Memorabilia fills the lobby and bar, a favorite local watering hole. Because the Pioneer Inn is at the center of Lahaina's popular Halloween party, rates are higher then and at Christmas.

Plantation Inn, 174 Lahainaluna Road, Lahaina, Maui 96761. 800-433-6815, 808-667-9225, fax 808-667-9293; info@theplantationinn.com (www.theplantationinn.com). $135–$215

A quiet oasis in the midst of bustling Lahaina, this inn combines turn-of-the-century plantation style with 21st-century amenities. All rooms have hardwood floors and brass or canopy beds, plus private baths, A.C., and VCR's. The pool and Jacuzzi are open 24 hours. Poolside breakfast is included, with a choice of French toast, poached eggs, or granola, and discounts are given at Gerard's, one of Maui's top-rated French restaurants, which occupies the front living room and porch. There are just 19 rooms at this popular inn, so book early.

Condominiums *and* Vacation Rentals

Maui has an abundance of condo rentals, only several of which are listed here since our concentration is on unique properties and many condo units tend to have a sameness about them. Many hotels have suites with kitchenettes (see above). For condos and home rentals, there is usually a minimum stay of two or three nights, sometimes a week.

Destination Resorts Hawai'i

Drawer 1138, Wailea, Maui 96753. 800-367-5246, 808-879-1595, fax 808-874-3554; info@drhmaui.com (www.destinationresortshi.com). $145–$710

Destination Resorts manages six luxury condominium complexes in Wailea and Mākena, either right on the beach, in lush gardens, or overlooking the fairways. All units, whether studios or three-bedroom condos, have concierge services, daily housekeeping, fully equipped kitchens, private lanais, and laundry facilities. A day camp program for children is available. Snorkeling, tennis, horseback riding, golf, and fine dining are just moments away. An amazing 40 percent of their guests are return visitors.

Wailea Ekahi Village is on a lushly landscaped hillside overlooking Keawakapu Beach.

Studios, one-, or two-bedroom units are available. There are four swimming pools plus a beachfront pavilion. This is their most popular condominium. $145–$390

Wailea Elua Village is an oceanfront property offering luxury one-, two-, and three-bedroom units, just steps from Ulua Beach, one of Maui's best snorkeling spots. There are two pools and a putting green. With spectacular architecture and expansive grounds, nestled between two grand resort hotels, this is a spectacular place. $270–$710

Wailea Grand Champions features spacious one- and two-bedroom villas with dramatic architecture, adjacent to the Wailea Tennis Club and Wailea Blue Golf Course. There are two pools, and beaches are nearby. $165–$265

Wailea Ekolu Village overlooks Wailea's famous Blue Course and features deluxe one- and two-bedroom apartments, most with ocean views. $155–255

Maui Polo Beach Club has one- and two-bedroom units in an eight-story high rise fronting the ocean. Exquisite interior decor features rich *koa* and marble accents. There is an oceanfront pool, and all apartments have ocean views. $310–$475

Maui Mākena Surf has one-, two-, and three-bedroom units right on the ocean. Each has a wet bar and whirlpool spa. There are four tennis courts and two swimming pools on the property. $360–$700

Ekena, P. O. Box 728, Hāna, Maui 96713. 808-248-7047; ekena@maui.net (www.maui.net/ ~ekena). $185–$600

Two private vacation homes on 9 lush acres, surrounded by exotic flowers and tropical fruit trees, can accommodate up to eight, but to maintain privacy the owners rent to only one party at a time (no children under 14). Both homes are nicely decorated and fully appointed; one of them, with 2,600 square feet, has two master bedroom suites. *Ekena* means Eden in Hawaiian, and that's just what these homes are.

Hāmoa Bay House & Bungalow P. O. Box 773, Hāna, Maui 96713. 808-248-7884; hamoabay@maui.net (www.hamoabay.com). House $250; bungalow $195

If you want to relax in the gentle breezes of heavenly Hāna, this secluded Balinese-inspired property, with a main house and bungalow, is an excellent choice. Conveniently located a short walking distance from lovely Hāmoa Beach, the property is reached by driving through a lush banana grove. Amenities in the cottage include a king-size

bed, Jacuzzi for two, full kitchen, and cable TV. The house has two bedrooms; the kitchen has a commercial gas range, and the master bedroom suite includes a steeping tub with a jungle view and an outdoor lava rock shower. Sheets and towels in both units are 100% cotton. (Note that the rate for the house is for two people; it is $350 for four.)

Hāna Aliʻi Holidays P. O. Box 536, Hāna, Maui 96713. 800-548-0478, 808-248-7742; info@hanaalii.com (www.hanaalii.com)

This company manages rentals for a number of Hāna vacation houses, ranging from a tiny cottage for $60 a night to spacious homes that go for over $250.

Hāna Bay Hale, P. O. Box 385, Hāna, Maui 96713. 800-327-8097, 808-248-8980, fax 808-248-7735; hanabay@hanamaui.net (www.hanamaui.net). $125–$195

Located on Hāna Bay in the heart of Hāna village, this new, nicely decorated triplex provides two one-bedroom units large enough for four and a two-bedroom unit that can accommodate up to six people. Each has a private entrance, but for family groups all can be interconnected. There are ocean views from the private lanais.

Hāna Cabana and Tradewinds Cottage, P. O. Box 385, Hāna, Maui 96713. 800-327-8097, 808-248-8980, fax 808-248-7735; hanabay@hanamaui.net (www.hanamaui.net). $110–$135

Two sweet guest cottages are located on the grounds of Tropical Island Flowers, on the airport road about 3 miles before the village of Hāna. Hāna Cabana is an airy studio, and Tradewinds Cottage has two bedrooms. Each has a hot tub on a private lanai, with views of the lush gardens and the blue Pacific beyond.

Hāna Kai Maui Resort 1533 Uakea Road, P. O. Box 38, Hāna, Maui 96713. 800-346-2772, 808-248-8426 or 808-248-7506, fax 808-248-7482; hanakai@ maui.net (www.hanakaimaui.com). $125–$195

Eighteen condo units occupy a spectacular setting on Hāna Bay. Studio and one-bedroom units are available for a maximum of four persons. Each is large and has a fully equipped kitchen. A spring-fed lava rock stream meanders around beautifully landscaped grounds. Daily maid service. Stay four nights and get the fifth free, and special weekly and monthly rates are available.

Ho'okipa Haven Vacation Services
P. O. Box 791658, Pā'ia, Maui
96779. 800-398-6284, 808-579-
8282, fax 808-579-9953; info@
hookipa.com (www.hookipa.com)

This business manages a number
of north shore vacation rentals in
all price ranges, from $45/night
apartments to luxury homes that
go for as much as $650/night. In
addition, they'll arrange for economical car rentals, adventure
hikes, and interisland travel—and
any other needs that might come
up during your vacation. Their
service is personal, and they try to
match vacationers with the right
accommodations. Check out their
website for last-minute specials.

Kahana Sunset, 4909 Lower
Honoapi'ilani Highway, Kahana,
Maui 96761. 800-669-1488,
808-669-8011, fax 808-669-9170;
sun2set@maui.net (www.kahana
sunset.com). $105–$290

This condo resort with its own
secluded white sand beach is one
of Maui's best values. Located
halfway between Kā'anapali and
Kapalua, the resort is minutes
from golf courses, shopping, and
fine restaurants. One- and two-
bedroom units are available, each
with a fully equipped kitchen.
Among the resort's amenities are
daily maid service and a heated
swimming pool. We like the

oceanfront units in buildings
A and F, where you can relax
on your private lanai for whale
watching and magnificent sunsets.

Kapalua Villas, 500 Office
Road, Kapalua, Maui 96761.
800-545-0018, 808-669-8088,
fax 808-669-5234. $195–$5,500

These vacation homes with one to
five bedrooms at Kapalua Resort
are the ultimate in luxury. The
most exclusive of them have whirlpool and steam baths, private outdoor pools and/or whirlpool spas,
and daily maid service. Shuttle
service takes guests throughout
the Kapalua Resort, to golf and
tennis, beaches and pools, fine
shopping and dining. Ask about
special packages.

**Maui Eldorado Resort Condo-
minium**, 2661 Keka'a Drive,
Kā'anapali, Maui 96761.
800-688-7444, 808-661-0021,
fax 808-667-7039;
reservations@outrigger.com
(www.outrigger.com). $195–$395

This low-rise condominium resort
is on one of Maui's best beaches.
Studio and one- and two-bedroom
units each have kitchen, washer/
dryer, private lanai, and daily maid
service. The landscaped grounds
include fitness facilities and
19 tennis courts. Be sure to ask
about packages and special rates.

Punahoa Condominiums
2142 'Ili'ili Road, Kīhei, Maui
96753. 800-564-4380,
808-879-2720, fax 808-875-9147;
PunahoaRes@aol.com
(www.Punahoa.com). $85–$175

This is one of the nicest condos
in its price range we've seen—
small, right on the beach on a
quiet street, walk to shopping,
dining, and tennis. Studio and
one- or two-bedroom units are
available. Each unit has an oceanfront lanai with breathtaking views
of the islands of Lāna'i, Kaho'olawe,
and Molokini (some of the photos
you've seen in *Sunset* magazine
just might have been shot here).

Walkus Home
1143 Front Street, Lahaina, Maui
96761. 800-621-8942, 808-661-
8085, fax 808-661-1896; relax@
mauiguesthouse.com (www.maui
guesthouse.com). $395

This elegant house with pool is
just seconds from a sandy beach
and within strolling distance of
Lahaina town. This fully equipped
house would be a great place for
a family reunion. Each of the four
bedrooms and the den (accessible
through one of the bedrooms)
have a queen-size bed, there are
two sleeper sofas in the living
room, and there are even a crib
and highchair. The rental agent
is Tanna Branum, owner of the
Guest House B&B (see below).

Maui Condominiums

There are simply too many condominium properties on Maui (well over 100) to list even all the best ones in these pages. Here is a listing of some other condos that bear checking out. Note that the Aston chain, based in Honolulu, has consistently honored the culture and environment of Hawaiʻi.

Kīhei

Aston at the Maui Banyan: 800-922-7866, 808-875-0004

Kamaʻole Sands: 800-367-5004, 808-874-8700

Mana Kai Maui: 800-367-5242, 808-879-1561

Maui Hill (Aston): 800-922-7866, 808-879-6321

West Maui

Aston at Papakea Resort, Honokōwai: 800-922-7866, 808-669-4848

Aston Kāʻanapali Shores, Kāʻanapali: 800-922-7866, 808-667-2211

Aston Kahana Reef Resort, Kahana: 800-922-7866, 808-669-6491

Kāʻanapali Aliʻi: 800-642-6284, 808-667-1400

Mahana at Kāʻanapali (Aston): 800-922-7866, 808-661-8751

Maui Kāʻanapali Villas (Aston): 800-922-7866, 808-667-7791

Nāpili Shores, Nāpili: 800-688-7444, 808-669-8061

Puamana, Lahaina: 808-661-3423

Whaler on Kāʻanapali Beach: 800-367-7052, 808-661-4861

Bed and Breakfasts *and* Cottages

Not all so-called B&Bs serve breakfast, or they may serve breakfast the first day only, or they may provide you with juice, coffee, and a bun. Be sure to ask. Most B&Bs have a two-night minimum stay, sometimes three nights. Cottage rentals, usually on the owner's property (and sometimes including breakfast), provide economical alternatives to hotels. For additional B&B options, see Reservation Services, page 232.

Aikane Oceanview Vacation Rentals

558 Kaleo Place, Kīhei, Maui 96753. 808-879-5454, fax 808-879-8824. $75–$125

This vacation rental, located in Maui Meadows, has two units, a studio and a one-bedroom cottage. There is a swimming pool, and the islands of Lānaʻi, Kahoʻolawe, and Molokini can be seen from the deck. Hosts Janna and Richard Hoehn welcome guests with a basket of local fruit.

Aloha Lani Inn

13 Kauaʻula Road, Lahaina, Maui 96761. 808-661-8040. $69–$79

This casual, modest bungalow situated at the south end of Front Street is away from the crowds, yet just a short walking distance to the beach and Lahaina's lively social scene. Two shared bathrooms accommodate the four guestrooms. The budget rates and convenient location are appreciated by visitors who want to spend less on lodging and more on Maui's many attractions.

Ann & Bob Babson's B&B

3371 Keha Drive, Kīhei, Maui 96753. 800-824-6409, 808-874-1166, fax 808-879-7906; babson@mauibnb.com (www.mauibnb.com). $90–$105

Just a mile from the ocean, this popular B&B home is in the quiet neighborhood of Maui Meadows, minutes from great swimming and snorkeling beaches. It has three stylishly furnished guestrooms with private baths. The Molokini Suite, the most luxurious of the rooms, has a spectacular ocean view and a Jacuzzi tub. A continental breakfast is served Monday through Saturday.

Anuhea B&B
3164 Māpu Place, Kīhei, Maui
96753. 800-206-4441,
808-874-1490, fax 808-874-8587;
anuhea@maui.net (www.anuhea
maui.com). $105–$115

Russell and Cherie Kolbo took
over this B&B in Maui Meadows, above Kīhei/Wailea, a few
years ago and have been remod-
eling since. Each of the five
rooms now has a private bath
and private entrance. A full,
healthy breakfast is served on a
large deck overlooking tropical
gardens and the hot tub. A health
retreat as well as a B&B, Anuhea
offers massage, body purification
programs, and reiki therapy.

B&D Vacation Hideaways
P. O. Box 616, Kīhei, Maui 96753.
800-635-1273, 808-879-3584,
fax 808-874-1939;
robinson@maui.net
(www.mauiscuba.com). $70

Dive operators Ed and Suzzy
Robinson have an *'ohana* cottage
on their property in a local Kīhei
neighborhood that appeals particularly to scuba divers. It has a
bedroom with a queen-size bed,
a fully equipped kitchen, and a
living room with a foldout futon.

Bamboo Inn, P. O. Box 374,
Hāna, Maui 96713. 808-248-7718;
hanahale@maui.net (www.hana
hale.com). $140–$185

See Hāna Hale Malamalama, below.

Bambula Inn, 518 'Ilikahi Street,
Lahaina, Maui 96761. 800-544-
5524, 808-667-6753, fax 808-667-
0979; bambula@maui.net
(www.bambula.com). $69–$100

Right in Lahaina town but away
from the hordes on Front Street,
this home is a 5-minute walk to a
nice beach. Accommodations
include two studios, each with
kitchen and bath, as well as a private room and bath. Innkeepers
Pierre Chasle and his wife, Irene
(he's from France and she's a
native of Tahiti), will help make
arrangements for fishing, diving,
golfing, etc., and will take you
for a free sunset cruise aboard
their sailboat *Bambula*.

**Bed and Breakfasts
and Cottages** are listed
alphabetically. By area they are:

Pā'ia/Upcountry Area
Banyan Tree House
Bloom House and Bloom
  Cottage
Country Garden Cottage
Haikuleana B&B
Hale Akua Shangri-la
Halfway to Hāna House
Hono Hu'aka Tropical
  Plantation
Kula Cottage

Olinda Country Cottages
  & Inn
Peace of Maui
Pilialoha Cottage
Silver Cloud Ranch
Tea House Cottage

Lahaina/Kapalua Area
Aloha Lani Inn
Bambula Inn
Blue Horizons
Garden Gate B&B
The Guest House
Old Lahaina House
Wai Ola

Kihei/Wailea Area
Aikane Oceanview Vacation
  Rentals
Ann & Bob Babson's B&B
Anuhea B&B
B&D Vacation Hideaways
Eva Villa
Mermaid's Palace
Sunset Cottage

Hāna Area
Bamboo Inn
Hāna Hale Malamalama
Hāna Lani Tree Houses

Banyan Tree House

3265 Baldwin Avenue, Makawao, Maui 96768. 808-572-9021, fax 808-573-5072; info@banyantree house.com (www.banyantree house.com). $75–$90

This old plantation house was once the home of Ethel Baldwin, of the Baldwin family who were among the first missionaries on Maui; family members later were instrumental in developing sugar and pineapple plantations. There are seven guestrooms, three in the main house and four cottages. A pool and spa have just been added to the beautifully landscaped lawns that boast exotic banyan and monkeypod trees. This quiet, restful area was once known as Sunnyside for its comfortable climate.

Bloom House and Bloom Cottage

229 Kula Highway, Kula, Maui 96790 (rental agent: Ho'okipa Haven Vacation Services, P. O. Box 791658, Pā'ia, Maui 96779). 800-398-6284, 808-579-8282, fax 808-579-9953; info@hookipa.com (www.bloom cottagemaui.com). $115–$140

The charming three-bedroom Bloom House, dating from the early 1900s, is on the highway, but there's a hedge and there is little traffic at night in this quiet country location. There are breathtaking coastal views and

heavenly gardens with roses and herbs. A trellised walkway leads to the two-bedroom cottage. Both have fireplaces for chilly evenings, fully equipped kitchens (with cookbooks), and are decorated with antiques. Close-by attractions include Haleakalā, horseback riding, hiking, Kula gardens, and the art galleries of Makawao. If you don't mind the cool 3,000-foot elevation and a half-hour drive down to the coast, this just might be the perfect place for you. Two-night minimum stay.

Blue Horizons

3894 Māhinahina Drive, Kapalua, Maui 96761. 800-669-1948, 808-669-1965. $79–$119

A beautiful B&B located in a quiet neighborhood between Kā'anapali and Kapalua resorts, the two-story cedar home has three nicely furnished apartments, each with bathroom and kitchen facilities. Guests have access to the rest of the house, including a gourmet kitchen and screened ocean-view lanai, where breakfast is served. There's a nice swimming pool and a barbecue for guests' use. Hosts Bev and Jim Spence, originally from Atlanta, epitomize warm Southern hospitality.

Country Garden Cottage

R.R. 2, Box 224-A, Kula Highway, Kula, Maui 96790. 888-878-2858, 808-878-2858. $120

Tucked away behind a tall hedge, this quaint cottage has its own secret garden, full of fruit trees and tropical plants. It features hardwood floors, a fireplace, and full kitchen. Candles and fresh flowers decorate each room, creating a cozy ambiance. The bedroom offers mountain and rose garden views; the living room has an expansive view of the West Maui Mountains and the ocean, a perfect vantage point from which to watch Maui's spectacular sunsets. Hostess Barbara Wimberly provides a continental breakfast. Three-night minimum stay.

Eva Villa, 815 Kumulani Drive, Kīhei, Maui 96753. 800-884-1845, 808-874-6407, fax 808-874-6407; pounder@maui.net (www.maui.net/~pounder/). $115–$125

This is one of the nicest B&Bs in Maui Meadows, an upscale subdivision on the slopes of Haleakalā, just above Wailea. Beautiful beaches and great restaurants are moments away. But, hey, you can swim in the inn's large heated pool, relax in the Jacuzzi, watch the sunset from the rooftop of the home of innkeepers Rick and Dale Pounds, and cook your own meals in the adequately supplied kitchens. The basic rate includes breakfast goodies left in the fridge each day and your own telephone line. All rooms have private bathrooms and separate living areas with cable TV.

Garden Gate B&B, 67 Kaniau Road, Lahaina, Maui 96761. 800-939-3217, 808-661-8800, fax 808-661-0209; jaime@garden gatebb.com (www.garden gatebb.com). $79–$110

There are a variety of rooms here, including a honeymoon suite, all with private baths and king or queen beds. A full breakfast is served in the pleasant garden, with birdsong to entertain. All rooms have TV's, phone, refrigerator, and A.C. They're one block from the ocean and two blocks from a beach. Hosts Bill and Jaime Mosley say "everyone is happy here." What better testimonial? Three-night minimum stay.

The Guest House, 1620 ʻĀinakea Road, Lahaina, Maui 96761. 800-621-8942, 808-661-8085, fax 808-661-1896; relax@mauiguesthouse.com (www.mauiguesthouse.com). $115

Divers and honeymooners make up most of the clientele here (perfect for honeymooning divers, we'd say). The owner, Tanna Swanson Branum, came to Maui for a two-week vacation some years ago and never left. Her friendly house has four private rooms, each with a bath and Jacuzzi or hot tub, refrigerator, and phone. A full breakfast is served in the dining room, and guests may use the large kitchen for cooking. In-house diving instruction is offered in the swimming pool. Seventy percent of their guests are repeats (which we hope doesn't mean repeat weddings!). Tanna is president of the local B&B association. If she doesn't have a room available, she'll probably suggest where you might find one. In addition, she runs Trinity Tours (see scuba diving in the Watersports section).

Haikuleana B&B
555 Haʻikū Road, Haʻikū, Maui 96708. 808-575-2890, fax 808-575-9177 (www.haikuleana.com). $100–$250

Just 12 miles from Kahului and 2 miles from Hoʻokipa Beach, Maui's windsurfing mecca, this quaint 19th-century plantation house was originally built for Maui's first doctor, who worked for the old pineapple cannery. The home, with 12-foot ceilings and hardwood floors, is tastefully decorated with tropical furnishings and antiques. The serene surrounding area is filled with lush vegetation and even a chicken coop. Each guestroom has a private bath, and guests can enjoy the relaxed atmosphere in the bright living room, where there is a TV, or on the front porch. Breakfast is served in the dining room.

Hale Akua Shangri-la
Star Route 1, Box 161, Haʻikū, Maui 96708. 888-368-5305, 808-572-9300, fax 808-572-6666; shangrla@maui.net (www.haleakua.com). $55–$150

If a clothing optional place puts you off, read no further. This is a healing retreat center, which also operates as a B&B. Guests can be au natural around the grounds and in the pool and hot tub area. There are a dozen accommodation options—with private or shared baths—from rooms in the main house to a private gazebo. There are daily yoga classes (included in the room rate) and on-site massage.

Halfway to Hāna House
P. O. Box 675, Haʻikū, Maui 96708. 808-572-1176, fax 808-572-3609; gailp@maui.net (www.halfwaytohana.com). $75

This private, secluded studio is a 20-minute drive from Pāʻia on the road to Hāna. It has a double bed, mini kitchen, and private entrance. A continental breakfast is provided for a small extra charge.

Hāna Hale Malamalama

P. O. Boxx 374, Hāna, Maui
96713. 808-248-7718; hana
hale@maui.net
(www.hanahale.com). $110–$195

This unique property on Hāna
Bay includes six rental accommodations, each an architectural
delight in a sumptuous jungle
setting. The Royal Lodge houses
the two-bedroom Royal Suite
and one-bedroom Garden Suite.
The Tree House Cottage and
the Pond Side Bungalow sit on
a bluff next to an ancient Hawaiian fishpond. The Bamboo Inn
has a two-story villa and a studio.
All are furnished in tasteful tropical style, with bamboo and teak
furniture, hardwood and tile
floors, and bamboo mats. Most of
the units have full kitchens; the
studio has a kitchenette. Several
have Jacuzzi tubs or private outdoor showers.

Hāna Lani Tree Houses

P. O. Box 389, Hāna, Maui 96713.
808-248-7241; hanalani@
maui.net (www.treehousesof
hawaii.com). $69–$89

In a jungle overlooking a flower
garden with the blue Pacific
beyond is a 20-acre compound
on which there are four tree
house rentals. If you dream of
sleeping on an open-air platform
or in a large room towering
above the jungle, or having a

torch-lit dinner beneath the
stars, this is the place for you.
Owner and architect David
Greenberg also operates tree
house resorts in Vietnam, the
South China Seas, and Fiji.

Hono Hu'aka Tropical Plantation

P. O. Box 600, Ha'ikū, Maui
96708. 808-573-1391, fax 808-
573-0141 (www.retreatmaui.com).
$90–$250

This 38-acre organic plantation is
located a short way off the road
to Hāna. There are tremendous
views of Maui's majestic north
shore as well as across the lush
tropical gardens of the plantation. Accommodations range
from single rooms to a poolside
gazebo to two very private cottages, one of which is perched
on the edge of a 150-foot cliff
overlooking the Pacific. Works
of art abound, with a kinetic
sculpture by George Rickey grac-
ing the entrance to the gazebo.
There's an emphasis on renew-
able resources here; the pool is
heated by solar panels and many
buildings are constructed of
sturdy, easily grown bamboo.
Massage, facials, and body work
are available on site. There are
facilities for spiritual retreats
(including a Hopi kiva)—an
aspect of the property that the
owner is encouraging. Breakfast
is provided the first day.

Kula Cottage

Kula Cottage, 206 Puakea Place,
Kula, Maui 96790 (mailing
address: 380 Ho'ohana Street,
Kahului, Maui 96732). 808-878-
2043 or 808-871-6230, fax 808-
871-9187; gilassoc@maui.net
(www.gilbertadvertising.com/
kulacottage). $85

The guestbook says it all:
"charming and comfortable";
"beautiful surroundings"; "cozy,
restful, quiet"; "a little bit of
heaven." All this and it's economical too for a one-bedroom cottage with full kitchen. Hostess
Cecilia Gilbert serves a continental breakfast with muffins or
homemade bread. There's a
fireplace for cool evenings, and
a small grocery is within walking
distance. Most people who
stay in this area come to hike
in Haleakalā crater or surf on
the north shore.

Mermaid's Palace

711 Mililani Place, Kīhei, Maui
96753. 808-891-0776, fax 808-
891-0776; mermaids@maui.net
(www.mermaidspalace.com).
$80–$120

Friendly innkeepers Feanna and
Koichi Ishii, who moved from
Kyoto to Maui several years ago,
welcome visitors to their island
home. The newly built wing for
guests includes four bedrooms, a
spacious living room, and a large
kitchen. Two of the bedrooms

share a hall bath. The grassy lawn, with a view to the Pacific and spectacular sunsets, is the perfect place for evening barbecues. The home is decorated throughout with the colorful marine artwork of Feanna and Koichi, both of whom are celebrated painters. It's a short ride to excellent swimming and snorkeling beaches.

Old Lahaina House

P.O. Box 10355, Lahaina, Maui 96761. 800-847-0761, 808-667-4663. $69–$115

If you could wave a magic wand and create a lovely and relaxing island B&B, this is the place you'd conjure up. Its location is ideal, two houses off Front Street at the quiet south end, within walking distance to restaurants, shops, and night spots. There are a variety of rooms, all with A.C. and some with private baths. Breakfast is served daily in a tropical courtyard next to a wonderful pool. Hosts John and Sherry Barbier create a warm and relaxing atmosphere for their guests.

Olinda Country Cottages & Inn

2660 Olinda Road, Makawao, Maui 96768. 800-932-3435, 808-572-1453, fax 808-573-5326; olinda@mauibnbcottages.com (www.mauibnbcottages.com). $120–$130; cottages $175–$195

Recently featured as inn of the month by *Travel & Leisure*, this Upcountry B&B offers a quiet, romantic alternative to busy tourist destinations. The Tudor-style main house, furnished with antiques, has two guest bedrooms, each with private bath, and the Pineapple "Sweet," which also has a kitchen and living area. A continental breakfast is served each morning. Also on the property—along with a protea flower farm—are two country cottages. At the Hidden Cottage, you can bathe outdoors in a bathtub for two on the very private deck. Olinda is located at 4,000 feet on the slopes of Haleakalā, where the air is crystal clear and the evenings are cool. There are cozy quilts on the beds and fireplaces in the cottages.

Peace of Maui, 1290 Hāli'imaile Road, Makawao, Maui 96768. 888-475-5045, 808-572-5045; pom@maui.net (www.peaceof maui.com). $40–$75

For $45 per night for a room for a couple, these accommodations can't be beat. There's a full kitchen and a living room for guests; bathrooms are shared. Hosts John and Tammi Cadman provide morning coffee. Also, they'll pick you up at the airport and arrange for good car rental rates. There are spectacular views of Haleakalā and Maui's north shore. This is an ideal location for surfers, windsurfers, and hikers. There's also a private one-bedroom cottage on the property that sleeps four—for just $75/night! You can check the swell and wind conditions for the entire north shore from the deck.

Pilialoha Cottage

2512 Kaupakalua Road, Ha'ikū, Maui 96708. 808-572-1440, fax 808-572-4612; cottage@pilialoha.com (www.pilialoha.com). $100–$140

This cute two-bedroom cottage, located in lush farmland a few miles from the cowboy/artsy town of Makawao, is truly away from the madding crowd. Roses bloom in the yard, and horses graze in the next-door pasture. There are a full kitchen and a pretty patio in back. Breakfast items are replenished daily by the hosts, who live next door. The closest beach is Ho'okipa, world famous for windsurfing. Swimming and snorkeling beaches are about half an hour's drive. Area activities include hiking and horseback riding. In the winter, temperatures can drop below 60 degrees here, which is cold by Hawai'i standards. Daytime temperatures range from 77 to 88 in the hottest days of summer.

Silver Cloud Ranch
Old Thompson Road, R.R. 2, Box 201, Kula, Maui 96790. 800-532-1111, 808-878-6101, fax 808-878-2132; slvrcld@maui.net (www.SilverCloudRanch.com). $85–$160

Originally home to the historic Thompson Ranch, this Hawai'i-style plantation now offers six B&B guestrooms in the main house, each with bathroom; five studios with kitchenettes in the Bunkhouse; and a romantic private cottage with full kitchen. Unlike most B&Bs, there is no minimum stay here, though there is a $15 surcharge for one night; a 10 percent discount is given for four or more days. At 3,000 feet, the ranch is an hour's drive from Haleakalā's summit.

Sunset Cottage
3371 Keha Drive, Kīhei, Maui 96753. 800-824-6409, 808-874-1166, fax 808-879-7906; babson@mauibnb.com (www.mauibnb.com). $125–$155

The owners, Ann and Bob Babson, also run a B&B on the property (see above). The cottage has two bedrooms, each with a full bath, and can accommodate four guests. There are a full kitchen and a living room. Seven-night minimum stay (breakfast not included).

Tea House Cottage
P. O. Box 335, Ha'ikū, Maui 96708. 808-572-5610; teahouse@maui.net (www.mauiteahouse.com). $110

Off the road to Hāna, toward the ocean on a one-mile country road, the Tea House Cottage is truly away from it all. Electricity is provided by solar, and the bedding and towels are all cotton. Breakfast is provided daily. The cottage includes a living room, bedroom, screened lanai, and a separate open-air bathhouse.

Wai Ola
1565 Ku'uipo, P. O. Box 12580, Lahaina, Maui 96761. 800-492-4652, 808-661-7901, fax 808-661-7901; tai@maui.net (www.maui.net/~tai/WaiOla). $95–$135

Run by friendly Julie Frank and her equally friendly black labs, this guesthouse caters primarily to couples. There are two private apartments, one with over 1,000 square feet, plus a single room. All have private baths and are nicely decorated and immaculate. Julie welcomes guests with a fruit basket and supplies coffee and condiments in the apartment kitchens. The single room has a coffeemaker and fridge. There's a large pool area (perfect for spreading out diving equipment) with a Jacuzzi, grill, and tables. Julie prides herself on making sure her guests have everything they need at no extra cost. Wahikuli Beach is two blocks away.

Hostels, Cabins, and Campsites

In addition to Banana Bungalow, listed below, there are at least two other Maui hostels, the names of which we'll give you, but we know nothing about these places. They are: Manuel S. Molina's Sports Bar and Rooms, 197 North Market Street, Wailuku (808-244-0141), and Patey's Place Maui Hostel, 761 Waine'e Street, Lahaina (808-667-0999).

Banana Bungalow Maui Hostel
310 North Market Street, Wailuku, Maui 96793. 800-846-7835, 808-244-5090, fax 808-244-3678; info@mauihostel.com (www.mauihostel.com). $16–$35

Luxury it ain't, but this place offers safe, clean accommodations with a large communal kitchen. The lowest price gives you a dorm bed; private rooms start at $29. You don't even need a car. There's a beach shuttle, and the manager, James Heine, leads *free* daily tours, including a rainforest hike, an all-day tour to Hāna, and other adventures. If you're over 30 you might feel uncomfortable here, unless of course you're into tie-dye.

Camp Keʻanae

13375 Hāna Highway, Keʻanae, Maui 96708. 808-248-8355; YMCAcampkeanae@aol.com. $15

One of Maui's most attractive camps and perhaps one of the island's best-kept secrets is Camp Keʻanae, located cliff-top overlooking the remote and lush Keʻanae Peninsula on the road to Hāna, a 2-hour drive from Kahului Airport. Here individuals and groups have the option of pitching tents or staying in spacious cabins. Visitors should plan to bring their own food, towels, and bedding (the beds have bare mattresses) and fill up the gas tank prior to leaving Kahului. Outdoor hibachi grills and community bathroom facilities, with hot showers, are the only amenities. The camp is adjacent to a lush rainforest, and downpours are not infrequent, especially in winter months.

State of Hawaiʻi

Division of State Parks, 54 South High Street, Room 101, Wailuku, Maui 96793. 808-984-8109. Free–$45

The state of Hawaiʻi manages cabins and campgrounds at two locations. At Waiʻānapanapa, a remote beach in Hāna, there are twelve comfortable cabins as well as safe and clean tent-camping areas. The cabins are well furnished with bedding, towels, cooking and eating gear, hot water, showers, refrigerators, and electric stoves. Each cabin will accommodate up to six people.

Polipoli Springs State Recreation Area, in Upcountry, has one cabin that can accommodate up to ten, furnished with bedding and cooking gear but with no hot water or electricity. Tent camping is also available here. Polipoli is reachable by four-wheel drive. At the 6,000-foot level on the side of Haleakalā, this is a challenging place to get to, so don't forget anything essential.

A permit is required for tent camping in both locations (no fee), and the maximum stay is five nights. Cabins are $45 per night; length of stay and number of occupants are limited. Make reservations well ahead of time.

U.S. National Park Service

Haleakalā National Park, P.O. Box 369, Makawao, Maui 96768. 808-572-9306 or 808-572-4400 (www.nps.gov/hale). Free–$40

The campgrounds and cabins inside Haleakalā National Park are surely among the most spectacular campsites anywhere in the world. Stays are limited to three nights, and group size is limited to 12.

Drive-in campgrounds are available at Hosmer Grove, near the summit, and Kīpahulu, on the coast outside of Hāna. Camping is on a first-come, first-served basis. No permit is required, and there is no fee. Grills, picnic tables, and restrooms are provided at both campgrounds. Hosmer Grove has water; no water is available at Kīpahulu.

Camping is allowed in the crater at Hōlua and Palikū, accessible only by hiking or horseback. Permits (required) are free and available on the day of the trip at park headquarters.

Three primitive cabins, at Hōlua, Palikū, and Kapalaoa, are available for $40 per night. The cabins are equipped with water, toilets, wood-burning stoves, firewood, and cooking and eating utensils. There are mattresses but no bedding, and it is necessary to bring a warm sleeping bag. Cabins are rented to one group of up to 12 people. These highly sought accommodations are obtained by a lottery system; applications must be made at least two months prior to the trip.

Reservation Services

Reservations services are knowledgeable about accommodations on each island and can assist in finding the right place to fit your budget and travel needs. These services charge a small fee, or rates are slightly higher than if you booked on your own to cover their commission, but they may save you a lot of time or help find a place at the last minute. If calling from the mainland, be aware of the time difference. Hawai'i Standard Time is 5 hours behind New York, 4 hours behind Chicago, 3 hours behind Denver, and 2 hours behind San Francisco. Add an hour to these when daylight savings is in effect.

Hawai'i's Best Bed & Breakfasts (P. O. Box 563, Kamuela, HI 96743; 800-262-9912, 808-885-4550, fax 808-885-0559; bestbnb@aloha.net; www.bestbnb.com) has listings of B&Bs, inns, and cottages throughout Maui, with a large selection in the Upcountry and Hāna areas. Owner Barbara Campbell has

been in the travel industry for years and has personally inspected each property. **Homes and Villas in Paradise** (116 Hekili Street, Kailua, HI 96734; 800-282-2736, 808-262-4663, fax 808-262-4817) specializes in upscale properties and has a large number of Maui listings. If your dream is for an elegant oceanfront home, these are the people to call. The following are additional reservation services:

Affordable Accommodations Maui, 808-879-7865

All Islands B&B 800-542-0344, 808-263-2342

B&B Hawai'i 800-733-1632, 808-822-7771

B&B Honolulu (statewide) 800-288-4666, 808-595-7533

Hāna Ali'i Holidays 800-548-0478, 808-248-7742

Hawaiian Islands B&B and Vacation Rentals 800-258-7895, 808-261-7895

Ho'okipa Haven Vacation Services, 800-398-6284, 808-579-8282

Dining

THE FOLLOWING LISTING is not intended to be inclusive. We figure most of you can find hotel and fast food restaurants without our help. Rather, we're telling you about some of our favorite places to eat on Maui, organized by regions of the island. We've classified our restaurants as inexpensive, moderate, and expensive. Bear in mind that when we say "expensive," we mean "expensive but worth every penny."

Since hours and days open are subject to change, we suggest that you call ahead even for those places for which no reservations are required.

Several special foods bear mention. The first is the refreshing treat known as **shave ice**, available from many roadside stands and refreshment vans parked near beaches. Finely shaved ice with flavored syrup poured over it, this cool thirst quencher closely resembles what is generally known on the mainland as snow cones, but it isn't the same. The texture of shave ice is much finer—more like actual snow—and the rainbow version is a delight to behold. On a hot afternoon this treat is ultra-refreshing. Some vendors will add a scoop of ice cream or sweet black beans under the mound of delicate ice shavings for an extra treat.

Also delicious, available from roadside vans, are **hot *malasadas***, rich, puffy Portuguese doughnuts that are best while they're still warm. **Kitch'n Cook'd potato chips**, made on Maui, have a strong following, as do **Cook Kwee's Maui Cookies**.

Unique to Hawai'i is the plate lunch, which consists of a meat, fish, or chicken entrée—teriyaki beef or chicken, deep-fried *mahimahi*, for example—plus two scoops of rice ("two scoop rice") and a scoop of macaroni salad. Plate lunch used to be served on a paper plate covered with aluminum foil to go, but these days it most likely comes in a styrofoam box. Even McDonald's serves plate lunch in Hawai'i.

Lahaina/Kā'anapali/ Kapalua *area*

Aloha Mixed Plate
1285 Front Street, Lahaina. 661-3322. Inexpensive

This beachside plate lunch joint, near Māla Wharf, has recently received the Kāhili Award from the Hawai'i Visitors and Convention Bureau in its Keep It Hawai'i competition. The most popular plate lunch is the Hawaiian Plate, which includes *kālua* pork & cabbage, *lomi* salmon, poi, mac (macaroni) salad, and two scoops rice. Try their award-winning appetizer:

coconut prawns with mango chutney. Open daily, 10:30 A.M.–10:00 P.M.

Ānuenue Room, Ritz-Carlton, Kapalua. 669-1665. Expensive

One of the most elegant restaurants on Maui, the Ānuenue Room is perfect for a great, romantic dinner. Hawaiian provençal cuisine features dishes like warm Keāhole lobster salad, *lomi* salmon, *imu*-baked pheasant with taro risotto, or grilled *'ahi* with Moloka'i sweet potatoes. Prix fixe menus are available ($65–$95, additional for wine). The adjacent Ānuenue Lounge features live entertainment. Dinner only, Tuesday–Saturday.

BJ's Chicago Pizzeria
730 Front Street, Lahaina. 661-0700. Inexpensive

This casual restaurant and bar is part of a Southern California chain. Situated in a prime second-story location overlooking Front Street, it offers great ocean views. The decor captures the ambiance of old Hawai'i, with walls full of historical photos of Maui and a bar replicating an Upcountry water tank. Sandwiches, salads, and pastas are available in addition to their award-winning pizza. BJ's mai tai is a favorite. Open daily for lunch and dinner.

Cheeseburger in Paradise
811 Front Street, Lahaina. 661-0830. Inexpensive

Many consider their trademarked cheeseburger the best in the islands. They serve great fries and tofu burgers and fish sandwiches for those who avoid red meat. Harbor and ocean views. Some of the drinks are serious, like Trouble in Paradise, their variation on a piña colada. Breakfast, lunch, and dinner daily.

Chez Paul, One Olowalu Village, Olowalu. 661-3843. Expensive

About 4 miles south of Lahaina, in a tacky strip mall with a phony brick facade, is one of the finest restaurants in all of Hawai'i, as attested by the limos in the dusty parking lot. Inside resembles a French country inn, intimate and charming. The menu is influenced by the south of France, where chef Patrick Callarec learned to cook, but the focus is on regional ingredients like Moloka'i sweet potatoes and Pacific snapper. Entrées ($28–$38) include *homard de Kona,* a locally grown lobster served out of the shell in a light saffron basil cream sauce, and *canard Tahitien,* which is boneless crispy duck served with a mango sauce. All are exquisite. The best dessert, if one had to select, is *gateau au chocolat*

chaud fondant, a hot and runny chocolate cake served with homemade ice cream. There's an excellent wine list. Service is lovely; Patrick will make sure you're satisfied and even comes to the door to bid you goodbye. Dinner only; reservations are a must. The paintings on the walls may look familiar; they're amazing reproductions of celebrated old master paintings by the likes of Renoir, Matisse, Manet, and Gauguin (you can have one shipped home to you for $1,500).

David Paul's Lahaina Grill
127 Lahainaluna Road, Lahaina. 667-5117. Expensive

Consistently ranked among Maui's top restaurants by national publications, David Paul's is right off Front Street in the center of Lahaina. Don't let the honky-tonk atmosphere of Front Street keep you away. The ambiance inside David Paul's is charming, and the service is impeccable. The cuisine, known as New American, features fresh fish and local ingredients. Signature dishes are Kona lobster crab cake, Tequila shrimp with firecracker (red chili) rice, *kālua* duck, and triple berry pie. At this writing, the restaurant has a new owner, and changes are possible. Dinner only; entrées: $22–$37. Reservations a must unless you want to eat at the bar.

Erik's Seafood Grotto, 4242 Lower Honoapi'ilani Highway, Kahana. 669-4806. Expensive

As its name implies, Erik's specializes in seafood, but the menu also has a few non-seafood entrées, such as filet mignon and rack of lamb. As many as 14 fresh fish entrées are available daily. Lunch and dinner are served. Early bird specials are featured from 5 to 6 P.M.

Gerard's
174 Lahainaluna Road, Lahaina. 667-9225. Expensive

Located in the Plantation Inn, Gerard's offers contemporary island French cuisine amid old world charm. Chef Gerard Reversade was tending his own vegetable garden in the Gascony region of France by the time he was eight and cooking by age ten. He opened Gerard's in 1982, focusing on fresh local produce and fish even before the Hawai'i regional cuisine movement took hold. Entrées ($26.50–$42.50) are spectacular and include dishes like roasted Hawaiian snapper with orange and ginger sauce or rack of lamb in mint crust. For dessert, try their signature crème brulée. Guests at the Plantation Inn receive a generous discount at Gerard's.

Guide to Fresh Island Fish

When a waitperson in a Hawai'i restaurant rattles off a selection of island fish on the menu, even we get confused. Here is a guide to a few of the most popular varieties.

'ahi yellowfin or bigeye tuna; a firm fish eaten raw, as sashimi, or broiled in thick filets, preferably rare; blackened *'ahi* is a favorite

aku skipjack tuna; firm red flesh

a'u swordfish or marlin, also known as *shutome*; a white flesh similar to *mahimahi*

hamachi yellowtail; also known as *kamanu* and rainbow runner; similar to salmon

kūmū goatfish; a light red reef fish; firm white flesh similar to red snapper

mahimahi dolphinfish (not the marine mammal); a firm white flesh with flaky texture and mild taste; probably the most popular on Hawaiian tables

moana goatfish; firm, sweet white flesh; similar to catfish

monchong also known as the bigscale pomfret; similar to halibut

onaga red snapper; firm and tender white flesh; sometimes used for sashimi; a very decorative looking pink fish when whole

ono also called wahoo; moist and flaky white meat that's *'ono* (delicious); similar to mackerel

opah also known as moonfish; firm pink flesh with a rich, mild flavor; similar to turbot or halibut

'ōpakapaka pink snapper; light pink flesh that is firm in texture

ulua a jackfish; white fatty flesh; similar to pompano; a small *ulua* is known as *pāpio*

Hula Grill, 2435 Kā'anapali Parkway, Whalers Village, Kā'anapali. 667-6636. Moderate–Expensive

Big Island chef Peter Merriman, a founder of Hawai'i regional cuisine, opened the Hula Grill in 1994. This casual, open-air beachhouse is decorated in vintage Hawaiiana with a "barefoot bar" just steps from one of Maui's most beautiful white sand beaches. There's entertainment nightly at the bar, where lighter fare is served for lunch and dinner, including *pūpū*, pizza, and salads. The dining room menu (entrées: $14.95–$24.95) features fresh fish and prime steaks grilled over a *kiawe* wood fire. The emphasis is on fresh local ingredients. This bustling establishment is not the place for a quiet, romantic meal, but it's perfect for watching the sunset after a day in the sun—or for lunch while shopping the many Whalers Village boutiques.

I'o, 505 Front Street, Lahaina. 661-8422. Expensive

Very New York, I'o offers contemporary Pacific cuisine oceanfront in Lahaina, steps away from a white sand beach. The chef/co-owner is James McDonald of Pacific'o fame.

He's received rave reviews for his innovative cuisine at both establishments. I'o serves only dinner. Entrées: $18–$57. For pre-dinner refreshments, there's a very cool martini bar decorated in what might be called postmodern funk.

Kimo's, 845 Front Street, Lahaina. 661-4811. Moderate

Situated right on the water on Front Street, this bar and eatery has been a Maui favorite for years. Consistently good food and superb location are the secret to its success. Lunch and dinner are served daily.

Kobe Japanese Steak House 136 Dickenson Street, Lahaina. 667-5555. Moderate

Located in the center of Lahaina, behind the Baldwin House, this restaurant resembles a Japanese country inn. Authentic artifacts include a three-hundred-year-old fisherman's kimono. Teppanyaki-style cooking is featured, with chefs preparing and cooking the meal at your table with great showmanship. Entrées include steak, chicken, and seafood dishes. Open for dinner only.

Leilani's on the Beach Whalers Village, Kā'anapali. 661-4495. Moderate

Casual beachfront dining with a menu of seafood, chicken, and burgers. This is an ideal place to watch the setting sun, with the islands of Moloka'i and Lāna'i in the distance. Lunch and dinner are served.

Longhi's, 888 Front Street, Lahaina. 667-2288. Moderate–Expensive

This longtime Maui favorite features Continental and Italian fare. Entrées include the likes of prawns Amaretto, veal Marsala, and chicken piccata. Open for breakfast, lunch, and dinner.

Okazuya & Deli, 3600 Lower Honoapi'ilani Road, Honokōwai. 665-0512. Inexpensive

This Japanese-style takeout deli offers excellent food at reasonable prices. It's convenient for those staying in the many condos in the Honokōwai-Kahana area.

A Pacific Café Honokōwai Marketplace, Honokōwai. 667-2800. Expensive

Chef Jean-Marie Josselin, who opened his first Pacific Café on Kaua'i in 1990, is one of the most celebrated of Hawai'i's chefs and a founder of what is known as Hawai'i regional cuisine—a sophisticated blend of European and Pacific flavors using ingredients from Hawai'i's land and sea. The menu varies depending on what fresh produce and fish are available (entrées: $18–$28). Everything is sublime, including desserts. A great dinner could include crab cakes with sweet chili sauce, a warm roasted tomato with freshly made mozzarella, wok-charred *mahimahi* with ginger-lime sauce (an award winner for Jean-Marie), and a heavenly chocolate soufflé. Wine by the glass complements each course. The decor is pleasing, with paintings by Maui artists on the walls and great furnishings (note the brass-topped tables). Open for dinner only. Honokōwai is between Kā'anapali and Kapalua, not far from the station for the Sugar Cane Train. Honokōwai Marketplace is on the *makai* side of the road.

Pacific'o, 505 Front Street, Lahaina. 667-4341. Expensive

With a great beach location and casual decor, Pacific'o is perfect for lunch or dinner. We can imagine nothing better in life than a leisurely meal on the porch here, with our only care being selecting from among the scrumptious offerings. You can't get fresher fish. Indeed, you're likely to see just-caught fish being carried through the dining room to the kitchen. Chef James McDonald has been lauded for his contemporary Pacific cuisine since he came to Pacific'o in 1993. Signature dishes include award-winning shrimp wontons and sesame seared fish. Entrées: $19–38. Try the banana-pineapple lumpia for dessert. Weekend evenings there's live jazz.

Pasta Penne

180 Dickenson Street, Lahaina. 661-6633. Moderate

Maui chef Mark Ellman (his now-closed Avalon used to be a favorite) has just opened a great pasta place, serving such specialties as *penne putanesca* with garlic *ahi* and whole wheat spaghetti with eggplant and feta. Sandwiches are on the lunch menu. For now, it's BYOB, but they expect to get a liquor license. Open daily for dinner; Monday–Friday for lunch.

Plantation House, 2000 Plantation Club Drive, Kapalua. 669-6299. Moderate–Expensive

Located on Kapalua's Plantation golf course, this restaurant has one of the best views of any on Maui, across wide pineapple fields to the Pacific and the island of Moloka'i beyond. The architecture is stunning, and the seating is exceedingly comfortable. Breakfast, lunch, and dinner are served daily. Chef Alex Stanislaw presents Maui-Mediterranean cuisine, featuring fresh fish with the warm, hearty flavors of the Mediterranean.

Roy's Kahana Bar & Grill and Roy's Nicolina Restaurant

4405 Honoapi'ilani Highway, Kahana. 669-6999 and 669-5000. Moderate–Expensive

Roy Yamaguchi brought Euro-Asian cuisine to Hawai'i. These side-by-side restaurants offer exciting menus with specials changing nightly. Specialties include island-style potstickers with spicy miso sauce and grilled Asian barbecued chicken with mango chili cabernet sauce. Dishes are beautifully presented and made with the finest fresh local ingredients. A signature aspect of all of Roy's restaurants, from Honolulu to L.A. to Tokyo, is an open kitchen and a high noise level. For an intimate, romantic evening, go elsewhere. But no Maui vacation would be complete without at least one dinner at Roy's.

Sansei

115 Bay Drive, Shops at Kapalua, Kapalua. 669-6286. Moderate

This seafood restaurant and sushi bar, owned by chef Dave Kodama, known as "D.K.," has received top awards since it opened in 1996, including Zagat's highest rating for food in the state for two consecutive years. The cuisine is Pacific rim, influenced by Kodama's Japanese heritage and his travels on the mainland and in Mexico and the Caribbean. The exotic entrées ($15.95–$22.95) include, for samplers, wok-seared fresh Hawaiian *opah* and tiger prawns with shiitake mushrooms, asparagus, and Japanese pepper sauce, or macadamia-crusted Australian rack of lamb with gorgonzola and garlic smashed potatoes and sweet miso sauce. Or you can make a meal from the extensive sushi menu ($3.95–$14.95), with such favorites as mango crab salad roll and panko-crusted *ahi* sashimi. There's karaoke Thursday and Friday nights from 10 P.M. till closing.

Swiss Café, 640 Front Street, Lahaina. 661-6776. Inexpensive

This European-style café (the plastic tables and chairs are strictly American) offers breakfast and lunch as well as a great cup of cappuccino and "Maui's best ice cream." It certainly is the best price for ice cream, with two scoops for $2. Favorites are melted cheese sandwiches and 8-inch pizzas, perfect for one. There's pleasant outdoor seating in a cool courtyard. Plus, the café provides internet access at 15¢/ minute ($2 minimum). Located across from the banyan tree on Front Street, next to Burger King. A menu in German is available.

Take Home Maui

121 Dickenson Street, Lahaina. 661-8067. Inexpensive

A store selling pineapples and papayas, Take Home Maui has a little deli on the side where they serve good sandwiches and salads plus the best smoothies in Hawai'i, made with fresh pineapple, bananas, and papaya (many places use frozen fruit). There are a few tables outdoors on the front lanai, where Kehau, an African gray parrot, speaks up from time to time.

Mā'alaea/Kīhei/Wailea *area*

Azeka's Ribs & Snack Shop

1280 South Kīhei Road, Kīhei. 879-0611. Inexpensive

Legendary ribs are made here Wednesday, Saturday, and Sunday and are served from 9:30 A.M. until they run out, usually around 1 o'clock. Azeka's is also popular for its plate lunch. Eat at outdoor tables next to Ace Hardware or, preferably, take out.

Bamboo Bistro, 300 Mā'alaea Road, Mā'alaea Harbor. 243-7374. Moderate–Expensive

Chef Peter Merriman, one of the originators of Hawai'i regional cuisine at his Big Island restaurant, recently opened this open-air bistro overlooking

colorful Mā'alaea Harbor, near the new Maui Ocean Center. Island-grown foods are featured. To encourage family-style dining, platter-size portions are available at this innovative dining room. Also, to reduce the high cost of dining out, you can order taster-size portions of all entrées ($3.95 for a taster of shrimp, macadamia nut, and corn fritters). Favorites are wok-charred 'ahi and sesame-crusted fish with spicy *liliko'i* sauce. The extensive wine list is complemented with carafes of house wine, in keeping with the bistro approach. Open daily for lunch (with a lower-priced menu) and dinner.

Bistro Molokini

Grand Wailea Resort Hotel and Spa, 3850 Wailea Alanui, Wailea. 875-1234. Expensive

This casual, open-air bistro, overlooking the Grand Wailea's pool and the Pacific Ocean, features creative Italian cuisine. Pizzas are prepared in a wood-burning oven. Open daily for lunch, dinner, and cocktails.

Coffee Store, 1279 South Kīhei Road, Azeka Place II, Kīhei. 875-4244. Inexpensive

This is one of our favorite spots for a cuppa Joe and a pastry. Sometimes the staff is the friendliest, most helpful this side of

the International Date Line (says a lot); other times they're downright surly. Internet access is available. The Coffee Store also has outlets in Kahului, Lahaina, and Mā'alaea (see Shopping, page 131).

Da' Kitchen, 2439 South Kīhei Road, Rainbow Mall, Kīhei. 875-7782. Inexpensive

This is a favorite local hangout and a good place to try Hawaiian-style food. Best bet is the Hawaiian plate, which includes pork *laulau*, *kālua* pork, chicken long rice, and *lomi* salmon—with of course two scoops rice and a scoop of potato/mac salad. Breakfast could be the loco moco: grilled burger, two eggs, rice, onions, and gravy. Calorie counters can make do with BBQ beef sticks and garden salad. Open daily. They also have locations in Wailuku at the corner of Market and Main (249-2326) and Kahului in Triangle Square, 425 Koloa Street, not far from K Mart (871-7782).

Five Palms Beach Grill

Mana Kai Resort, 2960 South Kīhei Road, Kīhei. 879-2607. Moderate

This beachfront open-air restaurant serves breakfast, lunch, and dinner. Happy hour starts at 2 P.M. with a creative *pūpū* menu.

Specialties: fresh fish, Black Angus beef, and rack of lamb.

Le Gunji, Diamond Resort, 555 Kaukahi Street, Wailea. 874-0500. Expensive

This intimate teppanyaki restaurant, situated in a lovely garden setting, features French-style Japanese cuisine. Zagat's rated the food "extraordinary to perfection." All menus are prix fixe and include appetizer, soup, salad, entrée, the famous garlic rice, and dessert. Reservations required.

Humuhumu
Grand Wailea Resort Hotel and Spa, 3850 Wailea Alanui, Wailea. 875-1234. Expensive

If you're looking for a refreshing tropical ambiance and excellent seafood, this "floating" restaurant at the Grand Wailea is the place, featuring contemporary Hawaiian cuisine. Named after Hawai'i's official state fish (*humuhumu-nukunukuapua'a),* the restaurant consists of a grouping of attractive thatched-roof huts, handcrafted from *'ōhi'a* and *koa* woods, perched over a picturesque saltwater lagoon. Open daily for dinner.

Joe's Bar and Grill
131 Wailea 'Iki Place, Wailea. 875-7767. Expensive

After Beverly and Joe Gannon successfully launched Hāli'imaile General Store (see page 241), they looked to the other side of the island for Joe's Bar and Grill, which opened in 1995 in a spacious, open-air dining room designed by a Hollywood set designer. Windows open to nature's best set: soft trades and views of Lāna'i in the distance. Bev is executive chef, and daughter Cheech does the desserts. The emphasis is on hearty home cooking—meatloaf, New York steak, and pork chops. But there are plenty of new cuisine–influenced dishes, like crispy Asian calamari and smoked duck tostada. Bev and Joe call it "home cooking from paradise," which is no exaggeration. Entrées: $17–$30.

Kihei Prime Rib and Seafood House, 2511 South Kīhei Road, Kīhei. 879-1954. Moderate–Expensive

Offering oceanfront dining in the heart of Kīhei, this attractive restaurant has a nice selection of American-style entrées, including Black Angus beef and fresh fish. Open for dinner only. Early bird specials between 5 and 6 P.M. offer a good value.

Maui Tacos, 2411 South Kīhei Road, Kama'ole Beach Center, Kīhei. 879-5005. Inexpensive

The crowds lining up at dinnertime will tell you this is the place to be. Founded by local chef Mark Ellman in 1993, this chain now has branches all over Maui and in Georgia, Florida, New York, and Delaware. Burritos, tacos, enchiladas, tostados, and quesadillas are the order of the day. Salsa, chips, and beans are made fresh daily. This is fast food with a sassy attitude— definitely worth a stop.

A Pacific Café, 1279 South Kīhei Road, Azeka Place II, Kīhei. 879-0069. Expensive

An architecturally stunning setting provides the backdrop for the celebrated food of chef Jean-Marie Josselin, whose distinctive cuisine has earned national accolades since he opened his first Pacific Café on Kaua'i in 1990. Signature dishes include "firecracker" salmon rolls, penne pasta with Kaua'i shrimp, and, for dessert, "Toasted Hawaiian," a mouth-watering combination of *haupia* and white chocolate cake with caramel sauce. Open for dinner only. Josselin has another Pacific Café in Hono-kōwai (see page 236). No Maui vacation would be complete without a meal at at least one of the two.

Pacific Grill, Four Seasons Resort, 3900 Wailea Alanui, Wailea. 874-8000. Moderate

East meets West at this casual Four Seasons Resort restaurant, which offers all-day dining, including a breakfast buffet, with both indoor or al fresco seating with a beautiful ocean view. This restaurant offers a creative menu and a romantic setting for dinner at one of Maui's most elegant hotels.

Pizazz Café, 1279 South Kīhei Road, Azeka Place II, Kīhei. 891-2123. Moderate

The draw here is the jazz band that plays at dinner, Tuesdays through Sundays. The menu reflects the jazz ambiance, with such Southern-style items as Bourbon chicken, seafood jambalaya, and collard greens. Entrées: $15.95–$22.95. The lunch menu includes sandwiches and pizzas.

Prince Court, Maui Prince Hotel, 5400 Mākena Alanui, Mākena. 875-5888. Expensive

Superb Continental and Pacific rim dishes are served in an elegant, quiet dining room. Service is friendly and attentive. The walls are hung with colorful paintings of Maui scenes by local artist Ed Lane, who "retired" from his Phoenix ad agency several years ago and moved to Maui to

paint. Entrées ($19–$33) include such specialties as Kona lobster stuffed with crabmeat and five-pepper spiced breast of duck, as well as delicious "smart dining" options for the health and diet conscious—after which the baked-to-order warm chocolate truffle cake with Kona coffee ice cream can be indulged. The Friday night prime rib and seafood buffet is a local favorite.

Sarento's on the Beach
2980 South Kīhei Road, Kīhei

As we went to press, this oceanfront restaurant, formerly Carelli's on the Beach, was scheduled to reopen in several months after extensive renovations. With Hawaii-born George Gomes as executive chef, it's sure to be a success.

Seasons, Four Seasons Resort, 3900 Wailea Alanui, Wailea. 874-8000. Expensive

This classy restaurant, located at the posh Four Seasons Resort, offers a sublime dining experience in an exquisitely romantic oceanfront setting. The menu is contemporary, with Hawaiian and Asian influences. Seasons recently won the coveted AAA Five Diamond Award, the first for any Maui restaurant and only the second in the state. Open daily for dinner.

Sea Watch Restaurant
100 Wailea Golf Club Drive, Wailea. 875-8080. Moderate–Expensive

Excellent island regional cuisine is served in an attractive and spacious setting with spectacular mountain and ocean views. Open daily for breakfast, lunch, and dinner.

Stella Blues Café, 1215 South Kīhei Road, Long's Center, Kīhei. 874-3779. Inexpensive

A varied menu with home-style cooking at reasonable prices makes this a good bet. Open daily from 8 A.M. to 9 P.M. with a traditional breakfast menu, imaginative sandwiches and salads, and entrées such as grilled ribs and vegetarian lasagna.

Pā'ia/ Upcountry *area*

Casanova
1188 Makawao Avenue, Makawao. 572-4978. Moderate

Housed in a 1938 building that was used for a USO during World War II, Casanova is a favorite local hangout for lunch and dinner. The food is Italian with a nod to Pacific rim with such dishes as *mahimahi* with *liliko'i* sauce or seared *'ahi* with tropical salsa. Classic Italian fare—pizza and pasta—is also served. Lunchtimes, the front porch is a great place to relax with a drink and sandwich. Unlike most Maui establishments, the place comes alive after 9 P.M. with live music and dancing (the likes of Willie Nelson and Richie Havens have played here).

Charley's, 142 Hāna Highway, Pā'ia. 579-9453. Inexpensive

This popular eatery serves breakfast, lunch, and dinner. Breakfasts are generous and reasonably priced, consisting of omelets, pancakes, and other standard fare. The lunch menu offers burgers, sandwiches, salads, and burritos. Dinner entrées ($9–$16.75) include chicken, *kiawe* smoked ribs, and fish. Local musicians often perform here, and the bar is a favorite relaxing spot.

Courtyard Café
3620 Baldwin Avenue, Makawao. 572-4877. Inexpensive

Healthy food with good-size portions is served at this casual Upcountry café for breakfast and lunch. You order at the counter, then sit at one of the few indoor tables or outside in the tree-shaded courtyard. Salads and sandwiches are delicious. Everything is homemade with fresh ingredients.

Grandma's Coffee House
153 Kula Highway, Kēōkea. 878-2140. Inexpensive

Grab a cup of coffee and enjoy the great views from the deck, overlooking all of south Maui. This is a good stop for food before embarking on the south-side road to Hāna. The muffins and cakes are homemade, and the coffee, grown by Grandma's grandson in Kula, is roasted at the back of the store.

Hāli'imaile General Store
900 Hāli'imaile Road, Hāli'imaile. 572-2666. Expensive

If you could have only one great meal on Maui, this is the place we'd recommend. The food is sublime, the sophisticated-casual atmosphere just right. Housed in a funky peach-colored 1925 plantation store, this restaurant has garnered top honors since chef Beverly Gannon opened it in 1988. (Her intention was to offer gourmet take-out, but customers wanted to eat in, so she had to add tables and hire staff.) Signature dishes include Bev's hot crab dip, Szechwan barbecued salmon, rack of lamb Hunan style, and piña colada cheesecake. Try to get a seat in the front room (unless you want quiet intimacy, in which case the back room is your place), and be sure to check out the great copper bar fabricated by local artist Tom Faught. Entrées: $17–$32. Open for lunch Monday through Friday and dinner nightly. It's close enough to the airport that you can stop by for lunch or dinner before your plane takes off, a perfect ending to a Maui sojourn, we think. How do you pronounce it? Ha-lee-ee-miley.

Kula Lodge Restaurant
Highway 377, Kula. 878-1535. Moderate

Prices are high for unmemorable fare, but you can't get a better view. On a clear day, there's a panoramic outlook across nearby flower farms to the West Maui mountains. Breakfast, lunch, and dinner are served (they open at 6:30 A.M.). Located on Haleakalā Highway, close to the turnoff for the Crater Road.

Makawao Steak House
3612 Baldwin Avenue, Makawao. 572-8711. Moderate

An attractive restaurant with a warm, pleasant ambiance and a nice lounge offering a cozy place to sit by the fire on cool Upcountry nights. The menu includes steak, chicken, and seafood. Open nightly.

Mama's Fish House, Kūʻau Cove, Pāʻia. 579-8488. Expensive

This South Seas oceanside restaurant, situated on Maui's picturesque windsurfing shore, has won highest praises since it opened in 1973. Although its prices are high, it continues to draw visitors, including many celebrities, with its excellent seafood. Open daily for lunch and dinner.

Moana Bakery & Cafe
71 Baldwin Avenue, Pāʻia. 579-9999. Inexpensive–Moderate

This is one of our favorites. Co-owners Don Ritchey and Thierry Michelier opened about two years ago; Don is the chef and Thierry the baker. The pastries, always available to go, are the best. The restaurant is open from 8 A.M. for breakfast (omelets and pancakes). Lunch is from 11 to 3 and dinner from 3 until closing at about 9 P.M. They serve terrific salads, fresh fish, and pasta. Dinner entrées: $8.95–$23.95. So far the crowds haven't found this place, which is fine by us (though we hope they have enough customers to keep going).

Pāʻia Fish Market
2 Baldwin Avenue, Pāʻia. 579-8030. Inexpensive

A popular spot, their lanai, where you can sit and watch the world go by, is always crowded. Menu choices, listed on a big blackboard, feature fresh fish plates, fish burgers, and seafood fajitas.

Picnics, 30 Baldwin Avenue, Pāʻia. 579-8021. Inexpensive

A favorite stopping place for a box lunch to take on a Haleakalā or Hāna jaunt, this small restaurant offers healthy sandwiches and salads as well as their famous spinach nutburger. They open

at 7 A.M., when you can get fresh pastries and hot coffee to steel you for the drive ahead.

Upcountry Café, 7 Aewa Place, Pukalani. 572-2395. Inexpensive

Breakfast, lunch, and dinner are served at this local eating place, whose decor focuses on a cow motif. Take the Old Haleakalā Highway to Pukalani. The Upcountry Café is on the left, after you pass Pukalani Terrace Center and McDonald's.

The Vegan, 115 Baldwin Avenue, Pāʻia. 579-9144. Inexpensive

This small restaurant, featuring freshly prepared vegetarian (vegan) cuisine, caters to the health conscious with reasonably priced meals and large portions. Lunch and dinner are served daily (but call ahead on Sundays to make sure they're open). The menu includes hot entrées with an international flavor, sandwiches, and salads.

Kahului/ Wailuku area

Bailey House Museum
2375 Main Street, Wailuku. 244-3326. Inexpensive

An authentic Hawaiian plate lunch is served in the garden of an 1833 missionary home. (For the museum, see pages 133–34.) Here's a chance to try such local specialties as chicken long rice, *laulau,* and *kālua* pork n' cabbage. Auntie Eleanor and Uncle Sol Kawaihoa not only serve the lunch, they play slack key guitar and dance hula on the lawn. However, the last time we checked, the lunch operation had closed temporarily, so it would be a good idea to call before you go.

Café Marc Aurel

28 North Market Street, Wailuku. 244-0852. Inexpensive

A coffee bar with seats on Wailuku's main drag, this place offers great espresso and cappuccino with top-quality pastries. They host poetry readings a couple of nights each month. Internet access available.

Kaka'ako Kitchen

Queen Ka'ahumanu Center, Kahului. 893-0366. Inexpensive

Located in the space previously occupied by Sam Choy's, this local-style eatery is a branch of the popular O'ahu restaurant, the brainchild of chef Russell Siu. Gourmet plate lunches are the buzzword here. Their signature dish and everyone's favorite is island-style chicken linguine. Entrées average $6, with nothing over $10. There's a full bar, and save room for dessert. Open for breakfast, lunch, and dinner.

Mañana Garage

33 Lono Avenue, Kahului. 873-0220. Moderate

Latin American cuisine imaginatively prepared and served, with only the freshest of ingredients, has made this newcomer to the Maui scene an instant success. Dinner entrées range from $11 to $26, with a much less expensive lunch menu. Look for the brightly colored table umbrellas at the corner of Ka'ahumanu and Lono avenues.

Mushroom

2080 Vineyard Street, Wailuku. 244-7117. Inexpensive

Local-style American/Japanese cuisine is served for lunch and dinner six days a week; closed Sundays. As at many Maui restaurants, lunch ends at 2 P.M.

Saigon Café, 1792 Main Street, Wailuku. 243-9560. Inexpensive

Vietnamese soups and noodles and other traditional fare are imaginatively prepared with the freshest ingredients. This restaurant is a favorite of Maui chefs on their nights off. Open daily for lunch and dinner. Located behind Ooka's Supermarket, this simple establishment is marked only by a sign that says "Open."

Sam Sato's, 1750 Wili Pa Loop, Wailuku. 244-7124. Inexpensive

This is the place to try saimin, a Japanese-inspired noodle soup. A large bowl of light broth filled with locally made noodles and vegetables, with your choice of chicken, meat, or fish, makes a heavenly meal. Another specialty here is dry mein, a noodle dish with small pieces of pork, bean sprouts, and green onions mixed with soy sauce and a little oil. Also try the *manju,* a Japanese pastry delicacy, here filled with lima beans following the traditional recipe. Lunch only, Monday–Saturday.

Siam Thai

123 North Market Street, Wailuku. 244-3817. Inexpensive

A favorite of residents and tourists alike (Robert Redford and Jimmy Buffet are among those who have discovered it), this unpretentious but pleasant restaurant has been serving delicious and modestly priced Thai cuisine since 1985. Menu items include coconut-chicken soup, green papaya salad, satay dishes, curries, and other traditional Thai fare. Open for lunch and dinner.

Wow-Wee Maui's Café
333 Dairy Road, Kahului.
871-1414. Inexpensive

This pleasant stop for coffee or a sandwich, not far from the airport, is home of the Wow-Wee candy bar, of which there is none better. Made on Maui, the bars come in milk chocolate, dark chocolate, and white chocolate and include such ingredients as macadamia nuts, caramel, coconut, and Kona coffee. Don't leave Maui until you've tried them all.

Hāna *area*

Dining Room, Hotel Hāna-Maui
Highway 360, Hāna. 248-8211.
Expensive

The chef has a way with local fish, combining it with sauces and vegetables that enhance, never overpower, the flavor of the fish. If there's a fish special

in addition to menu items, take it. The accompanying wasabi or sweet potatoes are tasty additions. Breakfast, lunch, and dinner are served, with reservations required for dinner. The lunch menu includes sandwiches and salads. Dinner entrées ($21.50–$32.95) include beef, lamb, fish, chicken, and vegetarian dishes. Casual, resort-style attire is recommended. From the architecturally striking dining room, with 35-foot open-beam ceiling and an enclosed lanai, there are stunning views of the hotel's meticulous grounds and the Pacific beyond. Hawaiian-style entertainment is offered two nights a week. Adjacent to the Dining Room, the Paniolo Bar features nightly entertainment and a light *pūpū* menu. The hotel also offers a beachside *lūʻau* and a *paniolo* cookout, though not on a regularly scheduled basis.

Kumulani Chapel on the grounds of the Ritz-Carlton, Kapalua.

Services

Island Weddings

Maui is a popular place for weddings, with about 7,000 ceremonies for nonresident couples each year. There are many beautiful beaches (free) that make heavenly sites for weddings. All of the resort hotels provide wedding services, arranging for everything from the minister to the champagne. Many hotels provide beautiful settings for weddings, including intimate gazebos and beachside pavilions. Just ask about wedding services. You may get more information by calling the local (808) telephone number rather than the toll-free number.

We particularly like the facilities at the **Ritz-Carlton, Kapalua** (see pages 218–19), where ceremonies may be performed oceanfront or at the historic fifty-year-old Kumulani Chapel, which once served as a place of worship for the surrounding plantation community. Wedding dinners can be in the acclaimed Ānuenue Room, or, for larger groups, a traditional Hawaiian *lūʻau* can be held on the Beach House lawn. And of course, what better place for a honeymoon than the Ritz-Carlton, Kapalua!

The **Grand Wailea Resort Hotel and Spa** (see page 215) has a seaside wedding chapel on its beautifully manicured lawns. Its magnificent stained-glass windows, designed by Hawai'i artist Yvonne Cheng, depict a royal Hawaiian wedding.

Equally romantic and luxurious, and more private, is the island of Lāna'i. **The Lāna'i Company** (800-321-4666) will help plan a wedding for up to sixty guests (though we bet Bill Gates had more than that when he married Melinda French at the 12th tee of the Challenge at Mānele golf course; he rented every room on the island for the occasion). The wedding coordinator will help you select a beautiful site at either the Lodge at Kō'ele or the Mānele Bay Hotel and take care of all the details. For a romantic setting, we like the charming lakeside gazebo at the Lodge (see page 271).

Trilogy Excursions (888-628-4800) also arranges romantic torch-lit weddings on the island of Lāna'i, ranging from an intimate affair for two up to a large party for two hundred.

Numerous local companies specialize in wedding arrangements. **Dolphin Dream Weddings** (800-793-2933, 808-661-8535;

dolphin@maui.net; www.maui.net/~dolphin) will take care of some or all of the details and doesn't mind last-minute calls. You might also want to check out the websites for **A Wedding Co.** (800-827-0391, 808-575-9225; www.aweddingcompany.com) and **Magical Maui Weddings** (800-472-5869, 808-879-8800; www.magicmauiweddings.com).

Marriage licenses are available from the State of Hawai'i Department of Health (54 South High Street, Wailuku, Maui 96793; telephone 808-984-8210). Licenses are issued immediately after application and expire after 30 days. They are valid only in Hawai'i, and the fee ($50) is payable at the time of filing.

Publications

The *Maui News,* a morning newspaper published daily, is Maui's newspaper of record. The weekly dining and entertainment section included in the Thursday paper is an excellent guide to what's happening all over the island.

Menu, a free publication available at tourist racks, has good restaurant reviews. *Maui Golf Review* and *Real Estate Maui Style* are also fine free publications on their respective subjects.

Laundry *and* Dry Cleaning Services

West Maui

Ali'i Dry Cleaners
910 Honoapi'ilani Highway, Lahaina (667-2544)

Donna's Laundry
Kahana Gateway, Kahana (669-7738) (self-service)

Kahana Koin-Op Laundromat
4465 Honoapi'ilani Highway, Kahana (669-1587) (self-service)

One-Hour Martinizing Dry Cleaning
3350 Lower Honoapi'ilani Road, Honokōwai (661-6768)

Valley Isle Dry Cleaners
Nāpili Plaza, Nāpili (665-0076)

Kīhei

Ali'i Dry Cleaners
2439 South Kīhei Road, Kīhei (874-8897)

Līpoa Laundry Center
41 East Līpoa Street, Kīhei (875-9266) (includes self-service)

Kahului and Wailuku

Happy Valley Laundry
340 North Market Street, Wailuku (244-4677) (self-service)

Kahului Laundromat
230 Hāna Highway, Kahului (871-6670) (self-service)

Maui's Quality Dry
Cleaning and Laundry
    210 Imi Kala, Wailuku
    (244-1945); also locations
    in Kīhei, Lahaina, Kahului,
    and Haʻikū
Valley Isle Dry Cleaners
    180 East Wākea Avenue,
    Kahului (877-4111)
W&F Washerette
    125 South Wākea Avenue,
    Kahului (877-0353)
    (self-service)

Pāʻia and Upcountry
Haʻikū Laundromat
    810 Haʻikū Road, Haʻikū
    (575-9274) (self-service)
Pāʻia Clothes Cleaners
    26 Baldwin Avenue, Pāʻia
    (579-9273)
Upcountry Laundry
and Dry Cleaning
    Pukalani Terrace Center,
    Pukalani (573-1818)
    (includes self-service)

Business Services

Kinko's at 395 Dairy Road in Kahului (871-2000) provides the most economical services for photocopying, small printing jobs, and PC and Mac rental stations. They're open 24 hours. FedEx packages may be dropped off here. **Aloha Business Centers** in Kāʻanapali (661-1145), Kapalua (665-0544), and Kīhei (891-0290) offer on-site PCs and Macs as well as equipment rental and a variety of business services. **Sandra's Secretarial Service** in Wailuku (244-0042) has been offering a wide range of business services for a number of years. Equipment may be rented from **BusinessWorks** (661-1705).

Medical Services

Maui Memorial Medical Center in Wailuku (244-9056) is a state-of-the-art facility with 24-hour emergency service. **Doctors on Call** (667-7676) provides same-day medical care seven days a week, 8 A.M. to 9 P.M., with three locations serving the Lahaina, Kāʻanapali, and Kapalua areas. **West Maui Healthcare Center** at Whalers Village in Kāʻanapali

(667-9721), open daily with evening hours, offers a full range of medical services. In Kīhei, **Urgent Care Maui** (879-7781) is open 365 days of the year. **The Maui Medical Group** (249-8080) has offices in Wailuku, Lahaina, and Upcountry and provides medical care in a number of specialized fields. **Kaiser Permanente** has clinics in Wailuku (243-6000), Lahaina (661-7400), and Kīhei (891-3000) —open only to Kaiser members.

For nursing care, **Action Med** (875-8300) will provide the services of LPNS, RNS, nurses' aides, and personal care attendants, all of whom have been carefully screened.

Medical equipment is available from **Gammie Homecare** (877-4032) and **Maui Home Care** (871-4663), both in Kahului.

Baby Sitters

There are two agencies on Maui that offer licensed, bonded, and insured childcare attendants: **Happy Kids** (667-5437) and **Nanny Connection** (875-4777).

The royal coconut grove near Kaunakakai (see page 257).

moloka'i

*T*he Pailolo Channel separates Molokaʻi from Maui, to whose county Molokaʻi belongs. Molokaʻi and her people embody much of what is known as the Hawaiian spirit and prefer to maintain the traditions of the old ways. Sometimes referred to as "the most Hawaiian island," Molokaʻi is the most laid back, least touristy of the islands. Tourists are not catered to here, which may bother some. Residents of Honolulu come here to relax and get away from it all, free from all the glitz and hype of many vacation spots. Other tourists come to see a view of Hawaiʻi beyond the luxury hotels and high-end shopping centers. The people who live on Molokaʻi are genuinely warm and engaging, more than living up to the island's "friendly isle" nickname.

Molokaʻi's population of less than 7,000 is predominantly native Hawaiian. Occupations include farming, ranching, and the limited tourist industry. There are no buildings taller than a palm tree, there are no traffic lights, and a traffic jam might consist of two cars at a stop sign.

The island is just 38 miles long by 10 miles wide, so you can manage to see much of it in just a few days. The northern coast has the world's highest sea cliffs, rising more than 3,000 feet. These steep windward cliffs isolate the peninsula of Kalaupapa on the northern shore, where, beginning in the 1860s, Hawaiians suffering from leprosy, or Hansen's disease, were forced to live, cut off from the outside world. The East Molokaʻi Mountains are a tropical rainforest; at their center is Mount Kamakou, 4,961 feet high at its summit. West Molokaʻi—much of which belongs to Molokaʻi Ranch, which owns one-third of the entire island—is generally dry and windy. One of Hawaiʻi's largest white sand beaches, Pāpōhaku, stretches 3 miles along the western coast.

Above: The north coast of Molokaʻi.   **Right: The island of Molokaʻi as viewed from Kapalua, Maui.**

Getting There

There are no direct flights to Moloka'i from the mainland. **Hawaiian Airlines** (800-367-5320) and **Island Air** (800-323-3345) both fly a number of round trips a day from Honolulu. Hawaiian also flies round trip from Kona, Hilo, Kahului, Lāna'i, and Lihu'e. Island Air flies from Kahului to Moloka'i. The main airport is Ho'olehua, better known as Moloka'i Airport.

Also, commuter flights to Moloka'i from Honolulu and Kahului are offered by **Pacific Wings** (888-575-4546) and **Moloka'i Air Shuttle** (808-567-6847). A splendid way to get to Moloka'i is aboard a 100-foot interisland yacht. The **Moloka'i Princess** (667-6165, 800-275-6969; www.molokaiferry.com) operates between Lahaina and Kaunakakai Harbor on Moloka'i, Monday through Saturday, making one trip a day each way. The fare is about $40; each person is permitted two carry-on items.

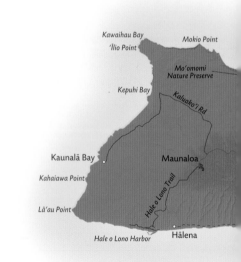

Kepuhi Beach, off the Kaluako'i Resort area on the west side. The hotel and golf course at Kaluako'i Resort, once a first-class vacation destination, have suffered hard times in recent years and are closed as of this writing.

Getting Around

A rental car is a must. **Budget Rent a Car** (800-527-0700) has a desk at Moloka'i Airport. Cars are also available from **Dollar Rent a Car** (800-800-4000) and **Island Kine Auto Rental** (808-553-5242).

Be sure to fill up before you return your rental car to the airport. The last service station before the airport is **Rawlins Chevron Service** (553-3214), located at the entrance to Kaunakakai. If you're coming from the west side, you'll have to drive into Kaunakakai before heading to the airport.

Accommodations

In addition to the accommodations listed below, the **Moloka'i Visitors Association** has a list of house and cottage rentals. Write to them at P.O.

Box 960, Kaunakakai, Moloka'i 96748, or call 800-800-6367, 808-553-3876, from a neighbor island 800-553-0404, fax 808-553-5288, e-mail: mva@molokai-hawaii.com (www.molokai-hawaii.com).

Also, there are a number of condo units available for rental through local real estate agents. Contact **Friendly Isle Realty** (800-600-4158, 808-553-3666), **Shirley Alapa Real Estate** (808-567-6363), or **Swenson Real Estate** (800-558-3648,

808-553-3648). One of the nicer condo developments is Wavecrest Resort at 'Ualapu'e, 13 miles from Kaunakakai on the east side of the island; the buildings are ordinary, but it is a beautiful spot and well maintained. There are one- and two-bedroom units, which are rented through real estate agents.

For camping at Pālā'au State Park, see page 259.

the island of **moloka'i**

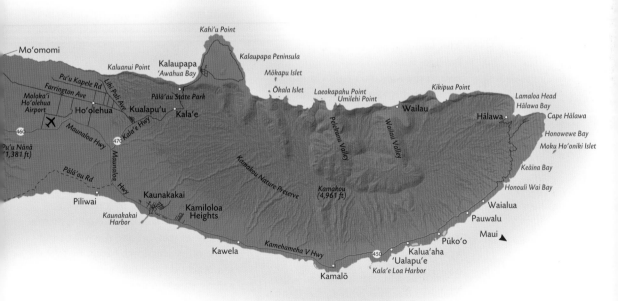

Hotel Moloka'i, P.O. Box 1020, Kaunakakai, Moloka'i 96748. 800-272-5275, 808-553-5347, fax 800-477-2329; info@hotelmolokai.com (www.castlegroup.com). $78–$133

The Hotel Moloka'i, just south of Kaunakakai, is a trip back in time. Although rooms have been recently redecorated, they still seem faded and somewhat dreary. However, service is as friendly as you'd get anywhere, and what the hotel lacks in amenities it makes up for with aloha spirit. There's a small swimming pool adjacent to the beachside restaurant and bar, where there's Hawaiian entertainment each evening.

Ke Nani Kai, P.O. Box 289, Maunaloa, Moloka'i 96770. 800-535-0085, 808-552-2761, fax 808-552-0045. $75–$199

This well-maintained condo complex has one- and two-bedroom units adjacent to the Kaluako'i Golf Course (closed at this writing). There are a swimming pool and spa, tennis courts, barbecues, and daily maid service.

Moloka'i Ranch, P.O. Box 259, Maunaloa, Moloka'i 96770. 877-726-4656, 808-552-2741, fax 808-660-2724; info@molokai-ranch.com (www.molokai-ranch.com). Kaupoa Beach Camp $205–$255; Lodge $305–$355

A welcome addition to Moloka'i, the Moloka'i Ranch is both a great destination vacation spot as well as an ideal place to stay while exploring the fascinating island of Moloka'i. Accommodations include the Kaupoa Beach Camp and the new Lodge in the village of Maunaloa. Whichever place you stay, you can take part in the many ranch activities, or you can just while away the time, listening to gentle breezes waft through the leaves of banana trees and tropical palms. Nights are magnificent. With little manmade light on the island to obscure the night sky, trillions of stars can be seen. Far off across the Pacific, the lights of Honolulu cast a glow on the horizon. The dawn is pink and gentle, with soft birdsongs to lull you awake.

Among the activities available to ranch visitors are horseback riding, mountain biking, hiking, ocean kayaking, ocean rafting, and snorkeling. Also, there are a ropes challenge course and a nine-station archery course.

Spread across manicured green lawns at Kaupoa Beach Camp are what are called "tentalows," basically, bungalows with canvas tops and sides. Each has a private bathroom with a hot shower, open to the sky. Solar energy powers the lights and overhead fan. This is camping in luxury, to say the least. Each unit has two tentalows joined by a redwood deck, ideal for families (though if there's just two of you, no one else will be put in the other tentalow). Meals are taken at a beachside pavilion, where there is nightly entertainment. There's a beautiful sandy beach, with beach umbrellas, chairs, and other beach paraphernalia.

You can snorkel or fish in the crystal-clear waters, take part in the many ranch activities, or just relax in a hammock, away from modern-day distractions. Included in the daily room rate are three meals a day and two ranch activities of your choice.

The new Lodge at Moloka'i Ranch has just 22 guestrooms, each spacious, beautifully furnished, and overlooking ranchland to the Pacific in the distance. Just outside the rooms, coffee trees and bananas grow vigorously, and you're close enough to the horses on the range to watch them romping in the cool mornings. The Lodge is an architectural gem, rustic but luxurious, nicely evocative of plantation architecture of the '20s and '30s. The two-story main hall has six large tree trunks as floor-to-ceiling support posts, 30 feet or so high, and the furnishings are a variety of appropriate period antiques. A painting by renowned Hawai'i artist Juliette May Fraser graces one wall of the great room, vintage photographs abound, and there are original prints in the guestrooms. The Lodge has one of the most magnificent swimming pools of any hotel in Hawai'i. The pool is small but never crowded. It's heated to perfection. There's also a spa with state-of-the-art exercise equipment and saunas. Massage is available. Lodge visitors may participate in all ranch activities for a fee. The only drawback to the Lodge, at least when we were there, is that the restaurant is expensive and the food is mediocre. There is, however, another

restaurant nearby (see below for the Village Grill) as well as a KFC (as in fried chicken) and a general store.

When making reservations, ask about special packages.

Rounding up cattle at Moloka'i Ranch, one of many visitor activities.

Pu'u o Hoku Ranch Country Cottage
P.O. Box 1889, Kaunakakai, Moloka'i 96748. 808-558-8109, fax 808-558-8100; hoku@aloha.net. $85

This rustic two-bedroom cottage near the end of the road in east Moloka'i is a bargain hunter's dream. There are a full kitchen and two baths. The living room has faded but comfortable wicker furniture, lots of books and games, and an amazing view to Maui in the distance. An hour drive from shopping and restaurants, this place isn't for everyone, but for those who like seclusion it's perfect. Activities include hiking, swimming and snorkeling, and horseback riding on the ranch. Also on the property is a lodge with 11 guestrooms that can accommodate 23 people for retreats and meetings ($750/night).

accompanied by *ipu*, drumlike instruments made of gourds. The modern hula, called hula *'auana*, is usually danced to songs with melodies. Its critics say that modern hula came about to please the tourists who started arriving in record numbers in the 1930s and wanted to see dances performed to songs they could understand. Most hula shows today present both ancient and modern forms of hula. The ancient traditions are kept alive by *kumu* hula, or hula teachers, who form their own *hālau*, or dance companies. Once a year, in April, *hālau* from all of the islands and the mainland come together at the Merrie Monarch Festival in Hilo on the Big Island to compete for prizes in hula *kahiko* and hula *'auana*.

According to one legend, Moloka'i was the birthplace of hula, the art form for which Hawai'i is best known. A dancer named La'ila'i is said to have come from the Marquesas to Moloka'i about A.D. 800, and for the next three hundred years the hula remained in La'ila'i's family on Moloka'i. The goddess Laka learned hula about A.D. 1100 from a descendant of La'ila'i and spread it throughout the Hawaiian islands. Thus Laka became known as the goddess of hula, and to this day dances are performed in her honor.

Today two forms of hula are performed. *Hula kahiko* is the traditional dance, performed to *mele* that are chanted in the Hawaiian language,

Dining

Because Moloka'i does not market itself as a tourist destination, there are few restaurants other than those frequented by locals, which generally offer inexpensive, home-style meals. Hours vary; it's a good idea to call ahead.

In the main town of Kaunakakai, the **Hotel Moloka'i** (553-5347) offers seaside dining for breakfast, lunch, and dinner. They have entertainment in the evenings. **Kanemitsu Bakery and Restaurant** (553-5855), located on the main street in town, has a great selection of Moloka'i breads and pastries. Their menu features local-style food. **Outpost Natural Food Store and Juice Bar** (553-3377), next to the Civic Center, has a snack bar that offers good health-food fare, including salads and smoothies. The best pizza on Moloka'i (possibly the only pizza) is at **Moloka'i Pizza Café** (553-3288) on the wharf road, a favorite stop also for sandwiches, pasta dishes, and fresh fish dinners. Kaunakakai's newest eatery is the **Moloka'i Brewing Co.** (553-3946), where a large window opens up to the brewery. Breakfast, lunch, and dinner are served daily.

The only fast food on Moloka'i is a **KFC** (552-2625) in Maunaloa on the west side. The **Village Grill** (552-0012) in Maunaloa offers Moloka'i's best meal, with such imaginative dishes as crisp egg rolls with sweet n' sour cherry guava sauce or wok-seared seafood in spicy Thai sauce. Their specialty is steak, fish, or chicken stone grilled right at the table. The *haupia liliko'i* cream pie is always a favorite. Entrées are reasonably priced ($13.95–$21.50), the staff is super friendly, there's a decent wine list, and everything is delicious. The Village Grill also serves lunch weekdays.

In Kualapu'u in central Moloka'i, **Kamuela's Cookhouse** (567-9655) has recently opened where Kualapu'u Cookhouse used to be. Serving breakfast and lunch every day but Monday and dinner four nights a week, this welcome addition to the Moloka'i scene has delicious food that's reasonably priced. Local-style favorites are served, such as loco moco for breakfast and plate lunches. Dinner entrées range from $7.95 to $14.95, with lower prices for *keiki* and *kūpuna*. Next door is **Coffees of Hawai'i** (567-9023), which has a small café for coffee, pastries, and sandwiches.

Traveling east, roadside stands are few and far between. Best bet is the **Neighborhood Store n' Counter** (558-8498) in Pūko'o between the 15 and 16 mile markers, which is open for breakfast, lunch, and dinner until 6 P.M. They serve plate lunches and sandwiches as well as homemade *malasadas* (Portuguese doughnuts). There are picnic tables for eating outside.

Exploring

Kaunakakai, the island's main town, is a short distance from Moloka'i Airport, on Highway 450 (the town was made famous by Alex Anderson's song "Cockeyed Mayor of Kaunakakai," written in 1935 and performed by Hilo Hattie).

Opposite: Chant and the traditional *ipu* (left photograph) accompany ancient styles of hula, as performed by a group of young girls (right).

molokaʻiʼs **beaches**

Ala Malama, the main street in Kaunakakai.

Kaunakakai is where the island's shops and services are located. The main street, Ala Malama, is lined with mom and pop stores selling groceries, clothing, and souvenir items.

The **Molokaʻi Visitors Association** (553-3876) is on the main highway (450) in Kaunakakai. Stop here to pick up a map and brochures on current activities.

The drive along the east side is truly spectacular. Along the way, 73 stone-walled fishponds line the southern coast. These ponds were built by native Hawaiians to raise saltwater fish, including mullet and milkfish. Many of the fishponds can be seen while driving along the coastal road; watch for stone walls built out into the ocean. Waters along this coast tend to be murky,

but swimming gets better the farther east you go.

At Kamiloloa, several miles outside of Kaunakakai, the endangered state bird, the *nēnē,* is being raised in captivity by **Nēnē o Molokaʻi** (553-5992), a nonprofit organization. Tours of the facility are free but must be scheduled in advance.

Just past the 10 mile marker, at Kamalō, is **Saint Joseph's Church**, built in 1876 by Father Damien. A bronze sculpture of Damien stands in the churchyard. Farther on, at ʻUalapuʻe, is **Our Lady of Sorrows Church**, built by Damien in 1874. Both of these churches are open and can be entered. They are still used for Catholic services and should be treated respectfully. Be sure not to leave any doors open. A

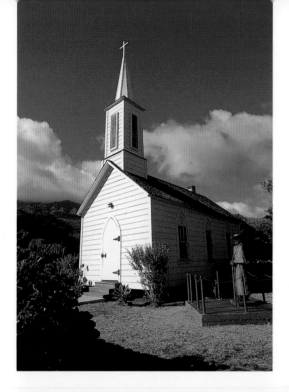

A bronze statue of Father Damien honors the Catholic priest who built tiny Saint Joseph's Church in Kamalō in 1876.

Just before Kaunakakai, on the *makai* side of the road, you'll pass the historic Kapuāiwa Coconut Grove. This royal garden was planted in the 1860s for Kamehameha V, known by his friends as Kapuāiwa. The trees provided a shady spot for the *ali'i* to relax at the beach. Originally 1,000 trees were planted; not all remain, but the grove is still a grand spectacle, especially at sunset.

Watch for falling coconuts; they can kill. This is a good place to collect a coconut or two to take home as a souvenir. Don't bother wrapping them; just keep the outer husk, an excellent natural packing that has served to float coconuts for thousands of miles across open oceans to be dashed by waves, unharmed, upon foreign shores. Not only that, they survive the rough handling of the U.S. Postal Service. Just write the address with a felt-tip pen on the coconut itself—unwrapped—and paste on the necessary postage stamps. The post office actually accepts these unorthodox parcels.

Hālawa Valley is at the end of the road in east Moloka'i.

Left: Bicyclists on the eastern coast.

fishpond across the road from Our Lady of Sorrows is easily seen.

After the 20 mile marker the road becomes very narrow and winding, at the edge of the sea, with no guardrails. At mile 23 it curves inland, continuing narrow and winding. The end of the road is past mile 27, at **Hālawa Valley**. On the final stretch of downhill road, you can see beautiful **Moa'ula Falls** at the back of the valley. Archaeologists

Moa'ula Falls are deep in Hālawa Valley.

Below: Waikolu Valley Lookout is in the Kamakou Nature Preserve.

have found evidence of settlements in Hālawa Valley dating to A.D. 600. Ancient *kalo* terraces and stone-walled enclosures can still be seen. A fairly easily hiked trail leads back to Moa'ula Falls. This 2-mile trail, which is on privately owned land, used to be open to the public. However, because of liability issues, the owner now limits hikes to those led by **Pilipo's Hālawa Falls Cultural Hike** (553-4355).

In the center of the island, Highway 470 (Kala'e Highway) leads to **Pālā'au State Park** on the north shore, over-looking Kalaupapa. Camping is available here at no charge. Permits may be obtained from the Division of State Parks, 54 South High Street, Room 101, Wailuku, Maui 96793 (808-984-8109).

You can hike down to Kalaupapa Peninsula from Pālāʻau State Park; it's a rigorous 4-mile round trip. However, before you set off, it's necessary to get permission to visit the area; the easiest way is to call **Damien Tours** (567-6171 or 567-6675), which charges a reasonable fee for a tour of the settlement (Damien Tours will also arrange air flights to Kalaupapa). The trail is wide though very steep; it descends 1,700 feet with 26 switchbacks. **Molokaʻi Mule Ride** (567-6088) offers guided tours down the trail by sure-footed mules. They'll take care of necessary visitors' permits. Also, fly-in tours by small plane are offered by **Molokaʻi Air Shuttle** (567-6847), **Pacific Wings** (567-6814 or 888-575-4546), and **Paragon Air** (800-428-1231). Children under the age of 16 are not permitted in the settlement.

Remote, windswept, and quiet, **Kalaupapa** is where Hawaiʻi's lepers were isolated before there was a cure for the disease. It is one of the most beautiful spots in the world. Seeing it today,

Above: Riding mules down to Kalaupapa.

Right: Seacliffs line the coast on Kalaupapa Peninsula.

Father Damien, known as the Leper Priest, cared for the lepers at Kalaupapa until he himself succumbed to Hansen's disease.

Top: The settlement at Kalaupapa, ca. 1895.

Called by the Hawaiians *maʻi pākē*, or Chinese disease, leprosy was brought to the Hawaiian islands about 1830, though whether from China or elsewhere is not known. At that time the sugar planters were bringing in workers by the thousands from all over the world, who toiled 54 hours a week to bring home about 50 cents a day in pay. These immigrants brought with them new diseases that the Hawaiian population was unable to fight. There was no cure for leprosy. The only solution was to isolate known lepers, and so men, women, and children with the disease were taken, often forcibly, to Kalaupapa, a remote peninsula on Molokaʻi's north shore, surrounded by 1,600-foot cliffs and the rough sea.

At Kalaupapa, lepers lived in government housing with little social structure or medical care. The criminal element, having nothing to lose since they were vanquished to Kalaupapa until their death, wreaked havoc in the community. The few doctors who came to treat the lepers avoided all personal contact. Eventually, moved by the plight of the lepers, Christian ministers, among them the Belgian priest Joseph Damien de Veuster, came to their aid. Father

Damien, a member of the Hawaiian mission of the Sacred Hearts, lived among the lepers for sixteen years, loving and caring for society's outcasts until he himself succumbed to the disease in 1889. A statue of Father Damien now represents Hawai'i in the Statuary Hall in the U.S. Capitol.

Leprosy became known as Hansen's disease after the Norwegian scientist who in 1873 identified the bacteria that transmitted it. It was not until the early 1940s, with the discovery of sulfa drugs, that Hansen's disease could be treated. Meanwhile, other people followed in Damien's lead to bring a better life to the residents of Kalaupapa. The settlement became no longer just a place to die, but a place where meaningful lives could be led.

Once there was a cure for Hansen's disease, there was no reason for sufferers of the disease to remain isolated. However, many people living in Kalaupapa wished to remain there for the rest of their days. Further, the Hawai'i state government did not officially recognize until 1969 that isolation was an obsolete treatment for leprosy. Today less than 100 people still live in the settlement. So that the area might be preserved, Kalaupapa became a National Park in 1980. It is not yet known what will happen to the simple wooden structures that were home for the 8,000 people who were forced to live out their lives separated from family and friends.

The cemetery at Kalawao on Kalaupapa Peninsula. Many graveyards line this beautiful coast.

it's difficult to imagine the awful despair that must once have overwhelmed its inhabitants. A trip to Kalaupapa should be high on every visitor's list. The experience is unforgettable.

At **Coffees of Hawai'i** (567-9023) in Kualapu'u (central Moloka'i), visitors can take a mule-drawn wagon tour of a working coffee plantation. There is a shop for coffee and related gift items

where Molokaʻi coffee is sold by the pound for a reasonable price. The espresso bar is a good place for a drink and snack. On Lihi Pali Avenue in nearby Hoʻolehua is **Purdy's Macadamia Nut Farm** (567-6601), where owner native Hawaiian Tuddie Purdy leads free tours through a seventy-year-old working farm; both fresh nuts and honey are sold.

The village of **Maunaloa**, a former pineapple plantation town, is being revitalized by the new tourist-oriented development of Molokaʻi Ranch. Now home to a movie theater with first-run films (552-2707), an art gallery and gift store, a colorful kite store, a gas station, and several eateries, the town is expected to grow as tourist activities pick up.

Kepuhi Beach on Molokaʻi's west side.

Pāpōhaku Beach.

Left: Jonathan Socher operates Big Wind Kite Factory in Maunaloa.

Along Moloka'i's western shore, **Pāpōhaku Beach** is a splendid, 3-mile stretch of golden sand. The extraordinarily wide beach is bordered by *kiawe* trees, with houses few and far between. Your own footprints are the only one's you're likely to see. Swim here with caution. In the winter especially the surf is high and currents are strong. O'ahu is visible less than 30 miles to the northwest.

Activities

Because Moloka'i has not been developed for tourists, the range of activities is limited. However, you'll find friendly, knowledgeable guides who will devote a great deal of attention to your needs since they are not likely to be overly busy.

For golfers, there's the **Ironwood Hills Golf Club** (567-6000), a 9-hole, par 34 course in central Moloka'i, in the cool upcountry town of Kala'e. The 18-hole Kaluako'i Golf Course, once a championship facility, has been closed and is up for sale.

Horseback riding is available at **Pu'u o Hoku Ranch** (558-8109), on the east side not far from the end of the road at Hālawa Valley. The countryside here is rugged and spectacular. The ranch offers 1- and 2-hour rides as well as adventure rides. An all-day excursion takes you

Right: Mountain biking along north shore cliffs led by Moloka'i Ranch Outfitters.

Below: A Moloka'i Ranch kayaking tour.

to a secluded waterfall where you can swim and picnic.

Moloka'i offers a variety of challenges for the biker, with steep climbs alternating with long stretches of level landscape. Roads are lightly traveled and most have wide shoulders. Biking information and rentals are available from **Moloka'i Bicycle** (553-3931 or 553-3931) in Kaunakakai. Mountain biking treks on the private Pu'u o Hoku Ranch on the lush east side of Moloka'i are offered by Phillip Kikukawa, a Moloka'i native and owner of Moloka'i Bicycle.

Moloka'i Ranch Outfitters Center (552-2791) offers a range of adventure activities, including horseback riding, mountain biking, cultural hikes, zodiac tours, whale watching and snorkeling, kayaking, and a ropes challenge course.

Moloka'i Ranch is fast becoming a mountain biking mecca. With over 100

miles of trails on the island's west side, the ranch attracts serious bikers from all over the world. An easy trail for novices goes about 7 miles from the ranch's headquarters in Maunaloa down to Kaupoa Beach. A full-day ride for experienced cyclists goes to the majestic north shore sea cliffs where there are panoramic views of the peninsula of Kalaupapa.

Also headquartered at the ranch is **Historical Hikes West Moloka'i** (553-9803), which offers 2- to 6-hour guided hikes ranging from easy walks focusing on archaeological sites to an all-day trek from the mountain to the sea on a five-hundred-year-old trail.

Snorkeling and whale-watching tours are available from **Bill Kapuni's Snorkel and Dive Adventure** (553-9867),

Kawākiu Nui Beach, on the west side, is known by residents as Make Horse ("dead horse") Beach, no doubt because a horse once found its grave here.

The setting sun at Kaunakakai.

Fun Hogs Hawai'i (567-6789), and also **Moloka'i Charters** (553-5852).

Charter boats are available for deep-sea fishing from **Alyce C.** (558-8377) and **Fun Hogs Hawai'i** (567-6789).

Several outfits offer guided hiking tours of various areas of Moloka'i, including **Moloka'i Outdoor Activities** (553-4477), located in the lobby of the Hotel Moloka'i. **Waterfall Adventures** (558-8464) offers hiking, rock climbing, swimming, bird watching, and photography tours for all levels.

Monthly guided hikes of the Kamakou and Mo'omomi nature preserves—one native rainforests and shrublands in the east, the other windswept dunes on the northwest coast—are offered by the **Nature Conservancy of Hawai'i**. Write the conservancy at P.O. Box 220, Kualapu'u, Moloka'i 96757, or call 553-5236 for information.

lāna'i

For privacy and romance swathed in luxury,
no place can top the island of Lāna'i. What Lāna'i lacks in tropical splendor it
makes up for with the peace and tranquility it offers in an unparalleled natural
setting. Fantasies come true at either of the two luxury resorts that dominate the
island, though even a day trip to Lāna'i will provide memorable experiences.

An arid volcanic rock in the lee of the West Maui Mountains (and part of Maui
County), Lāna'i today has a resident population of some 2,800. Never heavily popu-
lated by Hawaiians, the island was developed as a Mormon community in
the 19th century after Chief Ha'alelea allowed the Mormons to use his land free
of charge. In 1861 the Mormon Walter Murray Gibson bought most of the island,
using church money. A crafty fellow, he managed to put the land in his own name,
not in that of the church. His descendants sold the land to Charles Gay, who from
1902 to 1909 tried unsuccessfully to upgrade sheep ranching operations that had
been started by Gibson. In 1909 a group of local businessmen formed the
Lāna'i Company and purchased most of the land from Gay for a cattle ranch. Under
George Munro, brought in in 1911 to manage the ranch, it prospered. It was Munro
who planted the magnificent Norfolk Island pines that now cover the upland areas,
creating a watershed in the lush Lāna'ihale mountains.

The island was purchased by the Dole Company in the early 1920s for
a little over a million dollars. Dole turned Lāna'i into the world's largest pineapple
plantation, with a company town, Lāna'i City, as its centerpiece. Lāna'i then
became known as the Pineapple Island. But with the decline of U.S. pineapple
production, as cheaper Asian producers took over, Castle & Cooke, owners of
Dole, led by CEO David Murdock, closed the pineapple operation in the early
1990s and began to lure thousands of tourists to the island with the opening of
two luxury hotels. The Lodge at Kō'ele, with 102 rooms, opened in 1990, followed
a year later by the 250-room Mānele Bay Hotel. Both are consistently ranked
among the top hotels in the world, combining sophistication and elegance with
the gentle aloha spirit and easy lifestyle of a Pacific island. Currently under
development by Castle & Cooke are luxury townhouses and single-family
homes, clustered around each of the resort's two golf courses.

Although many residents initially opposed the hotels, they have proven a tremendous boost to the local economy, providing much-needed jobs and even bringing back young people who had moved away. Whatever they may think of Murdock, local residents go out of their way to welcome tourists with a warm aloha. People are as friendly here as anyplace in Hawai'i.

Lāna'i is usually sunny and warm around its shores and cool and misty upland. Temperatures average 71 to 77 degrees. If you're staying in the cool upcountry Lodge or the Hotel Lāna'i, you will probably want a sweater for cool evenings, when temperatures can dip into the 60s. Dress at the hotels tends to be more formal than it is at other Maui resorts. It's not unusual to see men in jackets, especially at the Lodge, where jackets are required in the Formal Dining Room.

Pages 270–71: A lovely gazebo on the grounds of the Lodge at Kō'ele.

Koi grace the ponds on the grounds of the Mānele Bay Hotel.

Getting There

Hawaiian Airlines (800-367-5320) and **Island Air** (800-323-3345) offer frequent flights from Honolulu, Hawaiian by jet and Island Air by twin-engine plane. The trip takes about half an hour. If you're going to Lāna'i directly from Maui, the trip takes more than 2 hours by air with a stopover in Honolulu. A happy alternative is to take the ferry from Lahaina.

The **Expeditions** Lahaina–Lāna'i passenger ferry (808-661-3756) makes several trips a day, leaving Lahaina Harbor at the public dock in front of Pioneer Inn. The hour-long ride offers magnificent views. If you can take the ferry back at sunset, all the better. As the sun sets over Lāna'i, it lights up Haleakalā across the channel and gives a warm pink hue to the mighty Pacific. The cost is about $25 each way (pay at the dock; credit cards okay). Reservations are required.

Unfortunately, leaving your car in Lahaina can be costly. Since most free parking is limited to 2 or 3 hours, and overnight parking is not permitted, the only sure option is a pay lot. The lot behind Burger King on Front Street costs $14 for 24 hours (pay in advance). There's a free public lot on Luakini Street in Lahaina, but it's usually full.

Pacific Wings (888-575-4546), a relatively new commuter airline, offers direct service from Kahului to Lāna'i, with two flights daily.

All scheduled flights and ferry arrivals on Lāna'i are met by shuttle service, for which there is a small charge. Private limousine service is available; ask about this when you make hotel reservations.

Getting Around

The two resort hotels offer a shuttle service from one to the other, with a stop in Lāna'i City. However, this is available only for hotel guests as well as guests of the Hotel Lāna'i. **Dollar Rent**

a Car has a desk at **Lāna'i City Service**, a gas station at 1036 Lāna'i Avenue in Lāna'i City (565-7227; or call Dollar at 800-342-7398). Cars and four-wheel drives are available; rates are high. Lāna'i City Service also offers taxi service. **Red Rover** in Lāna'i City (565-7722) rents out Land Rovers equipped with cell phones and beach gear, perfect for exploring Lāna'i's unpaved roads. Suburbans can be rented from **Adventure Lāna'i Eco Centre** (565-7737). Gas is pricey. You might want to consider renting a four-wheel drive just for an excursion and making do the rest of the time with taxis, bikes, and the hotel shuttles (should you be a resort guest).

the island of **lāna'i**

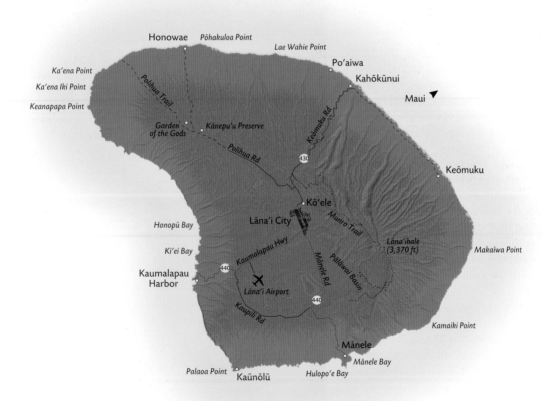

Accommodations

Central reservations for the Lodge
at Kō'ele and the Mānele Bay Hotel:
800-321-4666, fax 808-565-3868;
e-mail: reservations@lanai-resorts.com
(www.lanai-resorts.com). Reservations
also may be made through the Starwood
Luxury Collection. Guest privileges, such
as swimming pools, fitness facilities, and
the like, are shared by both hotels. Rates
at the Lodge range from $375 to $2,000;
at the Mānele Bay Hotel from $350 to
$2,500 for the presidential suite. Adven-
ture, golf, wedding, and honeymoon
packages are available.

The Lodge at Kō'ele (808-565-7300)
settles into the Hawaiian landscape as
if it had been there hundreds of years.
Situated at an elevation of 1,600 feet
and nestled among towering Norfolk
pines, it has 102 exquisitely decorated
rooms. The centerpiece of the Lodge
is the Great Hall, with immense stone
fireplaces at either end. Comfortably
and elegantly furnished with antiques
from the Orient and artifacts from the
Pacific, the Great Hall is a gathering
place for guests at any time of day. At
one side is the Terrace Restaurant, with
views to the gardens. Tucked away in a
corner is the very elegant Formal Dining
Room, where men don jackets at night.
While both restaurants are noted for their
gourmet cuisine, the Dining Room
appears consistently on lists of top restaurants in the world. Tea (complimentary

The Lodge at Kō'ele.

to guests at either hotel) is served in the afternoon, complete with cookies and scones. Each of the spacious guestrooms has a four-poster bed and is decorated with art and antiques.

The Lodge is designed to replicate an English country manor, complete with lawn bowling and croquet. Serpentine pathways meander through magnificent gardens, and wild turkeys strut across manicured lawns. The heated pool, rarely crowded, is a perfect spot to spend languid afternoons. A small fitness center adjoins the pool. The Greg Norman–designed championship golf course, the Experience at Kō'ele (see page 191), is adjacent to the Lodge, in a forested setting surrounded by tall pines and lush mountain vegetation. For ocean activities, Hulopo'e Beach is just a 20-minute shuttle ride away.

Wild turkeys strut across the lawn in front of the Experience at Kō'ele Clubhouse.

Right: Pathways meander through the Lodge's manicured English-style gardens.

The Lodge's carefully crafted image is that of a grande dame of hotels, the kind of place Rockefellers and DuPonts would have frequented. Today, dot.com millionaires, celebrities, and just ordinary folk find it a heavenly retreat from busy lives.

Mānele Bay Hotel (808-565-7700) sits on a cliff overlooking Hulopo'e Bay, amid lavish Hawaiian, Japanese, and Chinese gardens. Beautiful Hulopo'e Beach is just a short walk away. The architecture is a blend of traditional Hawaiian and Mediterranean styles.

The Mānele Bay Hotel with new town-homes in the fore-ground, overlooking Hulopo'e Beach.

Opposite, top: The Mānele Bay's swimming pool.

Bottom: Hulopo'e Beach, used by guests of both luxury hotels as well as other visitors and residents, is the best swimming beach on Lāna'i.

Guestrooms are large and lavishly decorated with art and antiques. You can even stay in a suite with your very own butler. Larger and more bustling than the Lodge at Kō'ele, Mānele Bay has an excellent spa and fitness facility where exercise sessions, massage, sauna and steam rooms, Swedish showers, and a full range of beauty treatments are available. One-on-one yoga classes are held in the hotel gardens. Also, there is a tennis center with six plexipave courts. For dining, there is the award-winning Ihilani Restaurant, along with several more informal choices. Surrounding

the hotel is a Jack Nicklaus–designed 18-hole golf course, the Challenge at Mānele (page 191). The course is built on 350 acres atop natural lava outcroppings and set among native *kiawe* and *'ilima* trees. Mānele Bay is consistently awarded top honors for its location, decor, and service. It is the best resort hotel in Hawai'i according to the readers of *Condé Nast Traveler*.

The resort's Pililaloha (Friendship) Children's Program is based at the Mānele Bay (a shuttle is provided for children from the Lodge). Activities include a Hawaiian *lū'au*, snorkeling,

tennis, even golf at the putting green at Kōʻele. Local children often participate in the program, providing a rich cultural experience for all.

A collection of ancient Lānaʻi artifacts collected by the Bishop Museum in Honolulu was returned to the island in 1991 and now can be seen at the Lānaʻi Conference Center, adjacent to the Mānele Bay Hotel. Included are implements reflective of Hawaiian culture—canoe parts, fishing and work tools, lamps, and weapons. The six-room Conference Center can accommodate up to 300 people for meetings.

Hotel Lāna'i, Lāna'i City, 800-795-7211, 808-565-7211, fax 808-565-6450; hotellanai@aloha.net (www.onlanai.com). This charming, cozy inn was built in 1923 to house guests of pineapple czar Jim Dole. From its veranda you can relax on white wicker furniture overlooking towering Norfolk pines surrounding the hotel and Lāna'i City's town square. Brightly decorated rooms have natural wood floors, old-style fixtures, and pretty quilts. Continental breakfast is included in the room rate. Rates are quite reasonable ($95–$105). Ideal for families, an adjacent plantation-style cottage ($140) features period furnishings and a four-poster canopy bed.

Owner Henry Clay Richardson took over the Hotel Lāna'i in 1996. A native of New Orleans and a graduate of the Culinary Institute of America, he has brought good country-style cooking with a Cajun twist to the hotel's restaurant, now named **Henry Clay's Rotisserie**. His herb-marinated rotisserie chicken, seafood gumbo, and pecan pie are favorites of visitors and locals alike. Open daily for dinner only; reservations suggested (565-7211).

There are several B&Bs in Lāna'i City offering rooms for under $100. **Momi's** (808-565-9520) is recommended by locals as being very clean with lots of flowers; she has two bedrooms, each with private bath. **Bed & Breakfast Pacific Hawai'i** (800-999-6026) has several listings on Lāna'i.

Dreams Come True B&B (800-566-6961, 808-565-6961, fax 808-565-7056; hunters@aloha.net; www.go-native.com/Inns/0117.html) has three bedrooms with private and shared baths in a plantation-style home amid tropical gardens. Innkeepers Michael and Susan Hunter live in a separate cottage. A continental breakfast with fruit and fresh-baked bread is provided daily. Also available from Dreams Come True are vacation rental homes with up to four bedrooms. Rentals are $198 to $350 per night.

Trilogy (888-628-4800, 808-565-9303; www.visitlanai.com), the folks best known for their first-rate snorkel/dive tours, offers three-night Lāna'i packages that include accommodations, a Jeep Wrangler, and a variety of ocean adventures, depending on the package. Prices range from $444 to $1,045 for three nights and include transportation from Lahaina. A five-day windsurfing adventure is $1,250.

Exploring

Lāna'i is 13 miles wide by 18 miles north to south, with elevations varying from sea level to nearly 3,400 feet. With only 30 miles of paved roads, a four-wheel-drive vehicle is necessary to explore the island's other 100 unpaved miles. Much of the landscape is arid and barren, with scrubby trees and fallow fields. High iron count gives the soil and rocks a rich palette of reds. The only lush tropical greenery to be found is at the resort hotels, where it is mostly in the form of

lāna'i's beaches

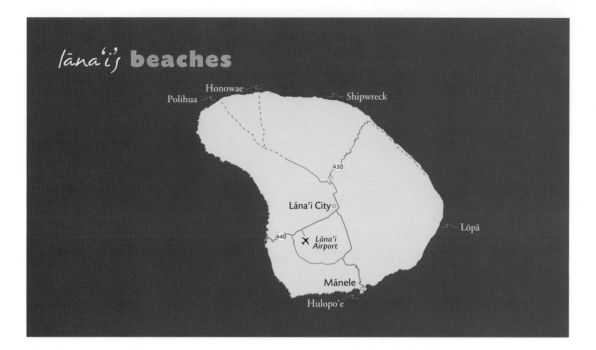

Honowae
Polihua
Shipwreck

430

Lāna'i City

440

× Lāna'i Airport

Lōpā

Mānele

Hulopo'e

transplants. However, there is a certain haunting beauty to Lāna'i's rugged landscape that beckons the traveler to explore it.

The Lodge at Kō'ele or the Mānele Bay Hotel will pack you a lunch before you set off on an adventure. Don't look for peanut butter and jelly and an apple; they'll provide a great gourmet feast complete with backpack.

Remember that this is private land and you are a guest of the owner. All efforts should be made not to disturb the natural landscape, and all refuse should be removed.

Hulopo'e Beach, site of the Mānele Bay Hotel, is an exquisite crescent of golden sand. Swimming is good, though the currents can be strong in winter.

Hulopo'e Bay is a marine conservation area abundant with tropical fish. At the left of the bay is excellent snorkeling, but you have to get there in the morning before the crowds of snorkelers brought in by tour boats leave the water too stirred up for good visibility.

The **Kānepu'u Preserve**, about 5 miles from the Lodge on an unpaved road, is maintained by the Nature Conservancy of Hawai'i. This rare native dryland forest has 48 plant species unique to Hawai'i, including *olopua* (native olive) trees, *lama* (native ebony) trees, and the endangered Hawaiian gardenia *(nā'ū)* and sandalwood *('iliahi)* trees, which are found nowhere else in Hawai'i. A self-guided trail introduces visitors to the preserve.

The awe-inspiring Garden of the Gods, an arid desert that changes colors with the passing of the sun, is the site of at least one petroglyph, a carving in stone of a human figure made by early Hawaiians hundreds of years ago.

Past the Kānepuʻu Preserve, the road becomes rugged and a four-wheel drive is required. About 6 miles from the Lodge is what is called the **Garden of the Gods**, an eerie landscape of huge boulders that takes on magnificent colors depending on the time of day. Small cairns erected by visitors, presumably as offerings to the gods, actually disturb the natural landscape, and volunteers are working to remove them. Another 5 miles leads to **Polihua Beach**, a nesting ground for green sea turtles. The white sand beach is an ideal place for a picnic, but the currents are strong and swimming here would be foolish.

Shipwreck Beach can be reached by hiking 8 miles from Polihua Beach or by a winding 8-mile road north from the Lodge at Kōʻele; a four-wheel-drive vehicle is necessary once the shoreline is reached. A shallow reef about 200 feet offshore holds the hulk of an abandoned World War II freighter. On the rocky beach is broken timber from the sailing schooner *Helene Port Townsend,* out of Puget Sound half a century ago. You can walk along this windswept, secluded beach for miles or take a Jeep on the 14-mile unpaved shoreline road. Warning: swimming on this shore is extremely hazardous.

Keōmuku Village, once a thriving sugar settlement, has been a ghost town since the early 20th century. The area, about 6 miles southeast of Shipwreck Beach, includes **Kaheʻa Heiau**, a native Hawaiian place of worship. According to local lore, the sugar company failed because its builders disrupted the *heiau* by removing its stones to build a railroad track, thus bringing on the wrath of the gods. A weathered wooden church, a reminder of the thriving community that once existed here, sits nestled amid palms.

Lōpā Beach is a remote beach beyond Keōmuku. Residents sometimes fish here with nets and spears, just as their ancestors did.

Polihua Beach is a nesting ground for green sea turtles. Molokaʻi can be seen across the Kalohi Channel.

Traveling on the
Munro Trail in a Jeep.

Below: A view of Maui
from along a Lāna'i trail.

Kaūnōlū, a deserted precontact Hawaiian village in southwest Lāna'i, was once a vigorous fishing community. Now a National Historic Landmark, it contains remains of house platforms, stone shelters, and **Halulu Heiau**, a place of refuge still in use at the end of the 18th century. Kamehameha I had a summer fishing place here in the 19th century.

The **Munro Trail**, named after naturalist George Munro who planted the magnificent Norfolk Island pines that line the trail, winds up an 8-mile dirt road from Kō'ele, through mountain grasslands and forests of native *'ōhi'a,* pine, ironwood, and eucalyptus. The highest point is the 3,370-foot summit of Lāna'ihale. From here on a clear day there are spectacular views of every Hawaiian island save Kaua'i. It's a 2-hour trip by four-wheel drive, or you can hike all or part of the trail. This trip should not be attempted in the rain, when parts of the road may be impassable.

The **Luahiwa petroglyph field** is at the base of a steep cliff overlooking the **Pālāwai Basin**, not far from the end of the Munro Trail; it is reachable from the trail or from unpaved roads through old pineapple fields. Boulders covered with petroglyphs are strewn over three acres. The area is said to be dedicated to the gods of fertility. Note that not all the carvings here are authentic. Many, such as those depicting dogs with leashes, were drawn by mischievous schoolboys at the end of the 19th century.

Petroglyphs—line drawings on rocks, carved hundreds of years ago by ancient Hawaiians—can be found on all the Hawaiian islands. These drawings offer an insight into the culture of the early settlers of Hawai'i, but they raise more questions than they answer. Probably no one will ever be able to unlock the meanings of these amazing drawings.

On Lāna'i, there is a large field of several hundred petroglyphs at Luahiwa, a three-acre field in the middle of the island at the base of steep cliffs. There is also a well-preserved field of petroglyphs on a short, well-marked trail near Shipwreck Beach, on the rugged north shore of the island. And in the Garden of the Gods, an awesome, windswept desert with wonderfully colored rock formations, there is at least one ancient petroglyph depicting a human figure.

The best viewing times are 7 to 10 A.M. or 3 to 6 P.M., when the sun is not directly overhead. Visitors should be careful not to walk directly on petroglyphs or to remove stones from their natural sites.

Many of the hand-painted ceiling, wall, and floor decorations at the Lodge at Kō'ele were executed by local artists in a unique program in which residents were asked to assist with interior decor under the direction of San Francisco artist John Wullbrandt and Lāna'i resident Sol Kahoohalahala, who acted as cultural advisor. Floral paintings on guestroom doors are by Loretta Pa'ahana Hera, who works as a teacher's aide in the Lāna'i school program. Descriptive calligraphy on the doors was executed by her daughter-in-law, Rohana Hera. Original oil paintings by local artists, including colorful depictions of Lāna'i's old plantation homes by Pam Andelin, hang in each guestroom. All artists were paid for their work. Continuing art programs for Lāna'i residents take place at the Lāna'i Arts and Culture Center in Lāna'i City (565-7503), where classes are held (visitors are welcome) and artwork by local residents is showcased.

Above: Pam Andelin,
Lāna'i City, oil on canvas.

Lāna'i City

Sleepy Lāna'i City was laid out in the 1920s with geometrically organized streets in alphabetical and numerical order. The heart of the town is a village green with towering Norfolk Island pines. Surrounding the green are a post office and two banks, a movie theater with double features five nights of the week, small shops, two general stores, and local eateries. Nearly everything is closed on Sundays, and shops often close midday for lunch. Residents live in colorful plantation cottages, many with small gardens of vegetables and flowers.

Blue Ginger Café at 409 7th Street (565-6363), open daily from 6 A.M. to 9 P.M., is probably the most popular eating place. They serve salads, sandwiches, pastries, plate lunches, and daily lunch and dinner specials. You order at the counter and eat inside on roomy oilcloth-covered tables or on the front porch.

Tanigawa's at 419 7th Street (565-6537) is another favorite for plate lunches and hamburgers. Open from 6:30 A.M. to 1 P.M., it's usually closed by the time we get there. **Pele's Other Garden** at 8th and Houston Streets (565-9628) serves deli sandwiches, pasta salads, and pizzas at nice tables on their lanai; also, they'll pack a picnic basket for your lunch. Lāna'i City has a new place for a great cup of coffee: **Coffee Works** at 604 Ilima Street (565-6962), around the corner from Blue Ginger Café, is open six days a week; they plan to have live music "once in a while."

Richard's Shopping Center at 434 8th Street (565-6047) is an old-style general store that sells everything from jeans to groceries to cold wine and beer; closed Sundays. **Pine Isle Market** at 356 8th Street (565-6488), also a general store, is closed Sundays too.

Akamai Trading at 408 8th Street (565-6587) *is* open Sundays, 9 A.M.–1 P.M. They sell mocha drinks, soft ice cream, gifts, toys, and good quality tee shirts made specially for them.

Several new shops have opened around the town square, the most exciting of which is the **Local Gentry** at 363 7th Street (565-9130), a clothing boutique with an excellent selection of bathing suits and casual and evening wear. Owner Jenna Gentry has brought big-city style to small-town Lāna'i. **Gifts with Aloha** at 363 7th Street (565-6589) is a family-run business, owned by Kim and Phoenix Dupree, with a good selection of local artwork and crafts. Adventure John of **Adventure Lāna'i Eco Centre** on 8th Street (565-7373) has opened a surf shop with swimsuits, board shorts, and dive and snorkeling equipment. Also new is **T&T Fragrance** at 431 7th Street, where owner Eva Batoon sells fresh flowers, leis, perfumes, and gift baskets.

Activities

This is what Lāna'i does not have: fast-food shops, traffic lights, nightclubs, shopping centers, buildings more than two stories high, tour buses—the list goes on. But don't be fooled. There's plenty to do, including golf, hiking, biking, sailing and ocean rafting, snorkeling and scuba diving, fishing, horseback riding, sporting clays, and exploring by four-wheel-drive vehicle.

Lāna'i's luxury resorts provide golf enthusiasts with two stunning courses (see page 191). There's also the free-to-residents, 9-hole **Cavendish Golf Course** just outside Lāna'i City, where there is a box by the first tee in which visitors are asked to leave a donation. Refreshments are by the honor system too; if you take a cold drink you leave payment in a small box. There are no tee times; you just show up.

The Lāna'i coast is rated among the ten best spots in the world for diving, and the best dive/snorkel tour of that coast is offered by **Trilogy** (565-9303 or 888-628-4800) aboard sailing catamarans with all gear provided. A half-day cruise departs daily from Mānele Small Boat Harbor. For first-time divers, Trilogy offers a daily complimentary scuba course at the Mānele Bay Hotel pool.

Trilogy also offers dolphin watches and ocean kayak adventures on the Lāna'i coast. **Windsurf Lāna'i**, for experienced sailors, is Trilogy's latest adventure activity (same numbers as

Trilogy's custom dive boat *Manele Kai* operates out of Mānele Small Boat Harbor.

above). If you're in reasonably good condition and can water start, they'll take you to remote north shore beaches where you'll have the sail of a lifetime. This seasonal activity (April–October) is available for groups as well as individuals. You can make a day trip from Lahaina, or, if you wish, Trilogy will arrange accommodations on Lāna'i.

Adventure tours of the island led by Adventure John (aka Kayak John) are offered by **Adventure Lāna'i Eco Centre** (565-7737 or 565-7373). They'll also rent you just about anything you'll need for your own adventure: camping gear, kayaks, mountain bikes, scuba and snorkeling gear, and 4x4 Suburban vans.

Spinning Dolphin Charters (808-565-6613) offers fishing and whale-watching trips on the 28-foot *Spinning Dolphin,* captained by local fisherman Jeff Menze (his wife, Sherry, is the harbormaster). Local game fish include Pacific blue marlin, silver and striped marlin, and yellowfin and bluefin tuna.

The Stables at Kō'ele (565-4424) offer 1- and 2-hour walking rides with Western tack. A private trail ride allows experienced riders to go at a faster pace. Lunch rides and lessons (both Western and English saddle) are also available. Rates begin at $40 for a 1-hour ride. Wear long pants and shoes; the stable provides helmets that are disguised as straw cowboy hats, so you needn't feel like a wimp wearing your helmet. Trails wind through Lāna'i's rugged countryside, offering a glimpse of the island's wildlife, trees, and flowers and sweeping views across the channel to the island of Moloka'i.

Lāna'i Pine Sporting Clays (565-4600) is a rustic 14-stand course in a pine-wooded valley above the Lodge at Kō'ele. The game of sporting clays has been around since the early 1900s when British gunmakers began playing sporting clays for informal target practice. The Lāna'i course is designed to appeal to both skilled and new shooters alike. Sporting clays can be enjoyed by individuals and groups, including families with children. Several different kinds of games are possible on the course—compact sporting, skeet shooting, and wobble trap—all of which utilize clays launched to simulate flight or running patterns of particular game species, such as duck, quail, dove, pheasant, or even rabbit. Introductory classes are available for those who have no idea how to shoot a gun, and a variety of shotguns are available for rent. Information is available from Lāna'i Company, 800-321-4666 or 808-565-4600.

The new **Lāna'i Pine Archery Range** (565-4600) serves novice, intermediate, and advanced players with 15- and 35-yard ranges. A sport for all ages, archery can be learned by any youth who can safely handle a light bow. Certified instructors offer private and group lessons. The 12-station archery range takes full advantage of the dramatic natural beauty of the surrounding countryside in Lāna'i's central highlands, a few miles north of the Lodge at Kō'ele. The range affords spectacular views of Moloka'i and Maui.

A stand for shooting, at Lāna'i Pine Sporting Clays.

Horseback riding at
the Stables at Kō'ele.

Lāna'i may be isolated, but it's no cultural backwater. Through the Lāna'i Visiting Artist Program, the Lodge at Kō'ele and the Mānele Bay Hotel serve as hosts to internationally renowned musicians, writers, performers, chefs, Hollywood personalities, and others. Informal programs are presented throughout the year by the visiting artists for the hotel guests as well as for the Lāna'i community, who have had the opportunity to meet and talk with such luminaries as André Watts, Garrison Keillor, Jane Smiley, and Dave Barry. All programs are free of charge. Chefs offer complimentary cooking classes as well as dinners at a fixed price, for which reservations are a must.

Glossary *of* Hawaiian *and* Local-Style Words

For fish served in Hawai'i's restaurants, see page 235.

ali'i	ancient Hawaiian royalty
aloha	greeting or farewell; love, kindness, affection, or goodwill
'aumakua	family or personal god
hala	pandanus, or screw pine, tree; it has long, narrow leaves
hālau	dance troupe; meeting house; house for canoes
hale	house, traditionally thatched with *ti* or palm leaves
haole	foreigner to Hawai'i
hau	lowland flowering tree, often with impenetrable thickets
haupia	coconut pudding or custard
heiau	place of worship
ho'olaule'a	celebration
hula *'auana*	modern style of hula
hula *kahiko*	ancient style of hula; also known as hula *'ōlapa*
hula *ku'i*	transitional hula form, combining the old with 19th-century European styles of dancing
imu	underground oven
kahuna	priest, minister, expert in any field (pl. *kāhuna*)
kalo	taro
kālua	to bake in an *imu*
kama'āina	native-born or longtime Hawai'i resident
kāne	man
kapa	tapa, barkcloth
kapu	taboo, forbidden

katsu	deep-fried chicken, fish, or pork with a savory coating (Japanese)
kaukau	food
keiki	child
kiawe	mesquite tree; the wood is often used for grilling
koa	large native forest tree, valued for its fine wood
koi	carp
kōkua	help, assistance
kou	tree used by early Hawaiians for cups, dishes, and calabashes
kukui	candlenut tree
kumu	teacher
kupuna	old person, grandparent (pl. *kūpuna*)
lanai	porch or balcony (*lānai* in Hawaiian)
lau	leaf
lauhala	pandanus leaf, used in plaiting
laulau	food, usually pork or fish, wrapped in *ti* or banana leaves and baked in the *imu* or steamed
liliko'i	passionfruit
limu	seaweed
loco moco	rice topped with a hamburger, fried eggs, and lots of gravy; a favorite local breakfast
lomi **salmon**	highly seasoned relish made with dried salmon and chopped onions and tomatoes
lū'au	Hawaiian feast, named for the *kalo* leaves always served at them

mahalo — thank you

maka'ainana — ordinary men and women

makahiki — annual celebration, with sports and religious festivals, at the beginning of the winter solstice; today the Aloha Festival

makai — toward the ocean; on the ocean side of the road (given as a direction)

malasada — Portuguese doughnut

malihini — newcomer, visitor

māmane — native tree; the hard wood was used for sled runners and shovels

manapua — steamed bun filled with barbecued pork

mauka — toward the mountains; on the mountain side of the road (given as a direction)

maunaloa — vine with blue or white flowers used for leis

mele — chant, song

milo — tree used for shade, wood, and medicine

mochi — Japanese rice cake

mokihana — shrub with waxy leaves and light green berries, used for leis

musubi — mound of sushi rice topped with a slice of Spam and wrapped with a strip of *nori* (seaweed)

mu'umu'u — long, loose dress for women, usually made of a bright, flowery print

nēnē — Hawaiian goose; Hawai'i's state bird

'ohana — family

'ōhelo — small native shrub in the cranberry family; its red or yellow berries are edible raw or cooked for sauce

'ōhi'a — native hardwood tree

'ono — delicious (there is a fish named *ono*)

paniolo — cowboy

pili — grass used for thatching houses

poi — food made from steamed and mashed *kalo,* a staple of the Hawaiian diet

poke — raw fish seasoned with soy sauce or seaweed (pronounced *pó-kay*)

pu'u — hill

pūpū — appetizer; a *pūpū* platter includes a variety of appetizers

saimin — noodle soup made with a clear fish stock and topped with a variety of foods, such as eggs, onions, and meats

tamure — Tahitian dance

ti — woody plant with narrow, oblong leaves; *kī* in Hawaiian

tūtū — grandmother

wahine — woman (pl. *wāhine*)

wiliwili — native tree found on dry coral plains and lava flows

Mahalo nui loa to the many individuals who provided invaluable information and assistance during the preparation of this book, most especially my sister Keven Richardson, Charlene Kaʻuhane of the Maui Visitors Bureau, Keoni Wagner of Hawaiian Airlines, Dale Madden of Island Heritage, and the following individuals:

Kathryn Acorda, Aston Hotels and Resorts; Akoni Akana, Friends of Mokuʻula; Barbara Allen, Sugar Cane Train; Pam Andelin; Laura Aquino, Current Events; Kelii Arruda, Old Lahaina Lūʻau; Kauʻi Awai-Dickson, Sheraton Maui; Nadine Awana Chase, Friends of Mokuʻula; Mark Barnes, Marriott & Renaissance Resorts Hawaiʻi; Jennifer Becnel, Grand Wailea Resort Hotel and Spa; Yvonne Biegel, Biegel Communications; Kaʻala Buenconsejo, Kapalua Resort; Patrick Callarec, Chez Paul; Patti Chevalier, Blue Hawaiian Helicopters; Sharon Dahlquist; Kathy Dziedzic, Outrigger Wailea Resort; Janice Fairbanks, Old Wailuku Inn; Sonja Fex-Rojo, Ritz-Carlton, Kapalua; Phil Freshman; Bonnie Friedman, Grapevine Productions; Julie Funasaki, PRWorks; Gary Gotling, Hyatt Regency Maui; Roxane Kozuma, Island Heritage; Diane and Ed Lane; Clarence and Elsa Lee; Michael Lee, Weston Maui; Michele Lee, Sheila Donnelly and Associates; Liz Marquez, Grand Wailea Resort Hotel and Spa; George Mason; Lori Michimoto, McNeil Wilson Communications; Michael Moore, Old Lahaina Lūʻau; Debra Morrill, Maui Classic Charters; Deanna Mukai, PRWorks; Donna Nabavi, Kapalua Resort; Clifford Naeʻole, Ritz-Carlton, Kapalua; Iokepa K. Naeʻole, Nature Conservancy of Hawaiʻi; Sweetie Nelson, Sheila Donnelly and Associates; Luana Paʻahana, Kāʻanapali Beach Hotel; Shae Page, McNeil Wilson Communications; Kennan Randolph, Sansei Seafood Restaurant; Lydee Ritchie, Maui Ocean Center; Don Robinson, Millennium Mapping; Charles St. Sure, Maui Lu Resort; Ken Schmidt, Hike Maui; Ray Serrano, Maui Downhill; Phil Sevier, Hotel Hāna-Maui; Wayne Shek, Color Station; Lynn Shue, Village Galleries; Jacque Smith, Limtiaco Company; Kimberly Mikami Svetin, Ritz-Carlton, Kapalua; Gigi Valley, Lanaʻi Company; Lorinda Waltz, Island Heritage; Mike White, Kāʻanapali Beach Hotel; Michelle Wilhelm, Hotel Hāna-Maui; and Caroline Witherspoon, Becker Communications.

Picture Credits

Veronica Carmona: pages 2–3, 35, 49 (top and bottom), 50, 52 (right), 58, 61 (top), 62, 65, 75, 76, 77 (top), 78 (top), 79, 80 (inset), 81 (top and bottom right), 86 (top), 87 (bottom), 105, 108 (top), 119, 125 (bottom), 135 (left), 152–53 (background), 157, 180, 182, 185, 193 (top), 247, 250, 253, 257, 258 (top), 259 (top), 260–61, 264, 265 (bottom), 266, 279 (top), 284 (bottom), 289.

Ron Dahlquist: cover (all except Kū image), pages 4 (all except petroglyph and palm fronds), 5–7, 8 (road to Hāna, Hulopoʻe Beach, Hāliʻimaile General Store), 9, 11, 12 (background), 13, 25, 26 (flower), 27, 30, 32–34, 37–39, 44–46, 47 (top), 48, 51, 52 (left), 60, 61 (bottom), 64, 66–72, 74, 77 (bottom), 80 (top), 81 (bottom left), 82–85, 87 (top), 88–90, 92, 93, 94 (top), 95–101, 103, 106, 107, 108 (bottom), 110–12, 114, 117 (bottom), 118, 121–23, 125 (top), 126–28, 130 (top), 131, 132, 134, 136 (top), 137, 139 (bottom), 142–43, 146–47, 148–50 (background), 151, 153–55, 158–63, 165–68, 170–72, 176, 178, 179, 181, 186–89, 193 (bottom), 194, 195, 197, 198, 201, 212, 232 (background), 241, 246, 248–49, 254, 256, 258 (bottom), 259 (bottom), 263, 265 (top), 267, 268, 278, 279 (bottom), 280, 282 (top), 283, 284 (top), 285, 287, 288, 291, 292.

Hawaiʻi State Archives: back cover (Kū image), pages 10, 14–16, 18, 19 (bottom), 20, 21, 42, 49 (David Malo), 156, 262.

Jim Wageman: pages 1 (inset), 4 (petroglyph, palm fronds), 26 (background), 91, 113, 135 (right), 138, 139 (top), 269–72, 274–77, 282 (bottom).

American Hawaiʻi Cruises: pages 130 (bottom), 207; courtesy **Pam Andelin:** page 286; courtesy **Sheila Donnelly and Associates:** page 8 *(ʻUlalena);* courtesy **Grand Wailea Resort Hotel and Spa:** page 78 (bottom); **Hawaiian Legacy Archive:** page 184; courtesy **Hotel Hāna-Maui:** page 117 (top); courtesy **Ed Lane:** page 116; courtesy **Ritz-Carlton, Kapalua:** pages 8 (top), 244; **Sugar Cane Train,** Lahaina: page 47 (bottom); courtesy **Village Galleries,** Lahaina: pages 57, 86 (bottom), 94 (bottom), 104, 136 (bottom).

index

Note to the Reader

Every effort has been made to provide accurate, up-to-date information. However, travel information is subject to change. We suggest that you call ahead when making travel plans. We also suggest that prudent care be taken whenever engaging in any outdoor activity and that you be aware of your own limitations. Neither the publisher nor the author can be held liable for errors or omissions herein or for loss, injury, or inconvenience resulting from the use of this book.

We welcome your comments. Please write to:

Essential Guide to Maui
Island Heritage Publishing
94-411 Kōʻaki Street
Waipahu, HI 96797

e-mail:
EssentialGuides@hawaii.rr.com